More What Works When | with Children and Adolescents

More What Works When

with Children and Adolescents

A Handbook of
Individual Counseling
Techniques

Ann Vernon

Research Press
2612 North Mattis Avenue, Champaign, Illinois 61822 | [800] 519-2707 | www.researchpress.com

RESEARCH PRESS
PUBLISHERS

Copyright 2009 by Ann Vernon

8 7 6 5 4   19 20 21 22 23

All forms and handouts referenced in the book are available for download at
www.researchpress.com/downloads

Copies of this book may be ordered from Research Press at the address
given on the title page.

Composition by Jeff Helgesen
Cover design by Linda Brown, Positive I.D. Graphic Design, Inc.
Printing by Seaway Printing Co., Inc.

ISBN-13: 978-0-87822-614-6
Library of Congress Control Number 2008942196

Contents

Activities   vii

Acknowledgments   xi

Foreword   xiii

Introduction   1

Chapter 1: Considerations in Working with Young Clients   7

Developmental Considerations   8

  Early Childhood   8

  Middle Childhood   9

  Early Adolescence   9

  Mid-Adolescence   11

Implications of Developmental Stages   12

Relationship Between REBT and Development   13

The Therapeutic Relationship   18

Building Rapport   24

  Strategies for Building Rapport with Children (Ages 5 to 10)   25

  Strategies for Building Rapport with Adolescents (Ages 11 to 18)   30

Establishing Goals   36

Chapter 2: Basic Principles of Rational Emotive Behavior Therapy   39

Basic Principles: The ABC's of REBT   40

  Rational and Irrational Beliefs   41

  Disputation   43

  Effective New Philosophy, Feelings, and Behaviors   44

Specific Applications to Children and Adolescents   44

  Problem Assessment   45

The ABC Process 64

   The A—Activating Event 64

   The C—Emotional and Behavioral Consequences 65

   The B—Beliefs 70

   The D—Disputing Irrational Beliefs 72

   The E—Effective New Philosophy (Thoughts) 79

   The F—Effective New Feelings 83

Homework 84

Evaluation 85

Chapter 3: Interventions for Internalizing Problems 89

Anxiety 91

Depression 114

Stress 130

Grief 153

Chapter 4: Interventions for Externalizing Problems 173

Low Frustration Tolerance 175

Anger 197

Acting Out 215

Bullying 245

Chapter 5: Interventions for Typical Developmental Problems 269

Self-Acceptance 271

Relationships 287

Transitions 305

Chapter 6: Applications for Parents and Teachers 325

Problem Assessment 326

Identifying Irrational Beliefs 329

Disputing Irrational Beliefs 335

Teaching and Parenting Styles 340

   Authoritarian Style 341

   Permissive Style 341

   Authoritative Style 342

Solving the Practical Problem 342

   Logical Consequences 344

Communication Techniques: What Doesn't Work and What
Does   345

Rational Emotive Education   348

Case Study   350

Summary of Case Study   354

Appendix: Game Board   355

References   359
About the Author   365

Activities

Chapter 3: Interventions for Internalizing Problems

Anxiety   91

What If?   94

Worry-Wart   97

Wanda the Worrier   99

Wash Away the Worries   102

Anxious About Being Anxious   104

Walk Away, Anxiety   107

Worry Management   109

Away with Anxiety   111

Depression   114

Sad, Sad, Sad   116

If You're Sad and You Know It . . .   118

Crying Takes the Sad Out of You   120

So Long, Sadness   122

Am I Depressed?   123

Don't Stay Depressed   125

Depression "Tool Box"   127

Spin Away the Blues   129

Stress   130

Where Is My Stress?   132

Stop Stressing   134

Stress Busters   135

Take a Deep Breath and Relax   139

Is It Stress?   142

Am I Stressed Out?   144

Away with Stress   147

De-Stressing Your Stress   149

Grief   153

It's Good to Grieve   155

Memory Mobile   157

Getting Through Grief   158

How to Heal   160

Living with Loss   162

Loss After Loss After Loss   164

Heal Your Heart   167

Beginnings and Endings   170

Chapter 4: Interventions for Externalizing Problems

Low Frustration Tolerance   175

I Can Stand It   177

Red Light or Green Light?   179

Fighting Frustration   181

I Think I Can   183

It's Frustrating to Be Frustrated   187

Talk Yourself Out of It   190

Deal with It   193

Is It Worth It?   195

Anger   197

Anger Antenna   200

Anger In? Anger Out?   202

Angry Annabelle   204

Adios, Anger   206

Expressing Your Anger   207

Angry Attitudes   209

Anger Is . . .   211

Anger—Any Advantages?   213

Acting Out   215

How Do I Act?   218

Stop or Go Behavior   222

What's the Consequence?   226

Me and My Actions   228

What's a Consequence?   231

I Am What I Eat   236

I'm Hurting   240

Pay the Price?   243

Bullying   245

What's Bullying?   247

Take Charge   249

Is It What You Think It Is?   251

Calling All Bullies   255

Bullying Can Be . . .   257

E Is for Empowerment   259

How Will You Handle It?   262

Emotionally Tough   266

Chapter 5: Interventions for Typical Developmental Problems

Self-Acceptance   271

Can I or Can't I?   273

No, I'm Not; Yes, I Am   277

The Whole Picture   279

Who, Me? Yes, You   281

Too Perfect?   283

Accept Yourself   286

Relationships   287

Finding Friends   288

Risky Relationships   291

Family Feud   294

Relationships Rule   296

Healthy or Unhealthy?   299

Reasons for Relationships   302

Transitions   305

Tough Times   306

Room for One More?   309

Switching Schools   312

Troubling Transitions   315

On My Own   319

Alone Again   321

Acknowledgments

For more than 30 years, I have personally and professionally practiced rational emotive behavior therapy (REBT) to the best of my ability, acknowledging that, as a fallible human being, I have not always done it perfectly, and that, under certain circumstances, it has been more of a challenge to apply the principles to my own life than at other times. Nevertheless, this theory has, beyond a doubt, profoundly affected me in positive ways too numerous to describe.

I owe a great indebtedness to the late Dr. Albert Ellis, who created this theory and devoted much of his life to promulgating it through his writing, his teaching, and the establishment of the Albert Ellis Institute, whose mission is, among other things, to train practitioners in the theory and practice of REBT. It was through my training at the Institute that I first began using this approach with children and adolescents and subsequently began publishing books and articles with the encouragement and support of other noted REBT practitioners, Drs. Virginia Waters, Richard Wessler, Dominic DiMattia, Ray DiGiuseppe, and Janet Wolfe.

Writing a book such as this takes persistence and patience, but, as I used various interventions with my child and adolescent clients and field-tested the interventions with other clinicians and school counselors, it reaffirmed for me how important it is to use nontraditional, developmentally, and culturally appropriate intervention strategies with young clients. Based on many years of clinical and school counseling experience with children and adolescents, as well as their parents, I remain strongly convinced that developing rational thinkers is the key to healthy development. Not only does this theory help young clients *get* better, not just *feel* better, but it teaches skills that they can use throughout their lifetime to cope with developmental, as well as serious situational problems, in constructive ways.

Last but not least, I would like to thank my spouse for his ability to tolerate my long hours at the computer; my editor at Research Press, Karen Steiner, for tolerating my perfectionistic tendencies in the preparation of this manuscript; and Russ Pence at Research Press for his enthusiasm for my projects.

Foreword

Well, Ann Vernon has done it again! With the addition of *More What Works When with Children and Adolescents* to her many books on how to help young people cope with the pressures of growing up, she provides the practitioner with a comprehensive guide to treating the emotional, behavioral, and developmental problems of children and adolescents. Counseling children, adolescents, and their parents is one of the greatest challenges facing psychotherapists and educators. This book certainly makes it easier for the practitioner to be more effective in the treatment of these challenging emotional and behavioral problems.

Ann's earlier publications—*Thinking, Feeling, Behaving* and *The Passport Program*—have provided teachers and counselors with excellent emotional education curricula to help young people handle life's daily challenges before they become too disturbed. These guides are widely used by educators around the world and offer excellent preventative approaches to assist young people in coping with the stressors of daily life. However, as we all know, there is always a need to help those youngsters who require individual attention. The first volume of *What Works When with Children and Adolescents* and now this companion volume provide counseling practitioners with an incredible number of creative, practical techniques and strategies to teach young clients how to handle their emotions and manage their behavior. Developed from years of clinical and supervisory experience, Ann has organized the best of these techniques into a user-friendly format.

Based on the principles and practices of Albert Ellis's rational emotive behavior therapy (REBT), Ann's techniques and strategies are theoretically consistent, and I am sure that if Albert Ellis had lived long enough to review this book he would strongly endorse it, as he did the first *What Works When*. She provides the reader with a solid background in the principles and practices of REBT as they relate to children, adolescents, parents, and teachers, and through vignettes, case studies, and numerous interventions, shows the reader how to apply the theory in a very practical manner. Many individuals have criticized REBT for being too intellectual and not applicable to working with children and adolescents. Ann certainly puts that criticism to rest with her creative approaches to applying REBT to younger clients. This book is filled with engaging techniques such as rational songs, stories, limericks, games, art activities, imagery and relaxation exercises, checklists, hands-on activities and experiments, and many other age-appropriate strategies that motivate young clients to participate in the counseling process and learn how to help themselves get better and feel better. In this book, Ann has developed 82 new techniques, including strategies that address bullying, stress management, low frustration tolerance, and grief, as well as anger, anxiety, acting out, depression, self-acceptance, relationships, and transitions.

There have been a few other REBT therapists who have written about applying REBT with children and adolescents, but I believe Ann's publications put her in front of the pack. No doubt she is the leading professional in the world at developing specific techniques and strategies for working with children and adolescents based on this therapeutic approach. This book and its predecessor should be part of every counselor's library if he or she works with children and adolescents.

In Australia, I have had the opportunity to work with Ann for many years conducting workshops for counselors and psychotherapists who counsel children and adolescents. Participants have been very enthusiastic about her ideas and are eager to try them with their clients. Each year, interest grows, and I am sure that you will also become as enthusiastic about Ann's ideas after you read this book.

Dominic J. DiMattia, Ed.D.
Professor Emeritus
University of Bridgeport
Former Executive Director
Albert Ellis Institute

Introduction

A 9-year-old was referred for counseling by her parents, who were concerned about their daughter's intense anxiety about bad things happening to their family. Megan's parents shared that they had taken their daughter to another therapist a few months ago, but it had not been very helpful, and they had stopped going after several visits. However, because the problem seemed to be getting worse, they were once again seeking help.

When I first met Megan, she appeared very hesitant and somewhat anxious. I sensed that it might be important to do at least one get-acquainted activity to help put her at ease. When I invited her to participate in a short exercise that would help us learn more about each other, she agreed to play "Who Are You?" (Vernon, 2002), where each person takes turns asking the other, "Who are you?" and responding with something descriptive, such as "I am someone who loves to read." After several rounds of this activity, Megan seemed more comfortable, and I felt I could ease into the counseling process. I shared with her that I understood she had been in counseling before because she worries about bad things happening to her family and asked her whether that was still something she would like help with. She nodded her head yes as tears welled up in her eyes. "I just want to get better. I worry so much that I don't know what to do. I know my parents are trying to help me, but they just don't understand. Only my dog understands, but he can't help me either."

After her tears subsided some, I assured Megan that I was there to help her and that I had worked with other 9-year-olds who also worried about their families. She said that her last counselor only had her talk about her feelings, and while that felt good at first, it didn't help her worry less. "This time I want something that really helps me get better," she explained. Although I was surprised that a 9-year-old could articulate her expectations so clearly, I definitely agreed with her. Counseling needs to do more than help clients "feel better"; it also needs to help them "get better."

This young client's seemingly simple statement showed unusual insight and intuition. In fact, Megan unwittingly stumbled on the central objective of rational emotive behavior therapy (REBT), a theory developed by Dr. Albert Ellis in 1955. REBT is based on the notion that how we think largely determines our feelings and behaviors (Dryden & Ellis, 2001). By helping individuals learn to identify and challenge the dysfunctional or irrational thinking patterns that create emotional disturbance, we can empower them to deal with a wide array of problematic situations.

Early in the practice of REBT, Ellis and his colleagues began applying the theory to children and, for several reasons, found it to be a highly effective form of therapy with young people (Vernon, 2009b). First, it is easily understood and is adaptable for children of most ages, cultures, and intelligence levels. Second, it is a short-term problem-solving form of therapy, which makes it particularly useful in school settings, where time for counseling sessions is limited and more traditional forms of therapy are inappropriate. The same time constraints hold true in mental health settings, where the number of sessions is limited by managed health care companies. That REBT is a brief form of therapy is also especially important for young clients because their sense of time is so immediate; they need something that will help them *now*. Additionally, this theory is widely applicable for work with children and adolescents who are in the concrete operational stage of thinking. The teachable concepts inherent in this approach offer a highly effective, concrete way of matching therapeutic style with youngsters' level of cognitive development. As young people mature into the stage of formal operational thought, this theory can easily be adapted to incorporate more abstract concepts.

Perhaps more important, REBT empowers individuals, making it a particularly relevant form of therapy for young people, who typically have very little control over most significant life events. Children are uniquely vulnerable to the decisions the adults in their lives make. For instance, most youngsters are not consulted about the death of a family member, parental divorce or remarriage, loss of family income due to a parent's unemployment, or parental substance abuse. REBT teaches behavioral and emotional self-control by helping children understand the connection between thoughts, feelings, and behaviors. In doing so, and in promoting psychological well-being, it helps them deal realistically with what they can and cannot change in their lives.

REBT is applicable to a wide range of normal developmental concerns such as self-consciousness during puberty, academic pressure, performance and competition issues, peer relationships, and developing independence. Whether the problems are situational, such as those mentioned in the previous paragraph, or developmental, this theory is more effective than many others because it immediately addresses the problem and teaches children how to think clearly and solve problems independently.

Finally, an integral part of this theory is its emphasis on teaching and prevention. In 1971, The Living School was established to help young people learn rational principles. Although The Living School no longer exists, the concepts introduced in that setting have been applied to children and adolescents across the United States and abroad through several emotional education programs. These programs, which promote emotional and behavioral health, are designed to help them apply rational thinking skills to the problems they face in their daily lives (Bernard, 2001; Knaus, 1974; Vernon, 1998a, 1998b, 1998c, 2006a, 2006b; Waters, 1979, 1980). These programs teach children the skills necessary for dealing with current problems and also enable them to acquire techniques they can use to prevent or minimize problems that arise in the future. The self-help emphasis that results from teaching these REBT concepts can facilitate problem resolution independent of regularly scheduled counseling sessions; this factor is especially beneficial for children and adolescents.

The purpose of this book, a companion to *What Works When with Children and Adolescents: A Handbook of Individual Counseling Techniques* (Vernon, 2002) is to describe more specific applications of REBT that help practitioners understand how to best use this approach with young clients. Chapter 1 discusses developmental considerations in working with younger clients and how REBT so aptly addresses developmental limitations that are characteristic of children and adolescents. A revised model graphically depicts how irrational thinking impacts children's ability to deal with both situational and developmental problems. The chapter includes several new strategies for establishing a therapeutic relationship with young clients, who are often referred to a counselor by others and do not always understand why they need counseling. Consequently, they may be apprehensive or opposed to counseling because it wasn't their decision.

Chapter 2 outlines the basic REBT schema and elaborates on the theory, putting major emphasis on the assessment process and problem conceptualization as they apply to young clients. This chapter has also been revised considerably from the first edition, with updated references and new techniques for employing the ABC therapeutic process with young clients.

Chapters 3, 4, and 5 of the book are all new and include creative cognitive, emotive, and behavioral interventions for internalizing disorders such as anxiety, depression, stress, and grief. In addition, there are developmentally appropriate interventions for externalizing disorders: low frustration tolerance, anger, acting out (including self-defeating behaviors such as self-injury, eating disorders, suicidal behavior, and substance abuse), and bullying.

Chapter 5 describes interventions for typical developmental problems such as self-acceptance, relationships, and transitions. Chapter 6 addresses REBT applications with parents and teachers.

Designed for counselors, social workers, and psychologists in school and mental health settings, this practical handbook offers developmentally appropriate, creative interventions for problems children and adolescents commonly experience. It includes games, art and music activities, experiential activities, imagery, bibliotherapy, behavioral rehearsal, and other strategies designed to motivate young clients to participate in their own therapy.

A few of these interventions involve the use of a game board or game cards. The point of using the game board is not to finish first or determine a winner but to encourage the client's self-disclosure and involvement within the familiar, comfortable context of playing a table game. You may create your own game boards, or you may photocopy the generic game board included in the appendix, glue or tape it to an open manila folder or a large sheet of tagboard, then decorate it however you wish. The game board in the appendix is a continuous loop with no finish line: You can play the game as long as you find it helpful and stop any time. Dot stickers of different colors are sometimes needed to color-code the game board and game cards.

For some activities, you will need dice; coins or buttons can serve as game markers. When an activity calls for the use of game cards, you will need to photocopy the page on which they appear, cut the items apart, and affix them to index cards or card-sized strips of tagboard. If you wish, you can also create your own game cards to fit your particular client and circumstances.

Many of the interventions include stories, songs, and poems that bring REBT principles to life by showing how other children and adolescents think, feel, and behave in various situations. You may read these materials aloud to clients, give them to clients to read, or read aloud while your clients read silently—whatever best suits the particular individual. Pages you may photocopy and give to your clients are included for all but the briefest of these items.

Additional materials accompanying the interventions in this handbook include photocopiable worksheets, checklists, and illustrations. If hands-on materials such as balloons or art supplies are called for in an activity, they are specified.

Although many of the strategies presented here can be adapted for use in small-group counseling or classroom settings, they are designed specifically for use in individual counseling and are based on my extensive experience applying REBT to children and adolescents. Practitioners using this book should find that this theory helps young clients strengthen their "emotional muscle" and equips them to deal more effectively with the normal challenges of growing up, as well as more serious problems. Consequently, these young clients will be better able to take charge of their lives and avoid self-defeating behaviors that are likely to have serious negative implications.

CHAPTER 1

Considerations in Working with Young Clients

Thirteen-year-old Lydia sat across from her counselor, alternating between staring out the window and fiddling with her book bag. Her nonverbal communication clearly conveyed her displeasure at being there, and attempts to engage her in even minimal conversation had failed. In desperation, the counselor bombarded her with questions, hoping for some response. With each question, Lydia withdrew even further, causing greater frustration for the counselor.

This scenario may sound familiar. For a variety of reasons, attempts to get young clients to open up are often met with resistance. These youngsters may not understand what the process of counseling entails, and they may be frightened or confused when a parent tells them they are going to see a counselor. This lack of understanding contributes to the fear that many children have that they are "crazy" or "bad" or that something is seriously wrong with them if they need professional help. Adolescents in particular resent being labeled "the problem," especially when they don't think anything is wrong with them. This same dynamic operates when an adolescent is a juvenile offender and is ordered by the court to receive counseling. Furthermore, many youngsters enter therapy without being told why by the adults who referred them. All of these factors can initially have a negative impact on the client–counselor therapeutic alliance.

Another factor contributing to these youngsters' reluctance to communicate is that they may not be adept at describing how they feel or what has occurred, so what seems like resistance is simply a matter of their not knowing what to say. Younger children in particular like to please adults, and it may be safer for them not to say much if they are not sure how to express themselves. One can imagine being in their shoes—being 8 years old and not having any idea what a counselor does: One day your mother announces that you are going to see Dr. Vernon, who will help you with your sad feelings. A week or so later, Dad loads you in the car and takes you to a strange office, where you sit in a waiting room with people staring at you. Finally, someone you have never seen before comes to get you, and you have to go all by yourself into another room. You really do not know what to say, and you want to avoid sounding dumb, so you just sit there. Should it surprise counselors that some young clients may initially give them the silent treatment?

During the past 30 years, helping professionals have gradually recognized that, in many respects, counseling children and adolescents is quite different from counseling adults. Fortunately, practitioners are now incorporating more child-oriented approaches into their work with young clients. In the field of rational emotive behavior therapy (REBT), however, there is a paucity of work that specifically addresses important developmental considerations and individual counseling interventions with children and adolescents. This book was written to fill that void.

DEVELOPMENTAL CONSIDERATIONS

Early Childhood

The world is a fascinating place for 4- and 5-year olds. These children are curious, energetic, and eager. With the help of their imaginations, anything is possible. As a result, it is often difficult for them to distinguish between real and make-believe, which is why the "monsters" under the bed seem so real (Vernon & Clemente, 2005). Preoperational thinking characterizes their cognitive development and limits the degree to which they can think logically or understand abstract concepts (Berk, 2003; McDevitt & Ormrod, 2002). By nature, preschoolers are egocentric; they assume that everyone thinks and feels the same way they do. Consequently, it is difficult, if not impossible, for them to see things from another's perspective. During this period of development, their self-esteem is quite high (Berger, 2003; McDevitt & Ormrod, 2002), and they tend to overestimate their abilities, thinking that they can do anything. Because they are developing so quickly and mastering so many tasks during this stage, their feelings of self-efficacy can be advantageous. They are also developing the ability to control their impulses.

Play serves an extremely important function at this age, and it is through this medium that children learn how to be cooperative and take turns (Owens, 2002; Rathus, 2004). However, they have difficulty understanding intentionality, so they are likely to misinterpret others' behavior and respond inappropriately (Vernon & Clemente, 2005). Because their emotional vocabularies are limited, they often express their feelings behaviorally. Toward the end of this stage of development, youngsters begin to acquire a better understanding of other people's emotions and can respond verbally or physically by, for example, apologizing or giving a hug when they think someone is sad.

Middle Childhood

During middle childhood, ages 6 to 10, physical growth is relatively stable, and children are able to master most motor skills (Bee, 2000; McDevitt & Ormrod, 2002). By age 8, children enter the concrete operational stage, which has a positive impact on their problem-solving abilities. For these reasons, many consider middle childhood to be the best period in a person's life (Berger & Thompson, 1991). As concrete operational thinkers, these children are able to think more logically, but they still do not reason abstractly or consider a wide range of alternatives—an inability that influences how they approach situations (Vernon & Clemente, 2005). For example, if their best friend does not sit by them on the bus, they might assume that they did something to make the friend angry rather than consider other possibilities.

During this period of maturation, children's self-understanding improves (Owens, 2002), and they begin to develop a stronger internal locus of control (Vernon, 2009c). As they enter school and compare themselves to others, they become increasingly self-critical and may begin to feel inferior.

The ability to socialize effectively with peers is a critical developmental task during these years, as children confront the issues of acceptance, rejection, peer pressure, and conformity. Peer interactions may elicit joy, concern, and disappointment, but friendships serve important functions as well. As children develop perspective-taking, they become more adept at interpreting social cues and are better able to employ social judgment as a means to resolve interpersonal conflict (Berger, 2003). The ability to recognize and communicate feelings more effectively also contributes to their improved social problem-solving skills.

Early Adolescence

Whereas middle childhood is generally thought of as the best period in a person's life, early adolescence (ages 11 to 14) is often considered the worst. It is during this period of development that young people feel increasingly vulnerable. Physical changes occur more rapidly during this time than at any other point in the life span, with the exception of infancy (Meece, 2002). Because the rate of maturity varies tremendously across genders and individuals, self-consciousness and anxiety are prevalent. Males and females alike may become clumsy and uncoordinated because the size of their hands and feet may be disproportionate to their other body parts. Their rate of physical change affects their self-concept (McDevitt & Ormrod, 2002); it is a factor that is especially relevant for early adolescents, who want to be like everyone else to gain social acceptance and are anxious about appearing awkward or different (Owens, 2002). Additionally, physical and hormonal changes can cause a great deal of confusion and discomfort as sexual thoughts and feelings arise, and they are often accompanied by feelings of guilt, shame, and embarrassment (Vernon, 2009c).

Although the shift from concrete to formal operational thinking begins during early adolescence, this process is gradual and is not completed until at least age 15 (Kaplan, 2000). As adolescents move into formal operational thinking, they begin to think more abstractly, develop the ability to hypothesize, reason more logically, and predict consequences (Wigfield, Lutz, & Wagner, 2005). However, they do not always apply these skills to themselves and often have difficulty linking events, feelings, and situations. Therefore, they may fail to make the connection between flunking a test and not studying for it (Newman & Newman, 2006). Because considerable variability exists in the degree to which formal operational thinking is attained and applied consistently during early adolescence, it is of critical importance not to assume that these youngsters are capable of more mature cognition (Cobb, 2001; Vernon, 2009c).

During this developmental period, early adolescents begin their search for self-definition and integration and push for autonomy (Cobb, 2001; Martin, 2003). However, because they are still immature and lack life experiences to guide them (Weisfeld, 1999), they often feel vulnerable and may be somewhat more dependent on adults. This situation is confusing to them (Vernon, 2009c). Adolescents in this age range tend to feel acutely self-conscious and assume that everyone is looking at them and that they are on display before what Elkind (1988) termed the *imaginary audience.* As a result of this type of thinking, adolescents fantasize about how others will react to them and are overly sensitive about their performance and appearance. Needless to say, self-esteem usually decreases during this period of development.

Another phenomenon that causes considerable concern during this stage is what Elkind (1984) labeled the *personal fable,* which is the belief held by many early adolescents that because they are unique, special, and invulnerable, bad things may happen to others but not to them. This type of thinking may explain in part why so many young people engage in risk-taking behaviors such as unprotected sex ("Others can get pregnant or contract sexually transmitted diseases, but it won't happen to me").

Peers play an increasingly important role in the lives of early adolescents, and, although teens look to one another as a source of support, they are also vulnerable to peer humiliation. Belonging and rejection are major issues at this age, and desire for one and fear of the other typically result in vulnerability to peer pressure. Because they are still egocentric and have difficulty taking others' viewpoints into account (Jaffe, 1998), young adolescents may be limited in their ability to deal effectively with these problems.

Early adolescents ride an emotional roller coaster during this developmental stage. Their emotional volatility is characterized by moodiness, emotional outbursts, anger, anxiety, shame, depression, and guilt. These negative emotions are typically overwhelming to adolescents and lead to feelings of anxiety about their vulnerability—an anxiety that is often masked by anger. This response in turn keeps people at a distance and can result in increased conflict with adults as well as peers.

Mid-Adolescence

Mid-adolescence (ages 15 to 18) is generally characterized by more stability than early adolescence, depending on when the onset of puberty occurs. Physical development is usually less rapid (McDevitt & Ormrod, 2002), resulting in a lesser degree of self-consciousness and fluctuation of emotions. Formal operational thinking continues to develop, and these new cognitive abilities allow adolescents to think and behave differently. Their thinking is more multidimensional (Owens, 2002), and they are better able to think abstractly, hypothesize, and consider future events and consequences (Newman & Newman, 2006). Additionally, they are less likely to conceptualize everything in either/or terms, the way younger adolescents typically do. However, inconsistencies in their thinking and behaving remain (Cobb, 2001). Although they may be able to see alternatives, older adolescents often lack the experience or self-understanding to make appropriate choices (Vernon, 2009c).

At this stage of development, adolescents are concerned about achieving independence and exploring various roles and responsibilities. Their interests may change, and they may engage in the process of self-questioning and experimenting as a way of establishing an identity. In addition, these older adolescents are generally more self-confident than they were in early adolescence (Vernon & Clemente, 2005).

Peer relationships continue to be very important and serve as vehicles to try out various roles and develop tolerance for individual differences (Broderick & Blewitt, 2006). Depending on their degree of formal operational thinking, mid-adolescents approach peer relationships with more maturity than they possessed in earlier years and consequently may not be as dependent on friends for emotional support as they were in the past (Dusek, 1996). As intimate relationships develop, new challenges, such as dating and sexual experimentation, emerge (Newman & Newman, 2006).

The degree to which a formal operational thought process has been attained is especially important because it has a strong impact on adolescents' emotional state. For the most part, adolescents during this stage experience fewer mood fluctuations than younger adolescents do. They also are not as overwhelmed by their feelings and are better able to deal with emotionally charged issues (Kang & Shaver, 2004). They are not as impulsive or as likely to behave erratically in response to emotional upset. The way they manage their emotions still varies widely, however, and is dependent on their level of cognitive maturation (Vernon & Clemente, 2005).

IMPLICATIONS OF DEVELOPMENTAL STAGES

Practitioners working with children and adolescents need to tailor their assessment and intervention strategies, using games with younger children and concrete techniques with children of all ages to illustrate their points. They need to remain aware of the ways in which self-development, as well as emotional, social, physical, and cognitive development characteristics, influence how youngsters interpret their world. Interpretations of such factors carry important implications for accurate problem diagnosis and selection of appropriate interventions.

Perhaps the most important factor to keep in mind is that cognitive development significantly affects perceptions. For example, although children in middle childhood have acquired enhanced problem-solving skills, they are still limited by their concrete thought processes. Not being able to see all sides of an issue, taking things literally, and not being able to reason abstractly all have major implications for how they process everyday occurrences. For these reasons, their perception of events is often distorted, and they frequently become upset because they have not judged problems accurately.

This phenomenon also pertains to the 11- to 14-year-old age group and often extends into mid-adolescence, depending on the rate of cognitive maturity. For example, children in middle childhood often are quite eager to please the teacher because they want the teacher's approval. If the teacher fails to call on them or reprimands them, they may wrongly conclude that the teacher does not like them or that they can never do anything to please the teacher. If appropriate intervention does not occur, they may become discouraged or act out in negative ways to gain attention. Because they also lack the ability to generate problem-solving alternatives, their behavior may be misunderstood and result in conflict with parents or teachers, who assume the children are able to recognize other possibilities. This type of behavior is exemplified by the 12-year-old who stayed for basketball practice and neglected to do her paper route. When her father asked her why she hadn't called home to ask her brother to deliver the papers, she said, "I honestly didn't think about it. The coach said we had to stay for practice or we would get kicked off the team, and that's all I thought about."

RELATIONSHIP BETWEEN REBT AND DEVELOPMENT

Because the stages of development, particularly cognitive development, play such a central role in how children and adolescents interpret their life experiences, therapeutic interventions must be developmentally as well as culturally sensitive if they are to be effective. REBT is uniquely suited for use with younger populations because it can be easily tailored for youngsters from various cultural backgrounds at any point in their development and employs a wide array of strategies that most appropriately address the problem. Furthermore, interventions aimed at correcting irrational thinking also help young clients gain cognitive perspective, which in turn enables them to deal more effectively with normal developmental problems as well as more situational factors.

The model shown on the next page illustrates the relationship between REBT and development. In the very center of the model (1) are the areas of development: self, emotional, social, physical, and cognitive. How clients respond to normal developmental problems such as relationships with peers and parents, performance in sports or music, typical developmental transitions, or identity and independence issues, which are depicted in the first circle (4), is influenced by their level of development. For example, a 6-year-old who is still quite egocentric and in the process of developing more prosocial skills, such as cooperating and compromising, will have more difficulty with peer relations than a 10-year-old who has more mature skills and is not as egocentric. Likewise, their level of development also affects how children respond to more serious situational problems such as abuse, death, parental divorce, or homelessness, shown in the outer circle (5). Because adolescents can think more logically and understand more complex issues, it would be easier for a 16-year-old, as opposed to an 8-year-old, to understand that it was not her fault that her father sexually abused her.

Not only does the level of development affect how children and adolescents respond to typical developmental problems—as well as to more serious situational problems that some youngsters experience—but their degree of irrational thinking also plays a major role. Listed in the outer square (2) are the core irrational beliefs: demands on self (self-downing), demands on others, and demands on the world, which

Relationship Between REBT and Development

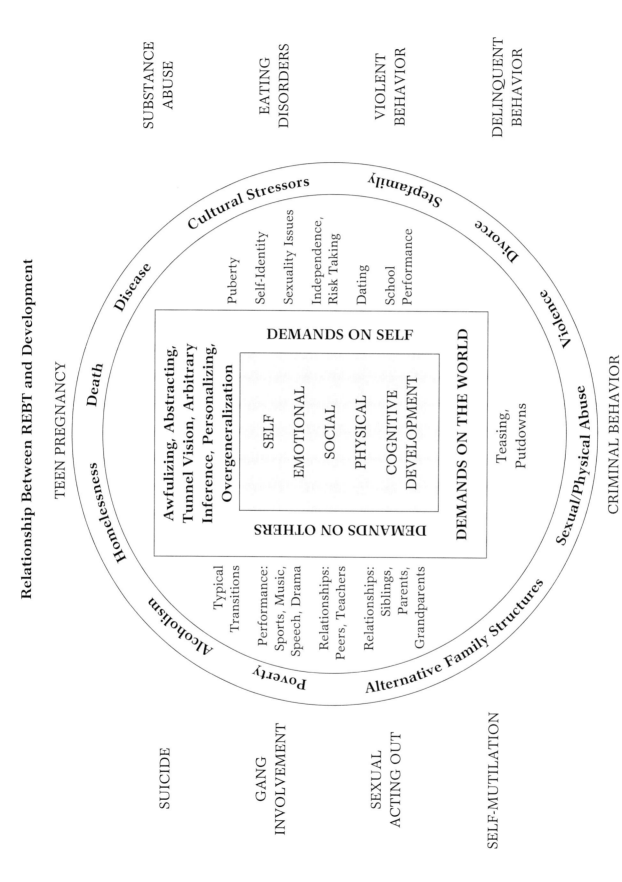

SUBSTANCE ABUSE

EATING DISORDERS

VIOLENT BEHAVIOR

DELINQUENT BEHAVIOR

TEEN PREGNANCY

SUICIDE

GANG INVOLVEMENT

SEXUAL ACTING OUT

SELF-MUTILATION

Cultural Stressors

Stepfamily

Disease

Divorce

Death

Violence

Homelessness

Sexual/Physical Abuse

Alcoholism

CRIMINAL BEHAVIOR

Poverty

Alternative Family Structures

Puberty

Self-Identity

Sexuality Issues

Independence, Risk Taking

Dating

School Performance

DEMANDS ON SELF

Awfulizing, Abstracting, Tunnel Vision, Arbitrary Inference, Personalizing, Overgeneralization

SELF

EMOTIONAL

SOCIAL

PHYSICAL

COGNITIVE DEVELOPMENT

DEMANDS ON OTHERS

DEMANDS ON THE WORLD

Teasing, Putdowns

Typical Transitions

Performance: Sports, Music, Speech, Drama

Relationships: Peers, Teachers

Relationships: Siblings, Parents, Grandparents

is often manifested in low frustration tolerance. For example, a youngster who has low frustration tolerance will experience more difficulty with a normal developmental issue such as performance in sports because he will give up more easily, thinking, "This is too hard. I can't do things that require this much effort. It's easier not to try at all." An adolescent who demands that others treat him exactly as he thinks he should be treated often ends up in unsatisfactory relationships characterized by anger and controlling behavior, and a fourth grader who engages in self-downing will make remarks such as "I'm so stupid; nobody is as dumb as I am" in response to missing several problems on a social studies test. This type of thinking can become problematic over time.

Listed around these core beliefs in the next square (3) are typical cognitive distortions that also can be problematic for children and adolescents, affecting how they react to developmental and situational challenges. As Bernard and colleagues (2006) noted, these cognitive distortions are characteristic of pre-concrete operational thought.

Awfulizing. Blowing things out of proportion and catastrophizing; thinking that nothing could be worse than fouling out of the basketball game, for instance.

Overgeneralizing. Drawing conclusions based on a single event, such as assuming that you will never get invited to a party because you didn't get invited to one this week.

Tunnel vision. Not seeing all aspects of a situation and therefore drawing erroneous conclusions; for example, assuming that your sister took your jacket when you looked in only one place for it.

Selective abstraction. Focusing on a detail out of context and ignoring other significant details; thinking, for example, that your mother favors your sister because she washed her laundry, but failing to remember that she didn't wash yours because you hadn't put it in the laundry room.

Arbitrary inference. Drawing a specific conclusion in the absence of supporting evidence; arbitrarily inferring something without examining all the evidence. For example, an adolescent assumes that her parents came home early from a party because they didn't trust her to be alone, when in reality they came home because they were tired.

Personalization. Relating external events personally, such as assuming that the neighbor doesn't like you because she asked you to get your dog off her lawn.

Magnification/minimization. Incorrectly evaluating the significance of an event; thinking it is the worst thing that could ever happen to you if you got picked up for speeding, or thinking that it is no big deal to get a ticket for driving too fast.

These cognitive distortions manifest themselves in various ways. For instance, problems are further compounded when young people take things out of context as a result of their tunnel vision or selective abstraction. Failing to see all sides of the issue can often result in inappropriate emotional upset, as in the case of a teenager who was furious at his coach for not letting him play in the football game, ignoring the reality that he had skipped practice the day before. Or, consider the 8-year-old who engages in personalization and worries that his teacher doesn't like him because she failed to call on him in class, or the self-conscious 13-year-old whose abstract thinking skills are limited who overgeneralizes and awfulizes about having to give a speech in front of a class. Instead of realizing that others probably feel much the same way—that everyone will not be staring at the barely noticeable pimple on her nose and that she can tolerate this embarrassment for a short time—she may see only one option: skipping class to avoid the situation. Not being able to think of alternative ways to deal with the issue or anticipating the consequences of her actions can have serious repercussions.

To illustrate further, consider how young people respond to moving, a situational factor that affects the lives of many children. Clients' level of emotional maturity, coupled with their ability to think rationally, will have a significant bearing on their level of distress. Twelve-year-old Kendra told her counselor that although she was not happy to be moving, it could be worse—she could be moving halfway across the country instead of only two hours away. Contrast this reaction by a logical thinker to that of a same-age classmate, who stated that he couldn't think of anything worse than moving because he would have to leave all his friends and he would never make new ones, he would hate his new school, he wouldn't be good enough to be on the basketball team, and he knew he could never be happy in this new town. In this case, his awfulizing and overgeneralizing resulted in depression. His failure to realize that his situation, although difficult, could definitely be worse had a negative impact on how he responded to this circumstance.

Having established that both their level of development and their irrational beliefs can influence how young people respond to typical developmental problems that they all experience in some form (as well as to more serious situational problems that far too many young people are subject to and have little control over), let's refer once again to the model on page 14. Around the outer edge of the last circle (6) are self-defeating behaviors such as self-mutilation, suicide, eating disorders, and substance abuse.

Consider the fact that irrational thinking and the inability to put things in perspective make problems—be they typical or more serious—seem insurmountable. If adolescents in particular, but children as well, misconstrue issues and make inaccurate assumptions, lack frustration tolerance, overgeneralize, catastrophize, personalize, fail to generate alternatives, and lack good coping mechanisms, they may resort to the behaviors listed around the outer circle as a way to escape or deal with their pain. The likelihood of this occurring seems stronger when they have both typical and situational factors to contend with. Of significant concern is that, once youngsters engage in these self-defeating behaviors, they often face other serious consequences that make it far more difficult, if not impossible, to remedy the problem. The following example illustrates this point:

> Jill, a high school junior, had been involved in a serious relationship with her boyfriend for more than a year. Her parents did not approve of Matt because they perceived him as emotionally unstable and were quite certain that he was a heavy pot smoker. They did whatever they could to discourage their daughter from seeing him, and the arguments they had were frequent and intense. Jill felt trapped because on one hand, she could see her parents' point, but on the other hand, she thought she loved Matt and could not consider the thought of breaking up with him; he had already threatened suicide when the topic had been raised. Jill also felt pressured to become sexually involved with Matt, which only added to her stress. In the midst of this, her grandmother became seriously ill.
>
> Because Jill felt much closer to her than she did to her mother, she became anxious and depressed. Her grades deteriorated, and that upset her parents. She dropped out of several activities and started drinking to forget about her worries. One night, after she had had too much to drink, she and her friends got picked up and charged with alcohol possession and intoxication. As a result, her infuriated parents grounded her for a month, during which time her grandmother died.
>
> After her grandmother's death, Jill became even more depressed. She felt that she had no support; she could not spend time with her friends because she was still grounded. She worried incessantly about her boyfriend's faithfulness because of how upset he was about not

being able to see her. As she sat alone in her room, waiting for Matt's phone calls, which seldom came, she felt worthless and rejected because she assumed he was out with another girl. All of this became too much for Jill, and she took an overdose of pills to "forget the pain." Fortunately for Jill, her mother found her and got her to the hospital before it was too late.

This case study underscores the potentially dangerous interaction of situational problems when coupled with irrational thinking and a lack of emotional and cognitive maturity. When Jill started counseling after her suicide attempt and discussed the events of the previous several months with her counselor, she described herself as feeling trapped and overwhelmed. She said she felt hopeless and thought that things would never get better. The fact that there were more effective ways to deal with this crisis than to attempt suicide had not occurred to her. She hadn't considered that she could eventually work through her grief over her grandmother's death and not feel so terrible, or that even if Matt rejected her and started dating someone else, she was not worthless and could get through it. It had not crossed her mind that her poor grades and her shaky relationship with her parents were problems that would eventually go away. And because, as a typical adolescent whose sense of time is in the "here and now," when she was weighted down with problems that seemed impossible to overcome, she reacted impulsively to stop the pain.

Understanding the characteristics of child and adolescent development and how irrational thinking and developmental levels affect so many aspects of young lives is critical in both assessment and treatment.

THE THERAPEUTIC RELATIONSHIP

Over the years, there has been considerable discussion among REBT practitioners regarding the nature of the therapeutic relationship. Ellis and Dryden (1997) recommended that therapists adopt an active-directive style with most clients, and they maintained that showing clients considerable warmth and caring may be detrimental because it can unintentionally reinforce their strong need for love and approval. Although Ellis strongly preferred the active-directive style, Dryden, DiGiuseppe, and Neenan (2003) encouraged counselors to be flexible and modify their approach to fit the client. Dryden (2002a, 2002b) stressed the importance of employing many different and equally effective therapeutic styles, noting that it is a misconception that being active and directive is incompatible with developing rapport. Dryden and Ellis (2001) emphasized that it is possible to vary the style and adhere to the theoretical principles at the same time.

Although there may be some difference of opinion concerning the nature of the relationship in the counseling of adults, REBT practitioners who work with younger clients definitely agree that it is essential to establish a good relationship with children and adolescents if counseling is to be optimally effective (Vernon, 2009a, 2009b; Young, 2006). According to Bernard, Ellis, and Terjesen (2006), "It has always been recognized by child-oriented and adolescent-oriented REBT practitioners that a warm, supportive, empathic relationship with young people is a necessary condition for the full benefits of REBT interventions to be realized" (p. 27). These professionals would also argue that being forceful is not appropriate when working with most young clients and that a slower pace and a gentler approach are essential.

Because children and adolescents usually are referred for counseling by their parents or teachers, their degree of resistance or reluctance may range on a continuum from extremely resistant and unwilling—with overt hostility and refusal to cooperate—to acceptance and compliance. Whatever the case may be, it is important to acknowledge what the children perceive, perhaps saying, "I sense that you don't want to be here, and that's all right. But because someone else thinks you have a problem, maybe I can help you deal with that." In the case of the child who is self-referred or willing to be in counseling, the counselor can reinforce this fact by remarking, "I understand that counseling was your idea; I appreciate that because it will make it easier for us to work together and find ways to help you deal with what is bothering you."

It is also a good idea to ascertain what young clients' understanding of counseling is in order to address any misconceptions. Young children may think they are going to a medical doctor, who will give them a shot; many adolescents may assume they are going to a "shrink," who is going to psychoanalyze them or tell them what they have to do. Explaining as succinctly as possible that you are here to help them resolve a problem or a situation that is disturbing to them or to others is important. Reassuring them that they are not crazy and that having a problem does not mean they are bad or ill-intentioned people also helps to alleviate some anxiety. It is often useful to explain to them that if they had a sore throat or a broken leg, they would go to a medical doctor for help, and when they have a social, emotional, or behavioral problem, they can get help from a counselor.

Some younger clients like to read what others their age have said about being in counseling, so sharing a few anonymously written testimonials from former clients often works well. If the parent reports that a child is exceptionally anxious or resistant, writing a short letter explaining who you are and what counseling entails has proven to be an effective way to help ease the child into counseling. Obviously, if the counseling occurs within the school setting, some of these issues will not exist because clients may be familiar with the counselor or at least feel comfortable with the school environment.

Regardless of where counseling takes place, many young clients are not sure what counseling is or why they need it. For these reasons, it is essential to address their preconceptions and reluctance in the first counseling session. In doing so, it is important to deliver explanations in an age-appropriate and nonpathologizing manner. For instance, you can explain that counseling is a safe place to explore thoughts and feelings and solve problems. The counselor should normalize the experience of problems of daily living in order to provide a sense of universality. Clearly stating that all individuals, including adults, have problems may provide an immediate sense of relief.

Because children's sense of time is more immediate, it is also important to let them know that this type of counseling will help them address the problem quickly and that you will teach them skills they can use to change their thoughts, feelings, and behaviors so they can get better in a relatively short amount of time. Suggest to them that you might be asking them to participate in some "experiments" between sessions that can provide them with additional ways to resolve problems. Using the term *experiments* is often better than using the traditional REBT term *homework*, because children and adolescents often assign a negative connotation to the latter, which they associate with schoolwork.

Following are additional ways of establishing a good therapeutic relationship with younger clients.

Learn about their interests and hobbies, things they enjoy, and what they think they are especially good at (Bernard et al., 2006). Also inquire about pets and family members. This information can be gathered in a variety of ways: by asking them to draw a picture or write a short story about one or more of these topics; by playing a game such as checkers and sharing something personal with each move; or by having them complete a name poem, in which they write each letter of their name down the side of the paper and write (or draw) a word or phrase describing themselves that begins with each letter:

R—Reads books about sports

A—Athletic

N—Nervous about taking tests

D—Drives with a permit

Y—Yells at the referee when something isn't fair

This information can then be used in several ways. For example, a young child shared during her first meeting with the counselor that she had a pet rabbit. In a subsequent counseling session, she expressed concern that her parents would think she was a bad girl because she accidentally wet the bed sometimes. Asking her whether she thought her rabbit was a bad rabbit if he ever went to the bathroom outside his cage was a concrete way to help this young girl see that her parents probably did not think she was a bad person if she wet the bed.

Knowing about interests and hobbies also helped a counselor working with a 16-year-old who thought he was a total failure because he had flunked math. Aware that Adam loved working on cars, the counselor asked him if he would think the car was a total piece of junk if it had a flat tire. "Of course not; the tire just needs fixing," Adam replied. "Then think of yourself as the car with the flat tire. You are not a failure; you just need to study harder in math," explained the counselor. This analogy seemed to be an effective way of getting the point across.

Take a nonjudgmental stance. Young clients generally will not disclose much if they think you are judging them. Therefore, even though you may not agree with them, you must nonetheless accept them unconditionally. Watch your body language and nonverbal behaviors so you don't gasp when a 14-year-old shares details about her recent sexual experience. At a later time, you may help the client look at the risks inherent in early sexual activity, but conveying disapproval, either verbally or nonverbally, will sabotage the counseling relationship. Adolescents in particular are sensitive about being judged. It can be helpful to explicitly state that "who you are is not what you do." For example, if they broke the law, they did something they should not have done, but that does not make them a bad person.

Be genuinely interested in their stories. It is too easy for adults to minimize children's problems, especially those of a typically developmental nature. To younger children, fighting with a best friend can be as upsetting as fighting with a spouse is to an adult; breaking up with a boyfriend can be as traumatic to an adolescent as a divorce is to a parent. It is important to remember that young clients may not have the ability to put their problems in perspective and therefore may overreact or act impulsively, responding in a way that can lead to significant negative consequences. For this reason, it is critical to listen carefully to their stories and see things from their perspective. Additionally, this nonjudgmental approach puts young clients in the position of being the expert on themselves, and you the expert in REBT, thereby creating a collaborative relationship. Doing so instills in them a sense of being respected and important. By being an active and interested listener, you will serve as a good role model and will be gathering important information that you will use later in problem resolution.

Whenever possible, normalize their issues and instill hope. Because of their developmental limitations, children and adolescents often do not understand why they think, feel, and act the way they do. Practitioners who understand what is typical for each age level often find themselves saying something like this: "You know, several other fourth graders I have seen have also been very worried about something bad happening to a parent, because at this age you are more aware of what can happen, but you sometimes don't understand all aspects of the situation. I think we can come up with some ideas about how to help you deal with this, and on this matter, you and I can discuss some things that have helped other kids your age." The only caution when using this approach is that you must be careful not to dismiss their problem with an offhand remark such as "Oh, that's nothing. All kids your age go through this."

Be honest with them about what you know about the issue. For example, you may know that Diana is no longer on the basketball team because her grades are too low, but there is a good chance that she won't share that news with you because she might be ashamed or embarrassed about it. Rather than trying to tease it out of her or wait for her to bring it up, you can introduce the issue in the following way: "Diana, I just learned that you aren't able to participate in basketball because of your grades. That must be very hard for you, and I assume you have lots of feelings about that. I can understand how hard this might be for you, and I would like to help you find a way to deal with it."

Explain the nature and limits of confidentiality, and discuss with clients how you will be communicating with their parents and teachers. Do not promise to hold in confidence things you will need to share later; by doing so, you are likely to destroy the therapeutic relationship. Explain to them that adults in their lives may be concerned about them and may be contacting you. Whenever possible, ask young clients whether there is anything they have shared with you that they do not want someone else to know. You may be surprised to learn that they put fewer limits on their sharing than you had imagined. In fact, they may appreciate your facilitating communication with adults on difficult issues. A 10-year-old recently asked me whether I could help her mom understand that girls her age like boys. "It's just a girl thing; I'm not going to do anything yucky with them like hold hands or anything, but I want her to know that girls just talk about boys. That's just the way we are," said Melissa. Of course, all clients aren't going to have requests of this nature, but asking them what you can share and being honest with them if you cannot honor their wishes because of your duty to warn, for example, puts the issues out in the open. Consulting with them about these matters can strengthen your client–counselor relationship.

Be genuine; be human. Young clients will respond to you better if you come across as a "real person." When working with this population, you may find yourself on the floor playing a therapeutic game with an 8-year-old, or you might spend the first few minutes of a session looking through a 14-year-old's yearbook or listening to a tape of her latest favorite song. This helpful tip does not mean that you should shed your professional role and become a friend to the child or adolescent, but it does indicate that by being more real, you have a better chance of establishing a good relationship.

Don't act like a parent! Even well-meaning parents may nag, over-control, and offer unsolicited advice at times. Adolescents in particular resent this intrusion. Your relationship with young clients should be more collaborative. Establish goals mutually, help them look at the consequences of their behavior, and zip your lip so you can refrain from saying, "I told you so" or giving them advice about what they should and shouldn't do. Your clients will be more likely to change if they initiate the process because they see a reason for doing it, not because they are being coerced. If you act like a parent, they will most likely put up greater resistance.

Be a salesperson. Just because you exist, don't expect that clients are going to want your services. Young clients may not have participated in counseling before; consequently, they have no idea what to expect. Parents, too, may feel ashamed because their child has a problem or is a problem for them. Selling clients on the idea of counseling can help in the rapport-building process. For example, you might say to 14-year-old Miguel that, because you have worked with other young adolescents who have had trouble completing their homework because it was boring and they had better things to do just like he did, you think you can help him, too. You can point out that if he gets his homework done, he can get his parents and teachers off his back. Be careful not to promise things you can't deliver, but keep in mind that many people think there are no advantages to counseling or that there is no need for them to get help for emotional problems. Selling them on the idea is often important. For clients who are particularly reluctant, contracting for a few sessions has proven to be a good way to initiate the process.

Be flexible and creative. Remember that it is not always easy for children and adolescents to pinpoint how they feel or describe what they are experiencing. If you are working with young clients who just will not talk, don't keep talking at them. Instead, shift gears. Play a game, read a story, engage in a role play, or invite them to write sentence completions.

Don't be afraid to self-disclose, but do so in a way that has therapeutic value. Young clients in particular are often curious about who you are. If you are playing a feelings game, share an appropriate experience related to that feeling. Or use yourself as an example: "I think I can understand why you are still so sad about your grandmother's death. I was also very close to my grandma, and it was a very sad time for me, too, when she died." Sharing in this way makes you human. Using common sense is important, however. Boasting to your adolescent clients about your teenage drinking escapades is obviously inappropriate. For one thing, it is easy for them to misinterpret this message as permission to drink; for another, it is a violation of the boundary that must exist between client and therapist.

Have patience and adjust your expectations for the counseling process. Sometimes the harder you push, the less you gain; this can be especially true when counseling adolescents. Although at times it may seem as if you are getting nowhere, in reality you are engaging in problem assessment throughout the rapport-building process. Accurate problem conceptualization contributes to more-effective intervention, which is the ultimate goal.

BUILDING RAPPORT

According to Walen, DiGiuseppe, and Dryden (1992), therapy actually begins with the first moment of contact with the client and develops as you establish a therapeutic alliance, initiate the assessment process, agree on the problem area, and establish treatment goals and strategies. They noted that it is important to delineate what clients can expect from therapy and what you expect from them; an understanding of these expectations can help ease clients' anxiety. This strategy imposes structure and ensures predictability, both of which are especially critical when working with young clients. The explanation needs to be simple: "I think we can work together to figure out ways to deal with what is bothering you. If you are open with me and will agree to try out the ideas we come up with, we should be able to make progress." Walen and her colleagues also emphasized that, although the goal of the therapeutic relationship is not friendship, demonstrating professional competence, credibility, respect, and commitment to helping the client are essential in building the therapeutic alliance. Young (2006) stressed the importance of warmth, empathy, and nonjudgmental regard.

Many REBT therapists believe that the best way to establish rapport is to engage in the therapeutic process—to begin working immediately on the client's problem. Although it is true that you can help clients believe in the process if they begin to feel better after the first session, it is important to remember that this quick approach may not work with younger clients, especially elementary-aged children. With this younger clientele, it is often necessary to ease into the process more gradually. The following activities have been helpful in breaking the ice with children and adolescents.

Strategies for Building Rapport with Children (Ages 5 to 10)

Because play is the language of a child, engaging younger clients in simple games or activities can be a good way to establish rapport. As you use these get-acquainted activities, it is important to interact with the client, ask extending questions to acquire more information, and be patient if the child chooses not to share. Although it may suffice to use only one of the activities during the first session, you may need to use more of them in subsequent sessions. Use your clinical judgment to determine how comfortable the child seems and to get a sense of how open she will be once you start working on the issues that prompted the call for counseling. Though the information gleaned from these activities may contribute to the assessment process, the actual intent is for the questions to be relatively nonthreatening and for you to build trust through mutual self-disclosure in a game format, which is a comfortable medium for young clients. Several examples of rapport-building activities for children follow.

Pick-Up Straws

This simple strategy involves putting the following unfinished sentences (written on tagboard and cut into very narrow strips) in plastic straws. Then have the client hold all the straws and randomly let them fall on a table. Next, you and the client take turns trying to pick up a straw without touching the others. If you are successful in doing so, take the slip out of the straw and finish the sentence. If one of you moves a straw other than the one you are attempting to pick up, you forfeit the turn.

Unfinished sentences

The best thing about being my age is . . .

The funniest thing I have ever seen is . . .

The best part about living where I live is . . .

The worst part of going to school is . . .

The best part about going to school is . . .

My favorite kinds of books are . . .

I don't like to . . .

I get frustrated when . . .

I don't think it is fair that . . .

I want my friends to . . .

I don't think friends should . . .

I like it when my parents . . .

I don't like it when my parents . . .

Teachers are . . .

I feel bad when . . .

Can You Do It?

For this get-acquainted activity, take three vegetable cans and label them as follows: *Can Do, Can't Do, Sort of Can Do.* Write the following tasks (which can be adapted depending on the age of the client) on individual index cards and place them in a pile. Then invite the client to select a card, decide if it is something he can do, can't do, or sort of can do, and read it out loud as he places it in the appropriate can.

Tasks

Count to 100

Count to 25

Read by myself

Dive off a diving board

Jump rope

Play soccer

Bake a cake

Sing a solo

Play the piano

Write in cursive

Recite the alphabet backward

Write left-handed

Speak another language

Take care of a younger brother or sister

Fix lunch for my family

Who Are You?

This is a simple activity that takes no more than 5 or 10 minutes. You begin the exchange by explaining to the client that this is a short activity designed to help the two of you become better acquainted. Indicate that you will take turns asking each other, "Who are you?" The person who is asked this question responds with something he is willing to disclose and in turn asks, "Who are you?" The other person responds and asks, "Who are you?" With younger children, it is often a good idea if the child asks the first question so that you can model a response. In this way, you can also establish some categories that you think will provide you with some good information about the client. This procedure can go back and forth for several rounds and can be repeated in subsequent sessions if needed. The following is a brief example of the activity:

Client: Who are you?

Counselor: I am a dog lover; I have two dogs. Who are you?

Client: I have a kitten named Fluffy. Who are you?

Counselor: I am someone who likes to read. Who are you?

Client: I'm someone who likes to roller blade. Who are you?

Button, Button

This activity can be completed in 10 to 15 minutes and works especially well with children who are 8 or younger. For this activity, you will need two buttons, one for the client and one for yourself, and some index cards with questions written on them. When it is your turn, you hide the button behind your back in one of your hands. The client tries to guess which hand the button is in, and, if correct, draws an index card and asks you the question written on the card (be prepared to read for the child). If the child's guess is incorrect, it is her turn to hide the button and your turn to guess and (if correct), draw a card to read to the client for her response. The following are examples of questions that might be asked:

What is your favorite place?

What do you like to do most on Saturdays?

What is your favorite television show or video game?

If you ever feel scared, what do you do?

If I had a magic wand and you could make a wish, what would you wish for?

What is something you don't like to do?

What do you like or not like about your friends?

If you ever feel mad, what helps you get over your mad feelings?

Flip the Coin

This activity can be handled in several ways. The easiest method is for you and the client to pick either heads or tails, take turns flipping a coin, and share something personal when it turns up heads on your flip (if you picked heads). Past experience indicates that this activity is often not structured enough for young clients. If this proves to be the case, you can have questions written on index cards and pick one when it turns up heads on your flip. Questions on topics such as the following can be geared both to younger and to older children.

For younger children

A favorite toy or game

A favorite and least favorite food

A happy memory

Something that makes you laugh

Something that scares you or makes you cry

For older children

Something you do or do not like about school

Something you have trouble with

One of your best memories

Something you think you do well

Something you feel sad about

People, Places, and Things

For this activity, take a piece of tagboard and cut out a circle, dividing it into three segments labeled *People, Places,* and *Things.* Using a tagboard arrow, make a spinner and fasten it to the center of the circle with a brass fastener so it will move. Explain the activity as follows:

Counselor: In order for us to get to know each other better, I'd like to have the two of us play this game for a few minutes. Are you willing?

Client: Sure!

Counselor: I'll start and spin. Oh, the spinner landed on *Places,* so I'm going to share one of my favorite places with you. I love to go to my cabin, which is on a lake. Now it's your turn.

Client: *(Spins.)* Mine landed on *Things.*

Counselor: What is one of your favorite things?

Client: I have lots of them, but I guess my favorite is my bike.

Counselor: Do you usually ride bikes alone or with someone else?

Client: Sometimes I go with my brother or my mom, but usually I go with my friend.

The game proceeds in this manner for a few minutes, with the counselor asking extended questions, when appropriate, to learn more about the client.

What's Your Bag?

For this activity, you will need two lunch-size paper bags, scissors, and several magazines. You and the client will each spend several minutes cutting out pictures of interests; hobbies; and favorite foods, clothes, cars, pets, colors, or places, for example. Next, each of you will place the pictures you selected in a separate bag, then take turns drawing them out of the bags and sharing them with each other.

It's Me!

This activity uses a game board and game cards. You may use the game board in the appendix or construct your own. Using three different colors of dot stickers, randomly place one colored dot on each space on the game board. Next apply twelve dot stickers, four of each color, to the same number of tagboard or index cards. On the other side of each card, write a question such as the following:

What do you like best about being your age?

What do you like least about being your age?

What do you think you would like to do when you are grown up?

What is your easiest subject in school?

What is your hardest subject in school?

How do you feel when you make a mistake?

How do you feel if you don't do well on a test?

What kinds of things do you and your friends argue about?

If you have a fight with a friend, what do you do to work out the problem?

If someone calls you a name, how do you react?

If you are not getting along with a parent or a brother or a sister, what do you do?

What is something that really upsets you or scares you? What do you do to feel less upset or scared?

To play the game, place the index cards, which have the colored dot stickers affixed to them, in separate piles beside the board. Give the client a coin and a colored button or marker and take the same for yourself. Explain that the two of you will take turns flipping the coin, moving a marker along the dots (a flip to heads is a one-dot move, to tails is a two-dot move), drawing a card from the pile that corresponds with the color of the dot you land on, and responding to the question on the card.

Alphabet Soup

For this simple activity, you will need a set of alphabet letters that you can buy or make out of tagboard. Put the letters in a box or a hat. You and the client then take turns drawing a letter of the alphabet and sharing something that applies to you or your family. For example, 9-year-old Juanito drew the letter *M* and stated that math was his favorite subject.

Fish for Feelings

This is a good game to use with younger children because it not only helps them build a feeling vocabulary that facilitates self-disclosure during the counseling sessions, but it also gives you more insight into the troublesome feelings that may have prompted the need for counseling. For this simple game, you will need to make a set of tagboard fish labeled with feeling words such as *happy, scared, mad, sad, worried,* or *excited.* Each fish should have a hole in its nose. You will also need a fishing pole (a short stick with a string attached to the end and a paper clip attached to the string). Place the fish on the floor. Take turns trying to snag a fish. Once you do, read the word on the fish and describe a situation in which you felt that way. By participating with the child, you can model self-disclosure, which makes it easier for the child to respond.

Strategies for Building Rapport with Adolescents (Ages 11 to 18)

Getting acquainted with adolescents may often be more difficult than it is with younger children. Although adolescents are better able to describe their problems, they also may be more defensive and reluctant to share them with you. It is important to keep in mind that adolescents are naturally self-conscious and vulnerable—and may feel even more so by merely entering a counselor's office and being asked to disclose things they may feel confused or uncomfortable about. It is sometimes helpful for adolescents (as it is for children) to have something to fiddle with during the session. Clay, stress balls, Slinkys, or other manipulatives may help put them at ease.

It is essential that you be empathic with those in this age group and imagine how you would feel sharing personal thoughts and feelings with an adult who may be a total stranger. A good idea is to address this concern by first asking the referring parent or teacher how the adolescent feels about coming to therapy. If the adult concedes that the adolescent does not want to see you, don't take offense. Instead, simply proceed with caution. Acknowledge to the client that you can understand why he might not want to be there, but reassure him that you are there to help him. Sometimes it may be necessary to contract for at least three sessions; then, if the adolescent still has a strong aversion to coming, you can reevaluate the situation. If you are a good salesperson and can begin to connect with your client, he will likely be more amenable to counseling by the third session and grudgingly agree to more therapy. If you cannot sell him on the idea, perhaps it will be necessary to confer with his parents and discuss whether he may be more open to counseling sometime in the future. Like some adolescents, he may need to hit rock bottom before he agrees to seek help. The downside to this scenario is that, in the meantime, he may act impulsively and engage in self-defeating behaviors that could have long-lasting ramifications. Therefore, you need to do your best in the first few sessions to convince him to continue in counseling.

When working with this age group, it is imperative that you be patient. Many adolescents may test you with their silence, seeing how long you can wait them out. A classic line you are likely to hear is, "I have to be here, but I don't have to talk." In response, you can acknowledge that, although that may be the case, it is also true that they probably won't have to come for as many sessions if they *do* start talking.

Another approach you can use is to permit them to remain silent. You can explain that, although you don't prefer this, you cannot force them to participate. You should casually suggest that it might be more beneficial to them in the long run if they did involve themselves in the process, because that could shorten the number of times they would have to come. By offering them the choice to remain silent, you will, in all likelihood, allow these adolescent clients to feel empowered and free to engage in counseling on their own terms.

Adolescents may also throw every obscenity in the book at you, anxious to see your reaction, be it verbal or nonverbal. Don't take the bait. Instead, let them finish their tirade and see what happens. In most cases, these clients will eventually back off. Even if you are offended by their language, the worst thing you can do is to react negatively, because that is exactly what they want. Once they see that they are not going to ruffle your feathers, you can request that they tone it down if you think your silence is condoning something offensive.

It is also important, when working with this age group, to maintain a sense of humor and perspective and not let them push your buttons. It may also be appropriate to use some humor with them, because they are better able, owing to their abstract thinking skills, to understand the intent. Without making fun of your clients, you can use exaggeration or humor to make a point or to help them see their situation in a different light. For example, a teenager was talking about how she threw fits to force her mother into giving in and letting her go to a dance. With a smile on her face, the counselor replied, "So, your 2-year-old temper tantrums worked rather well! Are there times when they don't, or when you feel rather foolish throwing a fit?"

Remember that adolescents will also try their best to engage you in a battle of wills, or they may test the degree to which you can be nonjudgmental by throwing out blatant statements or opinions. If you can refrain from overreacting, you can usually take the wind out of their sails, and they will ultimately be more amenable to counseling.

The following specific rapport-building ideas and activities may be useful with adolescent clients.

Music Collage

Because most teens enjoy music of some sort, an effective way to get to know them is to ask them to burn favorite songs onto a CD and as the two of you listen to it, invite the client to tell you what these songs mean to her.

Walk the Line

Younger adolescents may engage in this activity. First, put a strip of masking tape on the floor, designating one end as "like me" and the other end as "not like me." Invite the client to move to one end or the other as you read a list of characteristics such as the following:

Characteristics

More of a saver than a spender

Prefers sports over music or drama

Likes doing homework

Favorite subject is math

Is more of a leader than a follower

More of a loner than a joiner

Has a positive self-concept

Would rather spend time with family than with friends

Persists even when things are hard or frustrating

Thinks school is cool

Very concerned about world peace

Tries to be perfect at everything

Imagine Me As . . .

Young teens find this nonthreatening intervention intriguing, and it is a good way for you to learn more about them. Invite them to think of themselves in the following categories and either share this verbally or in writing. For example, "Imagine me as a TV program; what would I be?" The advantage of verbal sharing is that you can probe further and learn more about them or self-disclose, which may facilitate their openness.

Imagine Me topics

Imagine me as a restaurant . . . what would I be?

Imagine me as a country . . . what would I be?

Imagine me as a great athlete . . . who would I be?

Imagine me as a great musician . . . who would I be?

Imagine me as an animal . . . what would I be?

Imagine me as a school subject . . . what would I be?

Imagine me as a famous actor or actress . . . who would I be?

Imagine me as a dessert . . . what would I be?

Imagine me as a color . . . what would I be?

Imagine me as a sport . . . what would I be?

Imagine me as a hobby . . . what would I be?

Imagine me as a cause . . . what would I be?

Games

Depending on a client's developmental level, it is sometimes advantageous to play checkers or a card game, during which you engage in casual conversation that can help you get to know him better. Experience indicates that it is often better to induce casual conversation than to use a game that is more specifically geared to personal self-disclosure, because adolescents tend to resist activities of this nature. If you are initially low key, you can work into activities that are more self-revealing. For example, you can put feeling words or self-disclosing questions on checkerboard spaces and take turns responding as you and the client land on different spaces. Another game you can play is These Are a Few of My Favorite Things, in which you and the client write examples of favorite things (e.g., activities, hobbies, possessions, people, movies, music) on separate index cards. You then scatter the cards face down on the table and take turns flipping over a card, elaborating on the significance of the favorite thing as each of you turns over the cards. (These activities are generally more appropriate for younger adolescents.)

Read About It

Inviting teens to read about what their peers have experienced is another excellent way to help them see that they are not alone; consequently, they might be more open about sharing their problems. A 14-year-old who had been referred by her school counselor because she thought the student was depressed was in my office. Attempts to get her to share her concerns had been in vain. I suggested that it might be helpful if she would be willing to read about another teen struggling with shifting moods, and she agreed to read the following story (Vernon, 1998b, p. 187):

Like a Yo-Yo

I am 14 years old and in eighth grade. Since the end of last year, I have been feeling strange. Sometimes I am really happy, and I can joke around and laugh with my friends. Then I change, and I can't figure out why. I might get real angry or just depressed. Sometimes it doesn't even have anything to do with what's been going on. Like yesterday. I was walking down the hall with one of my friends, and all of a sudden I just went off on him. He hadn't even said anything, but I just got mad. When I'm like that I yell at my friends for no reason, and then they get mad at me. It happens with my parents, too. Sometimes I just want to be left alone, but they keep asking me what's wrong, and I just blow up. Afterward I feel really guilty that I treated them like that, and I don't even understand why.

Today I was walking home with a bunch of kids. We were just goofing off and having fun. I felt so good. Then later I was hanging out in my room and I just started to get depressed. Nothing had happened; my feelings just changed. I hate it, and I don't understand why this happens.

I know some of my friends feel like this, too, because some days they just go off for no reason. But, if I'm in a bad mood, I get ticked off at them, and then we get into big fights, so that creates more problems. It's like none of us knows what to do to stop this from happening.

I just wish I could feel the same way for longer than a few hours or a day. Sometimes I wake up and I know it's going to be a good day, but then it can change. Other days I wake up and I'm already in a super bad mood, and then things just get worse for a while.

When my client finished reading this, she immediately said that she felt exactly the same way and was relieved to know that she was not the only one who felt like this. She then proceeded to talk at length about what she was experiencing.

Artifacts

Other good ways to build trust include asking clients to bring in year-books, pictures, poems, artwork, or hobbies. Be genuine in showing interest in what they share with you, and don't suggest this activity unless you *can* be genuine. Not only can this interaction be a good way to break the ice with your clients, it may also be an excellent way to gain insight into their world.

Something You Can't Tell by Looking at Me

This simple strategy frequently yields some useful information. Indicate to clients that we often make assumptions about others, but there are many things that others can't tell just by looking at us. Volunteer to share an example or two to model the process: "Just by looking at me, you don't know that I like to sleep late" or "Just by looking at me, you don't know that I don't like comedy movies." Invite clients to do the same, then share back and forth for several minutes.

Inner–Outer Me

This activity can be especially effective with nonverbal adolescents who are reluctant to self-disclose. You will need an envelope, a pencil, and several strips of paper.

Explain that who we are on the outside can be very different from who we are on the inside, and that the purpose of this activity is for you to learn as much about your clients as they are willing to share. Invite them to write on the outside of the envelope words or phrases that describe how they appear to others. Then ask them to write on the strips of paper words or phrases they think describe themselves but that they do not readily share with others, and put these on the inside of the envelope. (Be sure to inform clients that they won't have to share these descriptions unless they choose to do so.)

One very angry adolescent wrote the following on the outside of her envelope: "Can be mean and snotty, smart, hateful, forceful, strong, loud." On the inside she wrote, "vulnerable, hurt, low self-esteem, and loner." Obviously, the discrepancy between the two lists generated good discussion and provided information for goal setting and therapeutic interventions.

Writing

Oftentimes it is less threatening for adolescents to write about what is bothering them than to share it verbally. Writing can take the form of a short paragraph; a letter to someone they think is "causing" their problem; a poem; or a "Dear Counselor" letter, in which they write to the counselor about their problems.

Sharing Information About Development

Most adolescents don't understand why they feel the way they do, so sharing information about typical adolescent development can be useful. For example, noting that it is normal for teenagers to feel confused, overwhelmed, angry, or moody often brings relief and can facilitate their self-disclosure. Be accurate and specific about what you share. If you are discussing their emotions, explain in simple terms why teenagers tend to be moody: their hormones are fluctuating and this turbulence results in a chemical imbalance that is usually resolved once they are past puberty. Or help them understand that, because they are still in various stages of developing more complex thinking skills, it is common for them to misconstrue things or make assumptions, some of which can have negative effects on their ability to solve problems. Indicate that, for these reasons, it is important for them to consciously consider all sides of an issue.

Experience suggests that clients are often very interested in their own development and tend to ask lots of questions. *Assessment and Intervention with Children and Adolescents: Developmental and Multicultural Approaches* (Vernon & Clemente, 2005) is one good resource for information on this topic.

How long it takes to build rapport with a client is not something you can easily predict. With some clients, you just click; with others, you don't. Sometimes it takes a long time to develop a trusting relationship. It is unrealistic to expect that you will like every client or that every client will like you—which certainly is not the goal of counseling, anyway. How you connect with children and adolescents, though, can have a major impact on how effectively goals can be accomplished. If you have good rapport with your young clients, they are generally less resistant or reluctant to come to counseling and more motivated to work on their problems.

ESTABLISHING GOALS

Most REBT therapists would agree that you should attempt to establish goals with your client within the first few sessions. With children and adolescents, this objective is sometimes more difficult to achieve or simply different than it is with adult clients—and for several reasons. First, it is not uncommon to hear young clients say they do not know why they are there, and that makes goal setting more complicated. Obviously, because of what their parents or teachers have shared with you, you have some idea why they are there; however, even though you may have an idea of a goal, the client might not see it that way.

Second, goal setting may be an alien concept to many young clients. They may be somewhat familiar with the term if it is used in school, but it may not be a household word. Therefore, you may have to do some educating about what goals are and why it is important to set them. You may even find yourself using simpler language, especially with younger children. For example, you might say to 7-year-old Tyler, "You and I talked today about how hard it is for you to keep your fists to yourself when you get angry at Tyronne. Should we try to think of some things you can do keep those fists from flying?"

Third, remember that children's sense of time is more immediate than that of adults and that you will want to set more short-term goals so that clients see that something is being accomplished.

Finally, keep in mind that, whereas setting unrealistic goals is discouraging for adults, it is even more so for children, whose thinking is still concrete. They tend to give up more quickly because they think they will never achieve the goal if they were unable to succeed the first time. This pessimism is exemplified by youngsters who are failing in school. If their goal is to pass all their classes, they find it easy to conclude that they will never be able to accomplish this goal and thus decide not to try at all. A more reasonable goal for these youngsters would be to pass at least one class each semester.

The goal-setting process should involve a partnership that encourages success. This success occurs much more readily if a good working relationship has been established, as this short case example conversation with a 17-year-old illustrates.

Counselor: Martha, in today's session we talked about your anger at your friends because they don't always include you in their activities. I'm wondering what you see as your goal for these counseling sessions.

Client: I don't know. I guess find a way to make them be better friends.

Counselor: That would be nice, but I'm not too sure exactly how to do that. How much control do you think you have over them?

Client: Probably none.

Counselor: I'm afraid you're right. But if you can't change them, is there something we could work on to help you?

Client: Not really—I can't think of anything if I can't get them to change.

Counselor: Let's look at it this way: When they don't include you, how do you feel and what do you do?

Client: Well, when I find out that they did stuff and didn't ask me, I usually get mad and yell at them. Sometimes I start rumors about them.

Counselor: And how does this work for you? Do they start including you more?

Client: No—it just makes them mad, and then they go off and do their own thing and leave me out again.

Counselor: So, it sounds like what you are doing now isn't helping with this friendship issue. Is this something you would like to work on?

Client: Yeah, I guess that makes sense.

Counselor: I certainly can't promise that if you change the way you react that your friends will change, but at least we can work on other ways for you to respond. With that in mind, can you think of a specific goal?

Client: I guess I need to stop yelling, but I don't know how.

Counselor: That's a good specific example. You say you don't know how . . . but are there times when you have been mad or hurt but haven't yelled?

Client: Yeah, a few.

Counselor: And what stopped you from yelling then?

Client: I don't know. Maybe I just realized that it wouldn't do me any good, so I didn't yell.

Counselor: So it sounds like stopping to think about how well yelling would work for you might be something you could try in order to achieve your goal. Is that something you would like to do?

Client: Yeah, I'll see how it goes. It won't be easy, but I'll try.

Counselor: I'll be anxious to hear how it works.

CHAPTER 2

Basic Principles of Rational Emotive Behavior Therapy

Albert Ellis, who lived to age 93, is considered the grandfather of cognitive-behavioral therapy and founder of rational emotive behavior therapy. Ellis introduced rational emotive therapy (RET) in 1955, distinguishing it as the first cognitive-behavioral therapy in clinical practice (Ellis, 1957). He later changed the name to rational emotive behavior therapy (REBT) because it more accurately describes the multidimensional aspect of the theory (Ellis, 2001a). For decades it has been and continues to be practiced throughout the world both with adults and children. In its over half a century of existence, REBT has been applied successfully to individual, group, marital, and family therapy (Ellis, 2001a), as well as to a wide array of problems such as fears and phobias, anger, depression, underachievement, lack of motivation, test anxiety, interpersonal relationship issues, low self-esteem, anxiety, impulsivity, cheating, aggression, and job performance (Ellis & Bernard, 2006; Ellis & Wilde, 2002; Vernon, 2009a). REBT is a well-established form of therapy that has been used in educational, industrial, and commercial settings and also in hospital and mental health facilities (Ellis & Dryden, 1997).

Moreover, REBT is a multidimensional form of therapy that enables practitioners to use many kinds of cognitive, emotive, behavioral, and interpersonal techniques to facilitate the problem-solving process (Ellis, 2001a). One of the unique features that distinguishes it from many other forms of therapy is its emphasis on problem prevention (Ellis, 2000, 2001a; Vernon, 2007b). REBT is designed as a self-help, educative therapy through which clients learn rational principles that will help them deal with present, as well as future, problems (Dryden & Ellis, 2001; Vernon, 2009b). Teaching people how to *get* better rather than simply *feel* better is a primary goal of REBT practitioners (Broder, 2001).

REBT is based on the notion that how we think determines how we feel and behave. Practitioners can empower clients to deal with a wide array of problematic situations by helping them learn to identify and challenge the irrational thinking patterns that create their emotional disturbance (Dryden & Ellis, 2001; Dryden, DiGiuseppe, & Neenan, 2003). In developing this theory, Ellis relied on teachings from philosophers such as Epictetus, who stated that "people are disturbed not by things, but by the views which they take of them" (Ellis, 1994, p. 64). Accordingly, Ellis (2001a) noted that disturbance is largely a function of our perceptions and evaluations. He maintained that humans have a biological tendency to think dysfunctionally and irrationally and that virtually all people exhibit major irrationalities (Dryden et al., 2003). Despite having given up some irrational ideas, even intelligent humans often adopt new ones or fall back into self-defeating habits, according to Ellis. However, human beings have the ability to see how they disturb themselves and, consequently, how to change their thinking (Ellis, 2001b). With knowledge and practice, they can overcome their dysfunctional thinking and behave in less self-defeating ways.

Ellis developed the ABC conceptual model to illustrate the theoretical concepts and the process of change (Dryden & Ellis, 2001; Ellis, 2001a; Ellis & MacLaren, 1998). In essence, the nature of emotional disturbance can be explained by recognizing that, as people attempt to fulfill their goals, they often encounter an *activating event* (A) that either blocks them from achieving their goal or helps them achieve it. Activating events may be either positive or negative; they may be past, present, or future oriented; they may refer to real or perceived events; and they may be caused by a person's own thoughts or feelings. In general, an A can be anything that a person judges or evaluates that elicits emotional and behavioral reactions. Because most activating events that bring individuals to therapy are adverse or unfortunate current events that have created some emotional or behavioral difficulties, most individuals enter therapy believing strongly that the activating events in their lives cause their emotional and behavioral reactions at C: A➤C.

According to REBT theory, people have thoughts or *beliefs* (B) about the activating events that influence their emotional and behavioral *consequences* (C). Although we commonly think that the events "cause" our reactions (that A➤C), this is usually not the case, unless the events are very powerful, such as a war or an environmental disaster. Hormonal or biochemical factors also may contribute to or cause the C (Ellis & Dryden, 1997). In reality, although activating events (A) may contribute to the consequence (C), beliefs (B) about the A actually cause the C and can be changed more readily than the activating event. Thus, instead of A→C, REBT theory maintains that the beliefs (B) about A→C. According to this theory, the A, the B, and the C are closely related and do not usually exist independent of one another; when you *think* negatively about an event or an experience, you usually *feel* bad and *act* dysfunctionally. Ellis (2001a) further noted that the B's not only include beliefs but also include aspects of the emotional and behavioral system.

This basic tenet of REBT theory may be difficult for individuals to grasp initially because we are so accustomed to linking emotional distress to upsetting events. However, once people understand that how one thinks affects how one feels, it will ultimately empower them because it gives them a method to gain self-control when faced with adverse events.

Take the case of an adolescent who interviewed for a job and was not offered the position (A): The fact that she didn't get the job did not *cause* her to feel angry; rather, her belief (B) that she should have gotten it and that it was unfair that they offered it to someone else triggered her anger. On the other hand, one of her classmates who interviewed for the same job and didn't get it was only disappointed. Although the classmate thought she had good qualifications and had hoped she would be selected, she recognized that employers have the right to hire the person who best meets their criteria. A third classmate was overjoyed when she was not selected because she did not want the job; her parents had insisted she apply for it, and the fact that she didn't get the job meant that she could spend more time with her friends. As this example illustrates, the same event resulted in three different emotional consequences (C) because of differences in thinking (B).

Rational and Irrational Beliefs

The beliefs that people hold may be rational and eventually lead to self-enhancing or self-helping behaviors, or they may be irrational and subsequently result in self-defeating behaviors. Irrational beliefs ultimately sabotage a person's goals and emanate from three basic "musts" that include the following demands (Dryden et al., 2003).

Demands about self: Thinking that one must be perfect and successful at important performances and relationships. The notion of doing well and being approved of by significant others can result in self-downing, which may lead to anxiety, depression, shame, and guilt.

Demands about others: Thinking that other people absolutely must always treat us well and considerately, and, if they don't, they are damnable and deserve to be punished. These beliefs are most commonly associated with anger, aggression, or passive-aggressiveness.

Demands about the world/life conditions: Thinking that conditions under which one lives absolutely must be comfortable, pleasurable, and rewarding—or else things are awful and unbearable. These beliefs are associated with self-pity, hurt, and lack of self-discipline.

These three basic irrational beliefs share four key elements: demanding, awfulizing, low frustration tolerance, and global rating of self or others. Irrational beliefs are rigid, inconsistent with reality, illogical, and detrimental (Dryden, 2003). They result in negative emotions (C) such as anxiety, depression, anger, resentment, self-pity, worthlessness, and rage. Withdrawal, avoidance, fighting, violence, procrastination, and addiction are typical behavioral manifestations. These irrational beliefs result in maladaptive behaviors and emotional upset, and therefore can interfere with a person's happiness.

In contrast, rational beliefs emanate from realistic preferences that typically result in moderate negative emotions and constructive behavior patterns. They are flexible and consistent with reality (Dryden, 2003). A rationally thinking student who studied hard for a test and got a grade lower than the A she was expecting would not feel elated about receiving the lower grade; that would be illogical. It would be understandable for her to feel disappointment—a moderate emotion that often is an outcome of rational thinking. Had she been thinking irrationally, she might have labeled herself a stupid person for getting an average grade and felt devastated, which would have been an overreaction to a disappointing outcome.

Dryden (2003) distinguished between healthy and unhealthy negative emotions: A person who thinks rationally about a negative event will experience a healthy negative emotion. A person who has an irrational belief about the same event will have an unhealthy negative emotion. For example, people who think rationally but have negative feelings feel concern rather than anxiety, sadness rather than depression, regret rather than guilt, disappointment rather than shame, and annoyance rather than anger.

To illustrate further, rationally thinking parents prefer to have their children perform well in school. But, if the children don't perform well, it doesn't mean that their children are complete failures and will never succeed in academic tasks or that the parents are doing a poor job of parenting. In contrast, irrationally thinking parents would magnify this problem by assuming that their children's poor academic performance was an indication of their failure as parents, that their children were deliberately performing horribly to spite them, and that their children will always be losers. Parents who think rationally would probably feel disappointed but not devastated, whereas the parents who think irrationally would most likely feel angry or depressed—reactions that could have a negative effect on the parent–child relationship.

Rational beliefs are logical and can be validly inferred from earlier premises. For instance, a young client says he wants to get an A in math and that studying for tests and doing the homework will help him achieve his goal. His rational conclusion is that he very much wants to get an A, and this conclusion is logical. Irrational beliefs, on the other hand, are illogical and are not validly inferred. In this example, the fact that the client wants to get an A and believes that studying for tests and doing homework will help him get the A does not validate the conclusion that he absolutely must get the A and that the teacher cannot give him anything except an A.

Disputation

Once these irrational beliefs and their emotional and behavioral consequences have been identified, the next step in the paradigm is to dispute the irrational beliefs (D). This step is accomplished by challenging or poking holes in the belief system, which can be achieved in a variety of ways: through modeling, Socratic questioning, didactic disputes (providing information), persuasion, humor, role reversal, rational emotive imagery, self-disclosure, and homework assignments (DiGiuseppe, 1999; Dryden, 2002b; Dryden et al., 2003; Ellis & MacLaren, 1998).

In the disputing process, a wide variety of cognitive, emotive, and behavioral techniques are employed. Asking how the irrational belief is helpful, how consistent it is with reality, and how logical it is can prove useful. Using the previous example of the parents who were angry and resentful that their children did not perform well in school, an REBT therapist would challenge their assumption that the children were doing poorly to spite them by asking for the evidence that this is true. The therapist might also have them make a list showing how their children's failure to perform well makes them bad parents. Asking them for examples of more horrible events could help them put this situation in perspective by showing them that this problem does not mean the end of the world for them and their children. If the parents are particularly resistant about giving up their irrational beliefs, the therapist could switch roles, playing the part of the irrational parent who is awfulizing about his or her children's performance and having the client assume the role of the therapist who is challenging the irrational beliefs. A homework assignment for the parents could involve writing a paragraph explaining how their children's failure doesn't mean they are failures as parents.

Effective New Philosophy, Feelings, and Behaviors

Because disputation is the heart and soul of this therapeutic process, it may take many attempts and several different forms of disputing before clients are ready to surrender their irrational beliefs and adopt a more rational perspective. Practitioners must remember that rational thinking does not imply that clients will feel wonderful about a negative event. Rather, as they give up their absolutistic thinking and consequent demand for perfection and comfort, clients will reduce the intensity of their negative behaviors and emotions, which is the goal of the therapeutic process. In doing so, they will be able to adopt a more realistic outlook based on rational beliefs. Ellis (2001b) described this as the E—effective new philosophy or effective rational beliefs. As clients begin to apply these rational beliefs to the problems of everyday living, they consequently experience less-intense negative feelings and behaviors (F), which results in a happier existence.

SPECIFIC APPLICATIONS TO CHILDREN AND ADOLESCENTS

Although the basic theoretical principles of REBT remain in effect with younger clients, there are considerable differences in the way the theory is applied to them and to adults. As noted in chapter 1, it is extremely important to establish a good therapeutic relationship with younger clients. It is also imperative that therapists working with youth be flexible and creative, taking into account the developmental considerations discussed in that chapter.

Furthermore, whereas Ellis and Dryden (1997) advocated the importance of helping clients change through the philosophic restructuring of irrational beliefs, this task may be more difficult or not always possible with younger clients because of their lower cognitive developmental level. In some cases, it may be impossible. For example, adults can arrive at the rational conclusion that it is sad, but not the end of the world, if their parents decide to divorce; they realize how futile it is to think that such a thing should never happen. However, because children are naturally more dependent on their parents for support and nurturance, it may take longer for them to understand that they can learn to adjust to a change so potentially devastating as a divorce, that they cannot control what their parents decide to do, and that life goes on.

Ellis and Dryden (1997) also noted that, in some instances, clients may make direct changes in the situation at A (the activating event). Although this is not the preferred way of practicing REBT, it is sometimes necessary with children and adolescents. For example, because of young people's concrete thinking, it can be difficult to dispute an 8-year-old's belief that a best friend should always be fair and loyal and never associate with other classmates. A practical solution to this problem might be to help the child expand his circle of friends and not rely on one best friend.

Although REBT practitioners are encouraged to use a wide variety of cognitive, emotive, and behavioral techniques when working with clients, practitioners working with children and adolescents must be even more flexible in order to connect in meaningful ways with this younger clientele and to employ the ABC process effectively (Vernon, 2009a, 2009b). Because younger clients are generally less skilled at expressing themselves verbally or may not be able to understand concepts as readily as adults, the practitioner's freedom to be creative and flexible allows him or her to target the problem more specifically and make the therapeutic process more interesting and engaging for client and counselor alike. The remainder of this chapter describes specific adaptations and effective strategies to employ with children and adolescents, beginning with the assessment process.

Problem Assessment

Accurate problem assessment is important not only in identifying the client's irrational beliefs and disturbing emotions, but also in determining whether this is a practical problem (e.g., not knowing how to make friends or how to study for a test) or an emotional problem (e.g., feeling anxious about interacting with peers or panicking when taking a test). Furthermore, it is imperative that the counselor assess whether the problem is representative of the child's age group and whether the child's emotions and behaviors are normal expressions, or whether the child is overreacting with an atypical response.

Because children and adolescents are dealing with normal developmental problems in addition to more serious issues requiring various degrees of intervention, professionals must examine the frequency, intensity, and duration of the symptoms to determine the exact nature of the problem. It is also critical that counselors identify who owns the problem: Is it the child's problem, or the parent's or teacher's problem about the child, that is the main issue? Counselors should keep in mind that parents and teachers sometimes refer a child who is exhibiting relatively normal behavior because they either don't understand child and adolescent development or are experiencing conflict with the young client.

Once it has been established that a problem exists, and once its ownership has been determined, the problem analysis phase occurs, resulting in a determination of the client's dysfunctional cognitions, emotions, and behaviors. From an REBT perspective, assessment is ongoing, and there is no clear distinction between assessment and intervention because, in every session, the therapist is constantly analyzing cognitions, emotions, and behaviors as they relate to the problem. Therefore, within the same session, an assessment of one aspect of a given issue may occur along with an intervention for another. In addition, it is not uncommon during an intervention for new information to surface that provides more assessment data.

An REBT assessment for children and adolescents has several distinguishing features:

▷ The relationship between the practitioner and the young client

▷ Parental involvement in the assessment process

▷ The developmental level of the client

▷ The assessment of problematic emotions and behaviors

▷ The assessment of irrational beliefs and cognitive distortions

In addition, because younger clients often are not very verbal or skilled at expressing themselves, assessment may be more challenging than it is with adults. Consequently, the counselor must be prepared to use a variety of approaches to identify irrational beliefs and accurately define the problem.

Relationship Between Practitioner and Client

Although it is a well-established notion that REBT counselors have de-emphasized the therapeutic relationship, this is indeed an overgeneralization. Ellis preferred an active and directive style, but he also emphasized that helping professionals must be genuine, empathic, and congruent (2001a). Dryden (2002b) noted that effective REBT counselors are flexible and vary their style to fit the client. Especially when working with children and adolescents, the importance of establishing a good therapeutic relationship is a crucial aspect of the entire counseling process, even though in and of itself, the relationship is not curative (DiGiuseppe & Bernard, 2006). Utilizing the rapport-building strategies described in chapter 1 may need to be the counselor's first step, particularly if the client is anxious or reluctant to share.

Parental Involvement

When working with younger children, it is often helpful to bring parents into the first session to explain the reason for the referral, if necessary, and to assist with the initial assessment. This approach is also beneficial because younger children may be more willing to go into an office with their parents if counseling is taking place outside the school setting. Even if the parents are present, however, it is preferable first to ask the client to explain why she is coming to counseling. If the child gives a typical "I don't know," then the counselor should ask the parent for input. Once the counselor has a clear picture of the issue from the parents' perspective and has discussed how he or she anticipates involving them in the counseling process, the counselor can usually excuse the parents and begin the relationship-building process with the child.

For several reasons, it is usually advisable for practitioners to see adolescent clients alone during the initial visit so they can get the client's perspective on the problem. First, to effectively join with a client, it is important to hear his version before anyone else's. Second, adolescents are generally more private than adults and don't want to share with their parents. Third, what parents share about their children may put adolescent clients on the defensive, causing them to be even less likely to open up with the counselor. In the case of adolescents, parental involvement in the assessment process often occurs with the initial phone call, when clients are referred. This contact allows the practitioner to hear parental perceptions and concerns, but at the same time honors adolescents by validating their perspectives without a parent being present.

When conducting problem assessment with parents, it is helpful to the practitioner to undertake a specific analysis that includes identifying

▷ The problem from the parents' perspective

▷ Individuals other than the parents who are involved (e.g., how the problem affects other family members)

▷ The duration of the problem

▷ Any specific precipitating circumstances or transitions

▷ Instances in which the problem is manifested

▷ Strategies that the clients, parents, and other key individuals have employed in previous efforts to address the problem

Developmental Level

With regard to the specific assessment strategies that are used, accurate assessment must take into account not only the developmental level of each client but also how the client's problem is conceptualized:

▷ Is this a typical problem for a child this age?

▷ Are the client's reactions typical for someone at this developmental level?

In addition, it is important for therapists to remember that children and young adolescents may have a myopic view of the problem because, as concrete thinkers, they may not be able to see all perspectives. Although it is always important that practitioners hear what these youngsters say and to accept their version of reality, they must keep in mind that a youngster's reality may be distorted. For example, it is not uncommon to hear adolescents claim that their parents *never* listen to them and that they are *always* unfair. In some cases, that may be true, but often these statements are overgeneralizations that result from adolescents' concrete categorizations and their inability to recognize exceptions or see all sides of the issue.

Because children and young adolescents may not be able to verbalize specifically how they are thinking, feeling, and behaving, it is often necessary to employ a variety of developmentally appropriate assessment strategies, such as the following.

Sentence Stems

Sentence stems can be adapted for all age levels and can be completed either orally or in writing. Because the goal of this activity is to stimulate discussion to get more information about a client, it is not necessary to use more than a few (eight to ten) sentences. If, on the basis of initial intake information, you have a general idea of the problem, you can develop sentences that elicit more specificity about the particular issue. If you are still unclear about the problem, you can use less-specific sentence stems. For example, if you know that the presenting problem of the client relates to problems with friends, you could use the following sentence stems to generate more information about the child's experience:

> When I am with my friends at school, I feel . . .
>
> When I am with kids in my neighborhood, I feel . . .
>
> When I play with other kids, I think . . .
>
> I think friends are . . .
>
> The best time I have had with a friend is . . .
>
> The worst time I have had with a friend is . . .
>
> My friends would say that I am . . .
>
> If I could change something about my friends, it would be . . .
>
> I think that my friends shouldn't . . .
>
> I can't stand it when my friends . . .

If you don't have a sense of the problem, the following sentence stems can elicit information in several areas:

> At home I feel . . .
>
> My parents are . . .
>
> School is . . .
>
> What I do best is . . .

What I'm not good at is . . .

What I like best about my life right now is . . .

What I'd like to change most about my life right now is . . .

When I am with friends, I am . . .

The following examples of sentence stems are designed specifically to assess rational or irrational thinking:

When I make a mistake, I feel . . .

I should never . . .

I must be . . .

When others make mistakes, I think . . .

When others don't approve of me, I feel . . .

Other people should . . .

I can't stand it when . . .

It would be awful if . . .

Writing Activities

Through various types of writing activities, it is possible to generate important assessment data. Diaries; logs; journals; and self-composed songs, poems, limericks, and stories are excellent sources of information. Examples of writing assignments that can be used to assess a variety of factors include journal entries that highlight key feelings about triggering events; written analyses of songs the clients think describe their circumstances or feelings; and original stories, poems, or letters to themselves or others that describe how they are thinking, feeling, and behaving.

Self-Monitoring Activities

Involving young clients in monitoring themselves often yields helpful information; the major drawback is that this approach is highly subjective, and results vary according to the clients' investment in the process and their level of honesty. Nevertheless, it is worth a try. Examples include behavior frequency graphs, on which clients plot a line to illustrate how often they experienced targeted behaviors during the week; worry boxes, in which clients write things they worry about on slips of paper and keep them in a box that they bring to share at the next therapy session; a troubling-times tin, for which they write examples of troubles and put them in a tin can to share during counseling; a feelings chart, on which, for a week or two, they identify the intensity of specific feelings such as anger, depression, or anxiety on a scale of 1 (low) to 5 (high) for each hour of the day; and a circle graph, on which they divide a circle into pie shapes representing as many different emotions as they experienced during a particular day, shading in each shape with a color to match the feeling (i.e., red for anger, blue for sad).

Assessment of Problematic Emotions and Behaviors

The first step in assessing problematic emotions and behaviors is to determine how accurately the clients are able to identify feelings and behaviors and how they define the feelings and behaviors they describe. One client's conception of anger, for example, may be another's description of irritation. A good clarifying question to ask is "When you say, 'irritated,' what exactly do you mean?" Suggest that clients be more specific by describing how they look, sound, or act when they are angry. What they were thinking or how others would know they were angry can give you a clearer idea of how they define terms. Role-playing how they act when they feel a certain way or drawing a picture of the feeling or behavior are good ways for clients who are less verbal to express themselves. Having younger children use puppets to convey feelings and behaviors is also effective.

With older clients, asking them keep a feeling/behaving journal is a good way to determine how they define terms. To initiate this activity, invite clients to take a few minutes each day to describe how they felt and behaved in response to incidents at home, at school, or with friends. (If they are willing to share what they have written, their descriptions will give you insight.)

Accurate emotional assessment also must include looking at all possible emotional reactions. I recall a case in which an adolescent was extremely upset because she hadn't been selected for an honor band. My immediate assumption was that she was upset with herself for being rejected and felt inadequate, but I was wrong. She was angry at the system and the band instructor, who deemed her unacceptable. A more specific question (e.g., "What do you mean by 'upset'?") might have gotten her to specify her anger. Then I would have asked her whom she was angry with—herself or others?

Assessing the behavioral consequences of different emotional reactions should not be ignored. Asking clients who report feeling angry to describe what they did when they were angry gives insight into the intensity of the emotional reaction and the accompanying thought process. If a client says she punched the wall, then obviously she was intensely angry. If she merely pouted, then she may have been more irritated than angry. These differentiations should be pointed out to clients. It is also important to assess whether their reaction is a common response to similar events, how much control they perceived that they had over their behavioral reaction, and how they felt about the way they behaved. Finally, you should inquire about clients' understanding of the consequences of their behavioral reactions.

Because younger children may not have a vocabulary adequate to describe their feelings, it may also be necessary to use the following techniques.

Feeling Flash Cards

Put feeling words on flash cards, and have clients define or act out the words described on the cards.

Feeling Chart (Featuring Pictures of Feelings and Feeling Words)

Invite young clients to select feelings from a chart that includes words or pictures that describe how they currently feel or how they felt during the time between sessions.

Behavior Chart (Featuring Pictures of Behaviors)

Ask clients to select pictures from a chart that depict their behaviors during the past several days.

Fabulous Feelings and Not-So-Fabulous Feelings

Fabulous Feelings and Not-So-Fabulous Feelings are games that help younger children identify positive and negative feelings. For these games, you will use the bottom half of two 1-quart milk cartons, one labeled Fabulous Feelings and the other labeled Not-So-Fabulous Feelings. In addition, you will need two sets of cards: one set consisting of Fabulous Feelings words and the other set consisting of Not-So-Fabulous Feelings words. The Fabulous Feelings cards should have the following feeling words written on them: *proud, happy, excited, calm, cheerful,* and *wonderful.* The Not-So-Fabulous Feelings cards should have the words *mad, scared, jealous, worried, furious,* and *sad.* (Each word—the fabulous and the not-so-fabulous—should be written on two separate cards.) You will also need the Fabulous Feelings scenarios and the Not-So-Fabulous Feelings scenarios.

Fabulous Feelings scenarios

You haven't seen your grandparents in a long time, and they are coming this weekend.

Your birthday is next week, and your parents have hinted that you will be getting a special present.

You just got your math paper back, and you got all the problems right.

You have wanted a kitten for a long time. Today your mom is going to take you to the Humane Society to pick one out.

Your cousins are coming over to play.

Your new baby sister is coming home from the hospital tomorrow.

Not-So-Fabulous Feelings scenarios

You are outside for recess, and one of your friends makes fun of the way you run.

You are at the market with your mother. She buys your sister some candy and won't buy any for you.

You are taking swimming lessons because you don't know how to swim.

You got your reading worksheet back. You didn't get very many right.

Your brother takes your roller blades without asking whether he can use them.

Your dad is in jail for selling drugs.

To play this game, mix up the scenarios and read them to the client, who then selects either a Fabulous Feelings card or a Not-So-Fabulous Feelings card and puts it in the corresponding milk carton. Once he has done so, discuss the meaning of the word on the card. Proceed with the activity, continuing to discuss the meanings of the words on the cards the client chooses to help increase his feeling vocabulary.

Feeling and behaving charts are also excellent assessment tools for measuring the frequency and intensity of emotions and behaviors. These charts can be easily made by writing the days of the week across the top of a sheet of paper and the hours of the day and evening down the side. Instruct clients to keep a record throughout the week by indicating on a scale of 1 to 5 how they were feeling or behaving (5 being very depressed, angry, or whatever feeling you are attempting to assess, and 1 being not very depressed, angry, and so forth. Or, for behaving, a 5 could be having lots of behavior problems, and a 1 could be having very few problems or behaving well). Invite them to bring this chart to the counseling session the following week. Using the data, ask more specific questions about what the feeling or behavior was like for them, how they feel about the ratings, and so forth. Note how many times a week they experienced certain feelings and help them draw connections between the feelings, behaviors, and any activating events to identify patterns. This information can also be used for goal setting: "Let's see whether you can reduce the intensity of the depression this week; how might you go about doing that?" Frequency can also be measured by asking clients to put toothpicks or small rocks in a jar each time they feel scared or have a temper tantrum, for example. This method is good for children who are more kinesthetic.

You can also measure intensity by using the subjective units of distress scales (SUDS) after the emotions and behaviors have been identified (Ellis & MacLaren, 1998). For example, if a client says she was mad at her teacher, ask her to pinpoint her degree of anger: "On a scale of 1 (not very mad at all) to 10 (extremely mad), how mad were you?" Asking what she did when she was that mad is also helpful, especially because there might be some discrepancy between how she rates her feeling and how she behaves. For example, if she says she was just a little mad but screamed and shouted at the teacher, you can confront this discrepancy and facilitate a more accurate labeling of the intensity of the emotion.

A visual method that can be used is a "thermometer of emotions," in which the client actually moves the scale from cold to hot emotions (using a tagboard thermometer into which a red strip of paper can be inserted and moved up or down) according to the strength of the feeling. This thermometer gives you and the client a specific indication of the intensity of the emotion.

Assessing the duration of the emotion or behavior can be accomplished by asking clients to show you on a clock how long they experienced the emotion or behavior: Was it minutes or hours? Another method is to have them color in a bar graph, divided into segments to represent units of time.

Practical Versus Emotional Problems. Differentiating between practical and emotional problems is also a distinctive aspect of REBT assessment (DiGiuseppe, 1999; Vernon, 2009b). Practical problems are realistic difficulties, whereas emotional problems are uncomfortable feelings about the practical problems that are generated by irrational beliefs. For example, if an adolescent is angry and ashamed because she lacks organizational skills that interfere with her ability to complete her schoolwork, then she might be irrationally thinking that she shouldn't have this problem and that she is stupid and incompetent.

An emotional problem frequently prevents clients from doing what they need to do at the practical level, so it is critical to deal with the emotional problem generated by the irrational beliefs first, or attempts at problem resolution will, at best, be temporary. A good example of this scenario is parents who try to coerce their AD/HD children into taking medication. Because parents, teachers, and many professionals don't deal with the emotional problems—the shame, guilt, or feelings about being different—the behavior management strategies that they frequently employ are generally effective only in the short term. Practitioners can expect far better results if they first address the underlying emotional issues before they attack the practical problem.

Secondary Problems. Another distinctive feature of REBT is that it assesses for secondary emotional problems, such as being depressed about being depressed or being anxious about being anxious. It is common for adolescents to feel ashamed or embarrassed that they are depressed. Thus, it is generally recommended that the secondary emotional problems be dealt with first, by asking certain questions, such as the following:

What does it say about you if you are depressed?

Where's the proof that others who aren't depressed are better than you are?

How will it help you get over your depression if you also have to deal with being depressed and angry about being depressed?

Helping clients dispute their irrational beliefs about their emotional disturbance is a critical step—indeed the first step—in dealing with the primary problem of anger, anxiety, or depression (Ellis & Dryden, 1997).

Appropriate Versus Inappropriate Negative Reactions. As previously noted, it is essential to differentiate between appropriate and inappropriate negative emotional reactions (Dryden, 2003). Concern, irritation, and disappointment are reasonable emotions that result from rational thinking, whereas anger, rage, and devastation emanate from irrational beliefs. You should keep in mind that, because young clients do not always accurately label their feelings, they may express irritation but, in reality, may be angry. For accurate assessment, it is important to probe further and uncover the beliefs as well as the behaviors, as the following example involving a sixth grader shows.

Counselor: So how did you feel when you found out your parents were getting divorced?

Client: Oh, I guess I was irritated.

Counselor: Irritated? In what ways?

Client: Well, it'll be a hassle to go back and forth between houses, and it won't be as much fun when I have to go to my dad's, since my pool and trampoline are at my mom's.

Counselor: So there are things you will miss by not being at one house all the time, and that can be irritating and certainly disappointing. I'm wondering whether there are other things you're irritated about regarding this situation or whether you have any other feelings about it.

Client: Not really.

Counselor: Well, can you share with me how you reacted when you first found out about this?

Client: I just shut myself in my room and stayed there for a long time.

Counselor: And when you were in your room, what were you thinking about?

Client: How I hate my parents for doing this. It's their fault that they are making my life so bad. They shouldn't have ever gotten married in the first place if they can't stay together now.

Counselor: So it sounds like you might have been more than just irritated—sounds like you were pretty mad.

Client: Yeah, I was.

One goal of treatment is to move the client away from the extreme emotional reactions that accompany irrational beliefs. Therefore, practitioners must assess the emotion accurately and not necessarily take what the client says at face value without probing further.

Assessment of Irrational Beliefs and Cognitive Distortions

Although the major objective of the REBT assessment process is to identify irrational beliefs, practitioners should keep in mind that not all beliefs are irrational. A major clue to the existence of irrational beliefs is the intensity or duration of the feeling or behavior. If, for example, a client reported that he felt sad when his dog died, and he cried himself to sleep for several nights, the practitioner should not assume that there is anything irrational about the client's behavior because it is normal to feel sad and cry when a pet dies. However, if he is still crying and can't sleep months after the event, the duration of the symptom is an indication that he is thinking irrationally that his dog's death is the worst thing that could ever happen, that he can never be happy without his dog, and that he can't stand this discomfort. It would also be normal for an adolescent to be upset when his girlfriend breaks up with him. But, if he is suicidal and thinks he can't go on living because the two of them are no longer together, he is thinking irrationally—that this is the end of the world, that he will never fall in love again, and that he can't stand the pain.

As described earlier in this chapter, irrational beliefs are distorted thoughts that result in self-defeating behaviors and intense negative emotions. Dryden et al. (2003) identified demands on self, others, and the world as core irrational beliefs. Waters (1982, p. 572) expanded on Ellis's core beliefs, identifying the following irrational beliefs for children:

It's awful if others don't like me.

I'm bad if I make a mistake.

Everything should go my way; I should always get what I want.

Things should come easily to me.

The world should be fair, and bad people must be punished.

I shouldn't show my feelings.

Adults should be perfect.

There's only one right answer.

I must win.

I shouldn't have to wait for anything.

Waters (1981, p. 6) enumerated the following irrational beliefs for adolescents:

It would be awful if peers didn't like me; it would be awful to be a social loser.

I shouldn't make mistakes, especially social mistakes.

It's my parents' fault I'm so miserable.

I can't help it—that's just the way I am, and I guess I'll always be this way.

The world should be fair and just.

It's awful when things don't go my way.

It's better to avoid challenges than to risk failure.

I must conform to my peers.

I can't stand to be criticized.

Others should always be responsible.

It can be difficult to explain the concept of irrational beliefs to young clients, so practitioners may want to use terms such as *junk thoughts, unproductive thoughts, muddy thoughts, insensible thoughts,* or *thoughts that cause problems.* Bernard, Ellis, and Terjesen (2006) suggested the terms *red light* and *green light* or *positive thinking* and *negative thinking* as opposed to using the words *rational* and *irrational.*

Children and adolescents also experience a variety of cognitive distortions. Helping them identify these distortions can be extremely important because distorted thinking results in problems with self as well as others. In addition to the distortions described in chapter 1, Merrell (2001, p. 92) listed the following additional examples.

Binocular vision. Looking at things so that they seem bigger or smaller than they actually are. This is similar to magnification or minimization: An adolescent is caught smoking pot and minimizes it by thinking it is no big deal even though it is against the law, or a child gets a bad grade on one test and magnifies it, thinking he will never pass fourth grade.

Dichotomous thinking. Looking at things as extreme opposites—things are all good or all bad.

Dark glasses. Looking at everything from a negative point of view and focusing only on the bad.

Fortune telling. Making predictions about what will happen in the future without having any facts to support it.

Labeling. Putting a negative label on something that is more complex, such as calling yourself a stupid fool because sometimes you don't do things right.

In assessing cognitions, it is important for therapists to distinguish between inferences and evaluations. Owing to their developmental level, children and adolescents often make inferences, which are automatic thoughts or interpretations, rather than evaluations that relate to the core irrational beliefs. For example, a young adolescent might state that his girlfriend doesn't like him; in actuality, that is an inference. The evaluation is that there must be something wrong with him (self-downing).

It is important to get to the evaluations, which may be more difficult with younger children. The therapist can accomplish this task by asking a series of questions such as "Suppose she doesn't like you—what does that say about you? Are you what she says you are? And suppose you are. Does that mean you are no good?" Using the analogy of peeling away the layers of an onion is a concrete way for practitioners to help young clients understand that the therapist is going to be asking them certain questions to get to the basis of what they are thinking.

Although it is preferable to identify young clients' core beliefs—if one is to practice the most elegant form of REBT—it is important that therapists be sensitive to each client's developmental level in the disputation of these core beliefs. It would be difficult, for example, for a first grader who was abandoned by his mother to understand that he is still lovable, even though his mother deserted him, and inappropriate to say, "Suppose it's true that your mother left because she doesn't love you—but how does that make you unlovable?"

Another factor for therapists to pay attention to is their young clients' ability to distinguish between facts and assumptions. It is characteristic for children and adolescents to make assumptions without checking the facts. They might assume that their best friend doesn't like them because the friend sat with someone else at lunch, or they might assume that their parents will not let them go to a movie because their parents said no the last time they asked. These assumptions result in negative emotions that can also affect behavior, as illustrated in the following example:

Nathan was irate because his girlfriend hadn't called him the night before, as promised. He told the therapist that he knew she hadn't called because she was out with another guy, and that this must mean she didn't like him anymore. He informed the therapist that he had waited over an hour for her to call, and when she didn't, he went out and picked up two female friends and rode around with them the rest of the night. When his therapist asked him whether there was any proof that his girlfriend was out with someone else or whether there were previous indications that she didn't like him, he admitted that there was no basis for his assumptions—and that he hadn't considered the possibility that maybe she hadn't called because of some other, extenuating circumstance. As it turned out, she had been grounded from using the phone, but when she heard from friends that Nathan had been out with other girls, she became angry with him, and a major fight ensued.

Had Nathan not jumped to conclusions and allowed his assumptions to rule his emotions and behaviors, the scenario would have been significantly different. This is why, as clients describe their problem, it is important to initially accept their perception of the circumstance but then help them to distinguish between facts and assumptions as you work through the ABC process. Teaching young clients this distinction is also an excellent prevention technique because, if they are able to differentiate between facts and assumptions, in the future they will have a clearer perspective of the problem. This fresh perspective can help alleviate some of their emotional upset and impulsive behavior. The following activities may be used to help clients learn about facts and assumptions.

Fact, Fact, Fact

An activity such as Fact, Fact, Fact (adapted from Vernon, 1980, p. 96) is effective in helping younger children distinguish between facts and assumptions. This activity can help children to understand that they have failed to take into account all perspectives of the situation. To play Fact, Fact, Fact, you will need an 8½ × 11–inch sheet of paper designed as a tic-tac-toe board.

Indicate to the client that you will be reading some statements, and that both of you need to think about whether what you are reading are facts (i.e., true statements that can be proven) or assumptions (i.e., statements that the client supposes are true but have yet to be verified). You and the client alternate turns and place an F for *fact* or an A for *assumption* on the board. Designate the client as 1 and yourself as 2, so when you put the letters on the board, you can also put a number beside each of them to indicate each player's response. As in tic-tac-toe, the first person to get three numbers in a row is the "expert" on facts and assumptions.

Some examples of facts

Broccoli is a vegetable.

Milk comes from cows and goats.

Lakes are smaller than oceans.

Pigs can't fly.

Arizona is a state located in the United States.

Some examples of assumptions

All third graders are smarter than all second graders.

Winter is the best season of the year.

Cats are better pets than dogs.

All presidents do a very good job.

Parents never have to do things they do not want to do.

Finding Facts

To teach clients to distinguish between facts and assumptions, prepare a fact-finding sheet by writing various age-appropriate facts and assumptions on a sheet of paper, instructing the client to circle all the facts.

Some examples of facts

An apple is a fruit.

Soccer is a sport.

George Washington was the first president of the United States.

The U.S. flag is red, white, and blue.

There are lots of different shows on television.

Some examples of assumptions

Everyone loves school.

All teachers are mean.

Red is the best color.

All kids love to play kickball.

Math is the easiest subject.

I See; Therefore, I Assume

Another short activity to help children as well as adolescents learn to distinguish between facts and assumptions is to engage them in I See; Therefore, I Assume. For example, you could say to the client, "I see that you are wearing glasses; therefore, I assume that you cannot see anything without them." Or "I see that you are wearing black; therefore, I assume that black is your favorite color." Then invite the client to indicate whether you assumed correctly or not. Switch roles and have the client make the assumptions and ask you to verify the facts.

Flip for Facts

To help children learn to distinguish between facts and assumptions, play this simple game. Using a coin, take turns flipping it. With each flip, the counselor and client take turns drawing an index card that lists different categories on separate cards, such as sports, school subjects, animals, food, music, friends, and games. If the flip is heads, the person who flipped identifies a fact relative to the category on the card, and, if the flip is tails, he or she identifies an assumption relative to that category. For example, a heads flip in the category of food might be that apples and bananas are fruits (fact); a tails flip (assumption) could be that everybody loves fruit. After playing this game for a while, help the client identify examples of facts and assumptions in the problem area that brought him to counseling.

The following strategies are effective in helping children and adolescents identify irrational beliefs and other cognitive distortions.

I'm a Believer

This strategy, adapted from Vernon (2006b, pp. 151–153) helps clients identify rational and irrational beliefs. On individual pieces of paper, write some examples of rational and irrational beliefs (can be adapted depending on age level), such as the following, and put them in an envelope:

Examples of rational beliefs

I wish I could get straight A's.

It is hard to run the mile, but I just have to keep practicing.

I hope I do well in the job interview.

I'd rather not have that part in the play, but I can do it if I have to.

I wish my parents would let me have more freedom.

Examples of irrational beliefs

I'll never speak to him again.

My parents never let me do anything.

I can't stand that teacher.

They're just doing that to annoy me.

If he breaks up with me I'll never be happy again.

Give the client a sorting board (sheet of paper divided into two columns with one column labeled rational, the other irrational), and ask her to sort the beliefs from the envelope into the appropriate piles.

Rational or Irrational?

This game helps adolescents learn to distinguish between rational and irrational beliefs. Before you start, you will need a set of rational beliefs and a set of irrational beliefs, with each set written on separate index cards.

Rational cards

I hope I get invited to the party.

If I miss one or two math problems, it isn't the end of the world.

It would be nice if I won the contest.

I really hope my friends call me to go skating.

If I don't get a good grade, I am still a worthwhile person.

If my parents don't let me use the car, it's not a big deal.

I'd like to get the new job I applied for, but, if I don't, I'll just apply for another one.

If I don't get elected to the student council, it doesn't mean I am a loser.

Irrational cards

I can't stand it if I don't get invited to the party.

I can't imagine anything worse than missing one or two math problems.

If I don't win the contest, I will be very upset and depressed for a long time.

I'll be devastated if my friends don't call me to go skating.

If I don't get a good grade, I might as well stop trying—it will just prove how stupid and worthless I am.

If my parents don't let me use the car, I won't be able to stand it.

If I don't get the job I applied for, it means I am a total loser.

If I don't get elected to the student council, it means I'm a loser.

To play, shuffle the cards well and put them face down, five in one row and five in another. Ask the client to turn over a card, state whether it is rational or irrational and why, and then turn over another card to try to find the first overturned card's rational or irrational counterpart. If he gets a match, those cards can be taken off the board. If there is no match, both cards are again turned over, face down, and remain on the table. Proceed until all cards have been matched.

Sentence Stems

Have the client complete these sentences: "When that happened, you were thinking . . ." "When you felt so angry, you were thinking . . ."

Inference as a Hunch

Ask the client something like "Some kids your age might think nobody liked them if they didn't get invited to a birthday party. What do you think about not being invited?"

Are You Thinking?

Although this technique should be used sparingly because it is better for the client to supply her own thoughts, it is effective with the younger client who has trouble expressing herself. The practitioner can ask, "Are you thinking . . . ?", then complete the sentence with a thought that would result in a dysfunctional emotion or behavior. Some examples: "Are you thinking that you can't stand it when you have something hard to do?" "Are you thinking that you are bad or different because you have to take medicine to help you control your behavior?"

If the client agrees that she was thinking along these lines, the practitioner can probe for other irrational beliefs related to the specific activating event.

Thought Bubbles

Eliciting irrational beliefs can be easier by using a visual of a head with thought bubbles surrounding it. After the client describes the activating event and the emotional and behavioral consequences, point to the head and ask what he was thinking. Write the thoughts in the bubbles and ask probing questions to generate additional thoughts. Often these thoughts are automatic thoughts or inferences, so it is important to continue to probe in order to determine the core irrational belief. For example, if the activating event is that the child got a bad grade on a test, one of the automatic thoughts might be that he didn't study hard enough. Asking what that says about him can lead to a core belief such as "It means I'm lazy and stupid." The counselor would follow up on that by asking what else it says about him, and so forth, to learn more about self-downing, demanding, and low frustration tolerance.

Think-Aloud Technique

Assign the client a task in the counseling session that is similar to one she is having trouble with, such as completing math homework. As she is working, ask her to verbalize what she is feeling and thinking to determine whether her beliefs are rational or irrational (Genest & Turk, 1981).

Expansion/Contraction Technique

As the client describes in his own words his thoughts or feelings about a problematic situation, the practitioner ask questions such as "When you said that you thought it was awful, what was it about that event that you thought was so awful?" or "I'd like you to describe for me the first thing that comes into your mind when you think about . . . " The purpose is to ask questions that help the client expand on his thoughts (Bernard, 1981).

Concentration

To help clients learn to distinguish between rational and irrational beliefs, write examples (which can be adapted according to age level) of both types of beliefs on index cards, making two copies of each. Then lay the cards randomly, face down, six per row, on a table. Take turns turning over two cards; when there is a match, the counselor or client identifies whether the card represents a rational or an irrational belief and why.

Examples for rational belief cards

It is nice to have a best friend.

I prefer to get good grades.

I like to do well in sports.

I hope my teacher likes me.

It is all right to make some mistakes.

I like it when things are fair.

Examples for irrational belief cards

I can't stand to make mistakes.

I have to be perfect.

It's awful if I don't get what I want.

I can't stand it when others act stupid.

Everyone has to like me.

If I'm not the best, it's awful.

After the game, discuss some examples of rational and irrational beliefs related to the issues presented in counseling.

Inference Chaining

Because younger children are not as adept at verbal expression as adolescents, the prompts "and . . ." and "because . . ." are useful for encouraging children to continue verbalizing. For example, if the child says she was angry when the teacher didn't call on her, you can say "because . . ." to help her complete the thought.

In My Hand

A visual strategy that helps clients identify distorted or irrational thinking is to have them draw around their hand. Then, ask them to write a distorted or irrational thought on each finger relative to a negative event.

THE ABC PROCESS

As noted earlier in this chapter, a distinct advantage of REBT is that its ABC model provides a framework that helps to structure the counseling process. This framework is especially helpful in counseling children and adolescents, because, as a rule, it is more difficult to keep them (as opposed to adults) focused and willing to work through the steps necessary to bring about change. In employing this model, practitioners have a mental map to guide them as they assess the problem and subsequently design interventions that help clients think rationally and behave sensibly.

The A—Activating Event

In conceptualizing the problem, REBT therapists can usually expect children and adolescents first to describe the A, or the activating event. This would be what the children experienced, what happened, or what they think happened or might happen. Occasionally, they may present a feeling, in which case the therapist would encourage them to discuss their emotions and accompanying behaviors and then identify a specific activating event.

Unlike less-directive therapists, REBT practitioners do *not* encourage children to elaborate extensively on the event because such detail is often unnecessary and time consuming. Practitioners need to judge how much to allow clients to elaborate on the activating event. Certainly, a traumatic event merits more time than a friendship dispute, and it is always important to allow some time for young clients to tell their stories because they may not have adults in their lives who are there to listen to them.

Unfortunately, many practitioners mistakenly believe that, because of the method's active-directive nature, listening isn't essential in the practice of effective REBT. In reality, listening is extremely important, as is the ability to ask well-directed questions that elicit information about clients' emotional and behavioral reactions and irrational beliefs. This strategy is especially important when working with resistant youngsters and those whose backgrounds differ markedly from the therapist's. In general, it is often during the initial session that more elaboration occurs, but once therapists have established rapport and acquired an overview of the problem, it is important to begin actively working on the problem.

Helpful techniques for eliciting the A include sharing with the clients what you understand the problem to be, particularly if they are quite young or reluctant to talk. This can be done simply by stating, "I understand you are being picked on at school. It might be helpful if you could talk more about this so that we can work together to figure out what to do about this problem." It is also helpful to ask the client to share a specific example: "Sara, you mentioned that you were having problems with your parents. Can you think about the last time you had trouble and describe what happened?"

If younger children have difficulty describing an activating event, inviting them to act it out with puppets or with toys can be effective. Other suggestions include asking the client to draw a picture or a cartoon of the event or to imagine that the two of you are watching it replayed on video: What would you see?

The C—Emotional and Behavioral Consequences

Although the core of the REBT problem-solving process is the identification and disputation of irrational beliefs, it is reached only after the emotional and behavioral reactions are assessed. Therefore, after the activating event has been described, the next step is to ask clients to discuss how they felt and how they acted relative to the particular event. The intensity of their feelings and behaviors is important in determining whether they are holding irrational beliefs, and their specific emotions help target the core belief. For example, if clients report feeling depressed and worthless, they are most likely engaging in self-downing, whereas those who are angry and resentful are probably engaging in demanding, "shoulding," and other-downing. So, not only do feelings and behaviors facilitate the assessment process, they also make up an integral part of the therapeutic process. Especially with younger children, it is important that therapists listen to their feelings.

Strategies for Eliciting the Emotional Consequence with Children

It is often difficult for children to describe their feelings, so it may be necessary for them to brainstorm a list of feeling words and select which ones apply to them relative to their current situation. Drawing a picture, acting out how they feel, demonstrating with puppets, or pointing to feeling faces on a chart of feelings are also effective strategies.

In addition, Feel Wheel (Vernon, 2006a, pp. 25–26) and other games, such Face the Feeling, are good ways to facilitate identification and expression of feelings.

Feel Wheel

Cut a large circle out of tagboard and divide it into 13 pie shapes, with each slice assigned a feeling word: *excited, grouchy, sad, happy, mad, angry, nervous, frustrated, upset, lonely, worried, scared,* and *furious.* Make an arrow out of tagboard and attach it to the center of the circle with a brass fastener so it will spin. Invite the client to spin the spinner. When the arrow lands on a feeling, have the client first explain what the feeling means, then have her discuss whether this particular feeling applies to the current situation that is troubling her.

Face the Feeling

Younger children are often better able to identify emotions if they are playing a game such as Face the Feeling. To make this game, attach four paper plates in the center of a large sheet of tagboard. On each plate draw a face showing one of those feelings: *happy, mad, sad,* and *worried,* and under each face put a colored dot: yellow for happy, red for mad, blue for sad, and green for worried. (Using yarn for hair, buttons for eyes, and so forth enhances the game board.) Finally, around the faces in a large circle, place multiple dots representing each color (but interspersed, so that the colors are mixed around the board), designating one dot as the starting point. The counselor and client take turns rolling a die, moving a marker around the circle the number of spaces identified by the roll of the die and describing a recent time when they experienced the feeling that corresponded to the color on which they landed.

Continuum of Emotions

Because younger children are active and like to move around, Continuum of Emotions is an activity that works well. Place a strip of masking tape on the floor and designate two opposite degrees of an emotion that relate to something the client is experiencing. For example, if he is angry, you could label one end "slightly irritated" and the other end "furious." After discussing the particular situation, identify the extreme emotions at either end of the continuum, and elicit from the client other emotions that would fit across the continuum (e.g., very angry, somewhat angry, pretty ticked off). Then ask the client to stand on the line at the spot that most accurately describes how he feels about various problems he is experiencing.

Strategies for Eliciting the Emotional Consequence with Adolescents

With adolescents, it may be necessary to share a chart of feeling words and ask them to select the term that describes them. You can also share excerpts from a movie that portrays emotions in a circumstance similar to theirs. Examples may include scenes from the movie *Dead Poets Society* that depict the relationship between a teenage male and his controlling father or scenes from the movie *Pump Up the Volume* that highlight the anger and confusion commonly experienced by adolescents.

Feelings Word Cluster

Adapted from Gladding (2005), this technique is especially helpful for adolescents. On a sheet of paper, draw a circle in the center and ask the client to identify the most significant negative emotion related to her problem. Then, randomly draw lines out from the circle with smaller circles at the ends, and more lines and circles from those. Invite the client to write whatever comes to mind relative to behaviors, events, people, or other emotions in the center circle. The information generated can facilitate exploration of the emotional and behavioral consequence.

Metaphors

Using metaphors can often facilitate identification of feelings: "Is the anger more like a rocket that goes off suddenly, or is it more like a pan of water on the stove—it slowly builds and then explodes?" "Is your depression like a dense fog, or is it more like fleeting clouds that come and go?" "Is your anxiety so intense that you feel like it's a wave washing over you, or is it just a little ripple?"

Reading About Other Teens' Feelings

Teens also seem better able to self-disclose and express their feelings if they have read about other teens' feelings. By reading about how others their age feel, they realize they are not alone, and they are relieved to discover that. Consider sharing the following story about growing apart from friends, written by a high school senior (Vernon, 1998c, p. 237).

I'm Lonely

When I refer to feeling lonely, I mean that I feel alone. But being alone and feeling lonely are very different. I've felt lonely, on occasion, when I am alone, but it is not a severe feeling. I am perfectly happy being with my own thoughts. When I do feel lonely, it is because I am remembering what it was like to have a real best friend who understood me well. Now I don't seem to have that. We've grown away from each other because our values have changed, I guess. But I really miss having that best friend, that kindred spirit.

At one point in time I lost respect for my peers. They wanted to do things that I didn't. They didn't understand the restrictions I put on myself. All in all, I grew away from them, and I guess that just happens. I'm a senior in high school, and I probably won't see these people much later in life. I miss the cohesive group that we had, but that is over.

What I think creates the most problems is not having a new group to fall into. In every class there are people who I should try to break down the barriers with so that I don't feel so alone. But that's hard. Slowly I am finding some people who enjoy "good clean fun" again, and I'm beginning to develop some new friendships. But in reality, I think I will still feel this loneliness until I move away next year and have a chance to start over again.

Another story written by an adolescent client, which is also helpful to share, is *The Emotional Roller Coaster* (Vernon, 1998c, pp. 43–44).

The Emotional Roller Coaster

I am 15. For the past several months I have been having lots of mood swings. I can wake up in the morning feeling excited about going to school to see my friends. But before I even get out the door I might be in a bad mood. Maybe it's something as little as not getting my hair to look right or not liking what I have to wear. But most of the time I just feel down for no apparent reason; there doesn't seem to be anything major that makes me feel the way I do. Oh, sometimes I may get in a fight with a friend, or I might get mad at my mom if she won't let me do something I want to do, but usually the moods just happen with no warning. Once I get to school I may snap out of it, but, if I don't, I don't even want to talk to anybody.

The bad part of it is that when I feel down, I get scared. Sometimes it seems like the bad feelings will never go away, and I feel like giving up. When I'm down I tend to think of other things that make me feel more down, and then it just gets worse. It confuses me that I can feel that bad, and then those moods can shift and I can feel real up and happy. That's how I'd like to feel more of the time. Then I can laugh, do crazy things with my friends, and just feel good.

Sometimes when I'm down I get argumentative. I'll yell at my mom or go off on my friends for no good reason. Then later I feel guilty because I acted like that. The last time I was with my dad I blew up at him in the restaurant. People started looking at me and I felt pretty embarrassed. It's not like I really planned to act that way; I just didn't feel like I had any control. The one thing that helps me get out of the bad moods is to force myself to get out and do something. It takes a lot of effort, but, if I do it, I usually feel better. I know that when I mope around I think about things that don't help my moods, so I try to stay "up" by getting involved in something other than myself. That isn't a guarantee that I'll stay "up," but at least it helps for a while. Doing things with my friends helps, too. We can have fun just hanging out.

I don't mean it to sound like I have a terrible life or am depressed all the time. It's not like that. I think I'm a pretty normal teenager. But sometimes no matter how hard I try, it just isn't quite enough, and the moods take over. I know a lot of my friends feel like this, too. I guess we just have to ride the "roller coaster" and try not to let things get to us. I keep trying to remind myself that this won't last forever, and that helps.

Strategies for Eliciting the Behavioral Consequence

It is generally easier for children and adolescents to identify behaviors than to identify emotions, but it still may be necessary to have them draw, pantomime, or, with younger children, act out with puppets how they behaved when they felt a certain way. Other techniques that might be helpful for both children and adolescents include the following.

Instant Replay

This technique, developed by Bedford (1974) involves asking clients to imagine that they are replaying the activating event as an instant replay in a sporting event. As they do so, ask them to describe how they behaved and what the consequences were.

Some Kids Might . . .

For less verbal children, or those who aren't able to describe their behavior, you can say, "Some kids in your situation might act or do . . .", then ask how they behaved with regard to the presenting problem.

Play the Part

Ask the client to reconstruct an event by role playing with you. The client identifies the role you will play and how you should act. He plays himself, depicting how he acted in the situation.

What Happened Next?

Take a sheet of computer paper and cut it into ten strips. Take one strip and ask the client what she did first relative to the problem being addressed. Write it on the strip and staple or tape the ends together. Then ask what she did next, write it on another strip, loop it through the first strip, and staple or tape it to form a chain. Continue in this manner to help the client identify a sequence of behaviors relative to an activating event.

Establishing the connection between feelings and behaviors is important, and this connection is something that children and adolescents may not think about. Questions that counselors might ask them are "So, when you were so angry, how did you behave? Were there consequences of those actions, and, if so, how did you feel about those?" Throughout the ABC process, the practitioner should strive to help clients understand how their behaviors help them or hinder them, how to assess the consequences of their behaviors, and how to control their behaviors.

The B—Beliefs

Once the disturbing emotions and behaviors have been identified and discussed, the practitioner uses the techniques previously described to help clients identify their beliefs. If, during the assessment process, it is determined that the feelings and behaviors are moderate and appropriate and the beliefs are rational, it is important for the therapist to acknowledge the feelings and reinforce the rational thinking, saying something like this:

> It is normal to feel sad about your best friend moving away. You said that you will miss her and that it might be hard to adjust to her being gone, and that is understandable. Had you been thinking that you can't stand this and can't imagine living in this town without your best friend, you would probably be depressed and more upset. But because you have told yourself that you can get along without her but at the same time wish she didn't have to move, you are able to cope with this situation even if you don't like it.

In this scenario, the counselor might then help the client learn to deal more effectively with her loss by having her write a letter to her friend, make a memory book, or compose a song or a limerick.

Regardless of whether the beliefs identified are rational or irrational, it is critical to help clients understand the connection between how they think, feel, and behave. Establishing the connection between the B (beliefs) and the C (consequences) is an integral part of the therapeutic process because clients must learn that they can reduce the intensity of the negative emotions and unproductive behaviors by changing their beliefs. This should be done even if the beliefs are rational, as the previous example illustrated.

There are several ways to help clients learn the B–C connection. First, the therapist might say something like this:

> Terrell, you have just shown me on the emotional thermometer that you are very angry when your sister comes into your room and plays with your Nintendo. In fact, you told me that you were so upset that you beat her up. Do you think that all of your friends would be just as angry as you are when that happens to them?

Depending on the age of the child, he might say yes, that all of his friends would be that angry. In that case, the therapist could say:

> Well, maybe all of your friends would be as angry, but, if we did a survey of all the kids in your class or in the whole school, can you think of a few who might not get as angry as you do?

Expanding the scope usually helps the child see that not everyone would be as angry. Once you have established this, help the client see that if everyone isn't as angry when they experience the same situation, then it must be what he is thinking about the event that creates his feelings and subsequent behavior. Engage him in a dialogue such as:

> So, Terrell, if everyone might not get as angry as you do when their sister invades their territory, how can you explain the difference?

Young clients might not be able to verbalize this, so the counselor can ask:

> I wonder whether they are thinking different things than you do about what their sister does. You shared with me that you think she shouldn't do this; that it's awful when she comes into your room, and that you can't stand it. If your friends weren't as upset, what might they be thinking?

The counselor should work with the client to identify what he might be thinking, then reinforce the notion that it is what he thinks that results in intense negative emotions and behaviors, and by changing his thoughts, he can change how he feels and behaves.

Once the B–C connection has been identified, the counselor establishes the therapeutic goal by asking the client whether he would like to learn more about how to change his thinking so that he won't be so angry and get into trouble for beating up his sister. After the goal has been set, move on to disputation.

The D—Disputing Irrational Beliefs

If it is determined during the assessment process that the beliefs are irrational, the therapist must now dispute them. With children and adolescents, practitioners need to be more creative in their disputation techniques than they are with adult clients and not rely solely on verbal challenging. Some suggestions that work well with both children and adolescents follow.

Just Pretend

For clients who deny that they have irrational beliefs, suggest that they just pretend that they do have such beliefs: What could they tell themselves? And what could they tell themselves that would help them be more rational?

Exaggeration

Used with some degree of caution, exaggeration can be effective in showing young clients how irrational their beliefs are. Before using this technique, be certain that your client is old enough to understand the concept of exaggeration. For a teenager whining about curfew, you could say something like this: "Maybe your parents should be locked up in jail because their crime of making you come in at 10 o'clock on a school night is so severe."

Reverse Role Play

In reverse role play, you play the part of the irrational student who, in this case, insists that it is the end of the world if she gets a failing grade. The client, meanwhile, attempts to help you dispute your irrational beliefs about this situation.

Humor

Humor, which is a strategy that can be somewhat similar to exaggeration, must also be used appropriately and cautiously so that it doesn't seem as if you are making fun of your young client. You might say to him, for example, "You, who has never made a mistake in your life, made one—and you are still alive to tell about it?"

Empty Chair Technique

This technique, which involves movement, is a graphic way to help children understand the disputational process. Use two chairs. Designate one chair as the irrational chair and the other as the rational chair. First, have the client sit in the irrational chair and verbalize the thoughts she has about a problematic situation. Then have her shift to the rational chair and attempt to dispute her irrational beliefs. The following transcript is from a 6-year-old who learned this process after it was modeled by the therapist for a different problem.

> **Irrational chair:** My mom never pays any attention to me. The only one she cares about is my baby sister.
>
> **Rational chair:** Just because my mom is paying attention to the baby doesn't mean she doesn't love me. My sister can't do anything for herself, so she has to help her.
>
> **Irrational chair:** I know she loves me, but it's not fair that she only reads one book to me before bed and rocks my sister for a lot longer.
>
> **Rational chair:** That's just the way it is. You can throw a fit about it or just read another book to yourself.

Paradoxical Technique

Suggest that the client set a time limit to be deliberately irrational. During this 10- to 15-minute period, she should think of all the awful things she can't stand, make lists of her mistakes, or create poems or songs about her irrational beliefs and behaviors. Once the time period is up, she should tell herself that she can't be irrational the rest of the day and will make every attempt to think rationally and act sensibly. During the next session, as she shares the results of her experiment, ask her to identify what changes she had to make in her thinking to be rational.

Best Friend Technique

This simple strategy can be an effective dispute, especially for children and adolescents who are hard on themselves and expect perfectionism. If the client has just told you that he is the biggest loser in the world because he failed a test, ask him what he would say to his best friend if this were his problem. In most cases, the client will say something rational to his friend. So ask him why he can't say those same things to himself. A variation is to have your client pretend he is his best friend: What would he say to a friend who was insisting that he always had to be perfect or thought he couldn't stand to be grounded for a day?

Bibliotherapy

Bibliotherapy is another excellent way to help children and adolescents understand the concept of rational and irrational beliefs and the disputational process. Waters' (1979) *Color Us Rational* stories are excellent for younger children. After reading one of the stories, involve your client in writing a story with a rational ending that relates directly to a situation in her own life. Recently, a 9-year-old client wrote that, although he was sad that his parents had gotten a divorce, he realized that it could be worse—one of his parents could have died: "I don't like what they did, but I know they both love me. I can choose to be mad and sad, or just accept it and try to be happy."

Instant Replay (Bedford, 1974) is also a good story to use. The concept of instant replay helps children think about their behavior and identify ways to replay the scenario and react more rationally. After children understand this concept, they can act out instant-replay scenarios with puppets or draw instant-replay cartoon scenarios.

Adolescents can learn more about their anger by reading *How to Control Your Anger Before It Controls You* (Potter-Effron, 1998). Also, children's books can be used effectively for both children and adolescents. For example, *The Little Engine That Could* (Piper, 1986) teaches about frustration tolerance and *What If It Never Stops Raining* (Carlson, 1994) helps clients learn how to deal with anxiety.

Change the Channel

Use the metaphor of changing the channel on the TV to help remind your client that if he is "tuned in" to an irrational channel, he can switch to a more rational channel by disputing his irrational beliefs.

Disputing Strategies Specifically for Children

Erase the Irrational

Activities such as Erase the Irrational (Vernon, 2006a, pp. 247–248) teach children and adolescents how to replace irrational thoughts with rational ones. After explaining the concept of rational versus irrational beliefs and discussing the idea of erasing something, give the client the following list of irrational beliefs and ask him to "erase" the following irrational beliefs and write rational replacements:

> I should be perfect in everything I do.
>
> My friends should always do exactly what I want them to do.
>
> If I make a mistake, I'm dumb.
>
> Everyone should like me. I can't stand it if everyone doesn't.
>
> I'm the only one around the house who ever does any work.
>
> The way I'm working on my project is the best way, and others should do it my way.
>
> I shouldn't have to go out of my way to make friends. People should come to me.
>
> It's not my fault that I'm unhappy all the time.
>
> Other kids shouldn't just stand there during a game—they should put in as much effort as I do.
>
> My friends should always listen to what I have to say.

Tunnel Vision

This intervention can help younger children develop a broader perspective and thus avoid the myopic thinking that characterizes tunnel vision. First, take a sheet of paper and fold it so that one end is narrow and the other is wide. Tape it so that the child can hold it and look through both ends. Next, arrange a series of objects on a table and ask the child to look at them through the narrow (tunnel vision) end and tell you what she sees. Then ask her to flip to the other end and look at the same objects, indicating what she now sees. Discuss with her that when she has tunnel vision she may miss important aspects of the situation. Apply this to her own issues and ask her to identify how she might look at the problem if she has tunnel vision versus a broader perspective.

Race to Rational

This technique teaches younger children how to think more rationally. First, write the irrational thoughts in the list below, each on a separate card. Next, you will need two small matchbox cars and two race tracks constructed on two large sheets of tagboard with a winding track segmented into 15 parts. Each track should have an identifiable start and finish. To play, the client draws two of the cards at a time and reads them, one at a time. Before moving the first car from the start position on the first track the number of spaces designated on the card, he has to state a rational thought in response to the irrational belief. Then he reads the second card he drew and follows the same procedure with the second card. After moving the car on the second track, he draws another two cards and continues in the same manner until one car has reached the finish line.

Cards

I'll never get this work done (2 spaces).

It's too hard (1 space).

I never do anything right (1 space).

I have to be perfect (2 spaces).

I have to have my way all the time (2 spaces).

It's awful if I have to share with my friends (1 space).

My parents should always let me do whatever I want to do (1 space).

I can't stand going to school (2 spaces).

Nobody likes me (2 spaces).

Everything is terrible (1 space).

I'm bad if I make a mistake (2 spaces).

I must always win (1 space).

Things should come easily to me (1 space).

Adults should be perfect (1 space).

It's awful if everyone doesn't like me (2 spaces).

Right to Rational

Read the following beliefs, one at a time, to the client. If the belief is reasonable and rational, the client raises her right hand. If it is irrational, she raises her left hand and thinks of a rational alternative.

Beliefs

I'll never have many friends.

It's okay to make mistakes.

I am going to study hard for the test and hope that I get a good grade.

I'll always be picked on.

Everyone makes fun of me.

My teacher doesn't call on me because she doesn't like me.

I don't have to be perfect.

My brother should always do what I tell him to.

It's awful if I can't have my way.

I hope I do a good job at the track meet.

I don't always have to win.

Sometimes I have to work hard at something, and that's okay.

Disputing Strategies Specifically for Adolescents

Challenging Irrational Beliefs

This activity (Vernon, 2006b, pp. 53–56) helps adolescents learn to challenge their irrational beliefs. Once your client has learned the process, she can substitute her own irrational beliefs and challenge them. Although the original version of this activity was intended for use in a classroom or small group, it can be adapted for use with you and a client. Use the following list of scenarios:

You have a chance to win the game for your team, and you miss the shot.

You don't get all A's on your report card.

Your best friend moves away.

You've got the flu and have to miss the only school party of the year.

Cheerleading tryouts are tonight, and you're nervous.

A teacher blames you for something you didn't do.

You have tests in four subjects tomorrow.

Someone you have a crush on ignores you.

Your parents are getting a divorce.

A group of kids has been giving you a hard time about your clothes being ugly.

Take turns reading the items aloud. When it is your turn, identify two irrational beliefs that could be associated with the particular situation; the client then identifies a challenge for each irrational belief. For example, for the situation of the best friend moving away, the irrational beliefs might be that you can't stand it and you will never find another best friend again. One challenge could be that you can stand it even if you think you can't. Another challenge could ask for evidence that you will never find another best friend ever again. After the client understands the process of identifying and challenging irrational beliefs, have her identify personal examples she can work on.

Put It in Perspective

This intervention is helpful for clients who overgeneralize, awfulize, and fail to put things in perspective. Invite the client to cut articles out of the newspaper that describe what he considers to be awful events, and then write his problem on an index card. Ask him to place the articles, including the index card with his problem, on a masking tape continuum, with one end representing the most awful and the other end, the least awful. Discuss where his problem is on the continuum and how to change his thinking so he doesn't blow problems out of perspective.

Survey Technique

The survey technique, which involves a homework assignment, works well for a client who stubbornly hangs on to her irrational thoughts. Suppose she insists that her parents are the worst in the world, *never* letting her go anywhere or do anything and *always* making her do all the work in the family. To help challenge her overgeneralizations, work with her in the session to develop a survey she can use to ask her classmates about their parents. For example, she could ask her friends whether their parents let them do anything they want, never have any rules for them, never make them do any chores, and give them as much money as they want. Just by generating the questions, the client usually sees how she is exaggerating her situation and, consequently, is better able to put it in perspective.

Advantages/Disadvantages

This strategy can be effective when clients have difficulty disputing irrational beliefs because they don't want to give up their demands. Invite the client to divide a sheet of paper in half. On one half, ask him to list all the advantages of holding onto his rigid thinking and on the other side, the disadvantages. Giving an example might facilitate the process: What are the advantages of continuing to smoke marijuana because you think it should be legal, even though you could end up in jail? Are there any disadvantages of holding onto this belief?

Verbal Disputing Strategies

Three types of verbal disputes (Bernard et al., 2006) that are effective with children and adolescents are the following.

> **Functional dispute:** How does it help you to think this way? Does thinking this way help you achieve your goals?

> **Empirical dispute:** Where is the evidence that this is true? Where is the evidence to support that you are an idiot? Where is the evidence that you are what they say you are?

Logical dispute: How logical is it for you to think this way? Does it make sense to insist that you shouldn't have to follow rules when you aren't the one who makes them?

More traditional disputing strategies involve challenging low frustration tolerance by asking whether it is unbearable (which most clients respond to by saying it is bearable—they just don't like it) or asking them to prove to you that they really can't stand it, when in fact they are still alive and functioning. Asking them to show you the rule or law that says that something "shouldn't" happen, but also acknowledging their preference (it would be nice if your parents allowed you to go to the movie, but does it make sense to think that you should always get your way?) is a useful technique for disputing demands. Asking whether anything could possibly be worse or whether this is the end of the world can help dispute awfulizing and catastrophizing. Using an analogy of junking a car if it had just a flat tire (Bernard et al., 2006) or asking them whether they are what others say they are (are you a pig because someone calls you one?) are disputes that help clients deal with self-downing.

Keep in mind that, when working with children and adolescents, you will usually not be as forceful in disputing as you would be with adults; it may take more effort and a combination of strategies before children and adolescents truly understand how to identify and dispute irrational beliefs. Using a combination of verbal disputes and more creative interventions and repeating disputes in several different ways are important. Because younger clients may never have heard of the terms *rational* and *irrational,* substituting terms such as *sensible, flexible,* and *helpful,* or *insensible, rigid,* and *unhelpful* is often necessary.

The E—Effective New Philosophy (Thoughts)

If the REBT process has been effective, clients should feel less disturbed and behave more sensibly because they will be thinking more rationally. Especially with younger clients, it is important to reinforce what they have learned so they can continue to handle the present situation, as well as future incidents, more effectively. To that end, the following strategies have worked well and can readily be adapted for children or adolescents.

Tape Recordings

Because most young people are technology junkies, tape-record the session with your client so she can hear herself working through the ABC process and can thus listen to how she learned to challenge her irrational beliefs.

Concrete Images

Teach your client concrete images he can use to help him dispute irrational beliefs. I recall working with an adolescent female who was frequently out of town on weekends visiting relatives. She claimed that she could not stop thinking about what her boyfriend was doing when she was gone. She admitted to letting her imagination run wild, picturing him meeting cool new girls, partying and dancing, and not missing her one bit. When she had those thoughts, she would get depressed, thinking that they would break up, that she wouldn't get over him, and that if they weren't together as a couple, she would lose her other friends as well. Despite my efforts to dispute her overgeneralizations, she was not able to develop a rational perspective.

Because she was a visual learner, it finally struck me that it might be effective to have her imagine her head as a giant "bug zapper" like the one hanging outside the office window. If she could visualize it as such, then—just as bugs would be eliminated when they hit the zapper—her irrational beliefs would be eliminated if she turned on her zapper each time she started to think irrationally. This concrete example was just what this client needed, as is so often the case with children and adolescents. They may find it helpful to visualize a stop sign in front of them when they start to make assumptions, engage in self-downing, or act impulsively. The stop sign can be a signal to stop and reevaluate.

Other examples that have proven useful include visualizing a superhero zooming in and snatching them away from situations when they are tempted to act out; imagining that there is a radio inside their head that switches to another channel when irrational thoughts are predominant; seeing a billboard with the words "Think sensibly, act smart"; or picturing a rearview mirror as a reminder not to dwell on past negative thoughts, feelings, and behaviors.

Rational Coping Self-Statements

Rational coping statements can be generated through a collaborative process with the client and involve identifying rational statements the client can use to address a variety of feelings and beliefs. This technique is especially effective with younger clients. These statements can be written on index cards that they can carry with them or post in lockers or on desks or mirrors to serve as a reminder to think rationally. Examples of rational coping self-statements include

> Everyone makes mistakes, and when I do, it isn't the end of the world.

> Even though it is hard, I can learn to swim.

> Getting mad will just make things worse, so I just need to take some deep breaths and walk away when I feel like exploding.

Rational Verses

Involve your young client in writing rational verses such as the following:

Jack and Jill went up the hill to fetch a pail of water.
Jack fell down and broke his knee.
Jill said, "This is bad, but not a catastrophe."

Rational Limericks

Teach your client to write rational limericks, in which the first, second, and fifth lines rhyme with each other, and the third and fourth lines rhyme:

There once was a boy named Larry
Who wanted to play with Mary.
But when he asked her to play
She said, "You're ugly—go away."
And Larry said, "I'm not ugly; I'll play with Terry."

Rational Songs

Teach your client to compose rational songs to familiar childhood tunes, or suggest to her that, for songs she frequently listens to, she rewrite them from a more rational perspective. A fourth grader who was upsetting herself about her best friend's lack of attention made up the following lyrics (to be sung to the tune of "Twinkle, Twinkle, Little Star"):

If my best friend plays with me, then I smile and
    sing with glee.
But, if she chooses someone else, I don't have to hate
    myself.
I just have to look around; other friends can surely
    be found.

Analyzing TV Shows or Movies

Suggest that your client analyze TV shows or movies for examples of self-downing, demanding, overgeneralizing and awfulizing, or low frustration tolerance and rewrite the episodes to reflect a more rational perspective.

Rational Bumper Stickers, Posters, or Banners

Invite your client to create rational bumper stickers, posters, or banners as a way of remembering rational concepts. A fifth grader who was having problems concentrating on schoolwork because he was anxious about his performance drew a two-part poster of himself surrounded by balloons with slogans such as "You can't do it," "If you miss one, you're a total loser," and "Nothing is more awful than doing a bad job on this test" on one side of the poster. On the other side he drew a picture of himself popping these balloons. He said the poster was a reminder that he could get rid of his negative thoughts.

Rational Books or Stories

Writing a rational book or a story is an excellent way to reinforce rational thinking. These can be modeled after Waters' (1979) *Color Us Rational,* where the main character experiences a disturbing event and thinks irrationally—but eventually develops a more rational outlook and less disturbed feelings.

Rational Advice Column

Suggest to the client that she write a rational advice column, in which she takes examples of problems she has been dealing with and writes suggestions about how to think more rationally and behave more sensibly.

Look Through the Lens

For this intervention, use two pair of glasses—one with clear lenses and the other with dark lenses. When the client talks about his problems, ask him to put on each pair of glasses and reflect on the situation from each perspective. For example, if he is extremely nervous about going to a party, he is probably reflecting on it through the darker glasses: "Kids will make fun of me," "I'll spill food all over my shirt," "No one will talk to me." If he is wearing the clear glasses, he might see that the party could be fun, that someone will probably talk to him, and that he won't have a terrible time. Encourage him to use this strategy to help him think more rationally and avoid awfulizing and overgeneralizing.

Picture This

This technique is especially helpful for adolescents with self-defeating behavior. Invite them to take pictures or cut them out of magazines to represent what their life will be like if they continue down the same path. After pasting these on one side of a sheet of poster paper, they then find or take pictures to represent what they would like their life to be like. An adolescent with substance abuse problems took pictures of a traffic ticket, a wrecked car, a high school diploma in flames, a substandard housing development, and herself behind the counter at a fast food restaurant to represent the consequences of continuing to drink. In contrast, the pictures of how she wanted her life to be included a nice car, a nice house, a diploma, and a good job. This concrete strategy served as a springboard for helping her develop the frustration tolerance she needed to stop abusing substances.

Words of Wisdom

Invite clients to interview others about how to tolerate frustration, accept imperfection, or give up demands. After the interview, have them write a "Words of Wisdom" song, short story, or a list of tips on what they learned from others about how to give up these irrational beliefs.

Scrap It

Have the client make a list of things she thinks she cannot stand and find pictures to represent each item. Have her paste each on a separate sheet of paper in a notebook. Encourage her to try doing each of the things she thinks she cannot tolerate, and as she does so, she can tear them out of the notebook to give her a visual representation of how she has overcome her discomfort anxiety.

Chain Reaction

This intervention is especially effective in helping clients understand the chain reaction of thinking irrationally or behaving insensibly. You will need multiple strips of paper and a stapler or tape. Start by asking the client to identify an irrational belief associated with a recent event. Write this on a strip of paper and fasten each end together to make a circle. Then ask what happened as a result of this thought. For example, if he thought, "I can't stand studying for this test, so I'm going to watch a movie instead," he might get a low grade on the test (write this on the second strip, loop it through the first, and fasten the ends together), have to stay after school (third strip), not be able to go out with friends (fourth strip), miss a fun party (fifth strip), and so forth. These strips, when fastened together like a chain, serve as a visual reminder of the negative results of irrational thinking and subsequent behavior. Invite him to tell you how he could think differently in order to break the chain.

The F—Effective New Feelings

One of the goals of REBT is to reduce the intensity of negative emotions—an objective that is particularly important for young clients, who easily become overwhelmed by their emotions and often don't know how to deal with them. The result of working through the ABC model is that clients can adopt an effective new philosophy that will consequently result in more moderate feelings. This is not to say that clients who have experienced a negative event that they were depressed about will feel elated, but they can feel less depressed, sad, or regretful. These moderate feelings facilitate problem solving and prevent the client from staying stuck.

HOMEWORK

Homework, which helps clients change more quickly and profoundly, is an essential component of REBT (Dryden et al., 2003; Ellis & MacLaren, 1998). The premise is that, through persistence and practice, clients can continue to work on getting better—independent of the counseling sessions. This form of self-help is empowering for children and adolescents and is often a good way for young clients to share what they are working on with parents and teachers. Various types of cognitive, emotive, and behavioral homework can be used: conducting short surveys or experiments, creating rational coping statements, making lists of advantages and disadvantages of maintaining unproductive behaviors, practicing self-talk in front of a mirror, or using bibliotherapy. Homework is usually assigned at the end of the counseling session, and when possible, it is a good idea to involve clients in the design of the task. The following example illustrates how the counselor involved Antonio in developing his homework task:

> For several sessions, 10-year-old Antonio had been working on his low frustration tolerance, noting that it negatively affected his ability to complete tasks. In his next session, the counselor had him read the ever-popular children's story *The Little Engine That Could* (Piper, 1986) to introduce the idea of positive self-talk. In this story, a little engine's goal was to get over the hill, but because he was smaller than all the other engines, he had to work harder to achieve his goal. As the story goes, the little engine kept saying to himself, "I think I can, I think I can," as he chugged up the hill, and "I thought I could, I thought I could," as he raced down.

After reading the story, the counselor and Antonio discussed how the little engine used positive, instead of negative, self-talk and how he had to work hard and be persistent in achieving his goal. The counselor asked Antonio what he thought he could do during the week to practice these ideas at school, and he came up with the idea of making an "I think I can" can to set on his desk to remind him of the message in the story. Together they came up with the idea that he could paste a list of the advantages of persistence on the can and look at that list several times a day as a reminder. The counselor suggested that, each time he persisted and completed something, he write it on a sheet of paper and put it in the can, reviewing the contents every few days to help him remember what he had accomplished.

In introducing homework to younger clients, it may be preferable to use the term *experiment* to avoid the negative connotation of *home-*

work. It is also important not to react negatively if they don't complete the homework, which is often the case with this age group. However, if the assignments are engaging and creative, there is a greater likelihood that they will complete the task.

EVALUATION

Evaluation can be accomplished as a monitoring process that occurs at various points during counseling or as an overall evaluation at the end (Ellis & Bernard, 2006). If it occurs periodically, the counselor can modify treatment as needed. Several forms of evaluation can be used: subjective client reports such as journals, feeling charts, sentence stems, and behavior graphs; objective measures such as depression inventories, anger checklists, feeling thermometers, and ABC self-help sheets; or input from parents and teachers. Parents and teachers, for example, can be asked to keep logs of behavior or evidence of feelings such as anger, anxiety, or depression in the child.

It may also be helpful for parents and teachers to complete standardized evaluation forms. Especially when working with younger children, evaluation from parents and teachers as well as the child is optimal, because, depending on the nature of the problem, younger children may tell you what you want to hear. If behavior at school is a problem, for example, they may be unwilling to admit that they haven't made much progress and therefore report that everything is fine, in which case teacher input is essential. This reluctance can also be the case with adolescents, particularly if they were not self-referred. If they don't want to be in counseling, their feeling charts or behavior logs may show dramatic improvement because they want to terminate counseling, not because there has been drastic change in their behavior. One way to get parental input without making adolescents feel defensive is to have clients write a note to their parents indicating specific improvements they've made and explaining why they think they can terminate counseling. My experience with these young clients has been that they are more honest about their own self-evaluation if they know that their parents may differ in their opinion of progress.

Regardless of which method is used, evaluation as an ongoing part of the therapeutic process results in data that can be used to reevaluate and revise goals and is a viable way to assess progress, both from the client's and the counselor's standpoint. In addition, frequent evaluation provides for accountability for all stakeholders. If, during this evaluation process, it appears that the client is making good progress, sessions can be scheduled less frequently, thus giving the client the opportunity to work on the problems and utilize homework assignments.

Evaluation conducted at or near the end of the counseling process compares the current functioning to criteria related to the goal. For example, if the goal was to decrease anxiety about spending the night away from home, evaluation in the form of self-report or parental input will indicate whether the goal has been achieved. This type of overall evaluation is important in determining what has been accomplished and whether termination is appropriate. If the client has made good progress, but the counselor senses that she is not quite ready to terminate, he or she can suggest decreasing the frequency of sessions but still doing some periodic checkups to see how well the client is maintaining her progress. In my experience, many young clients seem to like this approach because they can continue to have support and structure if they need it. Usually after one checkup, they are ready to terminate completely.

As part of the overall evaluation process at the end of therapy, it is particularly helpful to young clients to invite them to list both the changes they have made and what they need to continue doing to maintain those changes. Brainstorming together can often result in creative strategies that help keep them on target, as the following example illustrates:

> Eight-year-old Andrea, who had been in counseling to work on anxiety, made a list of the things she had been anxious or worried about before she came to counseling. After several sessions, she crossed off the things she no longer worried about. She was proud of her progress! When she first came to counseling, she had been asked to put a penny in a jar each time she felt worried or anxious during the week. After the first week, she had 50 pennies in the jar, but at termination, she only had 10, which was a nice visual way of reinforcing the hard work she had done. To help her maintain her progress, Andrea and the counselor brainstormed other things she could do, coming up with several suggestions: continue with the penny jar, make a list of the things she could do or think about when she started to worry, and play counselor. To do this, she would sit in one chair and talk to her doll, who would sit in the other chair. She would tell her doll what she was worried about, and then she would pretend that the doll was her counselor and the doll would "help" Andrea deal with her problems.

Evaluation, coupled with strategies intended to maintain progress and self-evaluation, is an inherent part of the counseling process.

Informal evaluative measures can be used with more formal procedures, as needed, to provide comprehensive treatment.

Interventions for Internalizing Problems

The challenges facing youth today are greater than in any previous generation, making access to high-quality mental health services more critical than ever. McWhirter and Burrow-Sanchez (2009) noted that it is more difficult than ever for families to provide healthy environments for their children as a result of numerous social, demographic, and economic factors. There is also considerably more stress on families, which can manifest itself in domestic violence, as well as numerous other problems. Changes in family composition (blended, step-, and single-parent families) and increased economic instability make it more challenging for some children to thrive. Social changes, coupled with technological advances, have exposed children and adolescents to new influences and experiences that are often overwhelming and inappropriate for their age level. Furthermore, they frequently see public figures model irrational risk-taking, sexual permissiveness, and violence as a way to cope with anger and frustration. It should come as no surprise, then, that we see an increase in these same behaviors in youth.

As a society, we are seeing the ramifications of these changes. Many children do not have much adult guidance in developing skills such as self-discipline and responsibility and, consequently, may be more prone to negative peer pressure. Children growing up in violent households, or those who have been physically or sexually abused, experience more stress and other related psychological problems such as anxiety, eating disorders, substance abuse, teen pregnancy, and lower impulse control (McWhirter & Burrow-Sanchez, 2009). Depression, once considered nonexistent until late adolescence or early adulthood (Evans, Van Velsor, & Schumacher, 2002), is now recognized as a prevalent problem for adolescents. In fact, Evans et al. postulated that "depression may be one of the most overlooked and undertreated psychological disorders of adolescence" (p. 211). Today about 20 percent of teens will experience depression before they reach adulthood and are at high risk for suicide, which is the second leading cause of death among youth ages 15 to 24 (McWhirter & Burrow-Sanchez, 2009). Unfortunately, even children and pre-teens are not entirely immune to depression. Although still quite rare, the age of onset is earlier and the prevalence progressively increases throughout adolescence (Koplewicz, 2002).

As noted in chapter 1, children and adolescents often lack the support and skills necessary to cope effectively with situational and developmental problems, and consequently feel anxious, depressed, or stressed. They may have very low self-concepts or engage in irrational risk taking or violence as a way to cope with their confusion, anger, or frustration. It is imperative for practitioners to identify effective interventions to help young people deal with life's challenges in self-enhancing ways.

The purpose of this chapter is to identify cognitive, emotive, and behavioral interventions to be used in individual counseling for internalizing disorders of childhood and adolescence. Merrell (2001) described internalizing disorders as problems that are developed and maintained primarily within the individual. He cited Reynolds (1992), who referred to them as a secret illness, which implies that they are difficult to directly observe. In this chapter, anxiety, depression, stress, and grief will be addressed. Although stress also manifests itself behaviorally and physically, it is initiated and maintained to a large extent within the individual. In a similar vein, grief is multidimensional and complex, comprising a variety of symptoms, many of which are internalized. Interventions both for children (ages 6 to 10) and for adolescents (ages 11 to 18) will be described. Many of the interventions are brief and are intended to be incorporated into the counseling session to reinforce concepts or help with disputing. Others are more detailed and will constitute most of the session.

ANXIETY

As Wilde (1996) noted, anxiety is not caused by events but rather by our perceptions of events. For children and adolescents, this idea is often complicated by their limited cognitive skills, which may interfere with their ability to perceive events correctly; they may naturally tend to extrapolate ideas from one context and apply them inappropriately to another situation that may be completely different.

There are different types and degrees of anxiety. For example, healthy anxiety helps us anticipate future misfortune—it is a concern or vigilance that helps people cope with difficult or dangerous situations (Foa & Andrews, 2006). Healthy anxiety is almost always based on a realistic fear, such as worrying about crossing the street at a busy intersection where there is no traffic light and there is a realistic chance of being hit by a car. In contrast, unhealthy anxiety is an "emotional response to perceived dangers that seem real but are mainly imaginary because so little probability of occurrence exists" (Wilde, 1996, p. 94). The fears associated with unhealthy anxiety are exaggerated, unrealistic, maladaptive, or irrational, such as being terrified about riding on a roller coaster for fear it could crash. Although it is *possible* that this could happen, the *probability* is very slight; it rarely happens. According to Ellis (1998), unhealthy anxiety frequently makes you restrict your activities when there is no need to do so, or it makes you lose control of yourself because the physical and psychosomatic symptoms of panic, phobia, trembling, or shaking interfere with your ability to cope adequately.

When children are anxious, they have negative and unrealistic thoughts. They assume something bad might happen in the future and that they cannot do anything to prevent it (Antony & Swinson, 2000). Furthermore, they irrationally believe that if the event were to occur, it would be so bad that they wouldn't be able to stand it. Thus, they not only minimize their ability to cope with very bad things, they also catastrophize, assuming that their worst fears will become reality. They may hear about something bad happening to someone else and assume it could happen to them. Their overgeneralizations or exaggerations increase their anxiety. They may become so anxious that they can't think about anything else and therefore often beg for a guarantee that their fears won't materialize. Even though the best way to deal with anxiety is to face the feared situation, anxious parents may inadvertently reinforce their children's anxiety by protecting them from this exposure. To further complicate things, when young clients feel anxious, they often experience secondary emotions. For instance, they feel anxious about being anxious or put themselves down for being anxious and then feel depressed.

According to Merrell (2001), anxiety disorders involve subjective feelings such as discomfort or fear, overt behaviors such as avoidance and withdrawal, and physiological responses such as nausea or shaking. Tight muscles and pain, such as headaches, are also common reactions (Antony & Swinson, 2000). Grieger and Boyd (2006) described two types of anxiety common in young clients. The first is ego anxiety, which is anxiety about one's self, resulting from the belief that she must do well and be approved of or else be considered a bad and unworthy person. Another type of anxiety is discomfort anxiety, in which the child may be fearful that bad things will happen that he would not be able to tolerate—if his comfort level is threatened, it would be awful to feel the discomfort.

It is important to understand that younger children become anxious because they have difficulty distinguishing real from imaginary dangers (Grieger & Boyd, 2006) and may lack the cognitive skills to put things in the proper perspective. The case I vividly recall is the one in which a father of a third grader called me because he had found his young son's will. The father asked me whether John had appeared anxious or depressed in our recent counseling sessions to discuss his parents' separation. Although I hadn't noted any anxiety or depression on John's part, I was concerned about what his father was reporting and scheduled an appointment with John for the next day. When John and I met, I explained that his dad had found the will and was worried. I questioned John about being very sad or anxious and worried about something, and he said the reason he had made the will was that, in his social studies class, they had been talking about how some kids his age had been trapped in a cave and had died. He was afraid that would happen to him, so he wanted to be sure his brother got his baseball glove and baseball cards and his friends could have his favorite toys.

This example clearly illustrates how children can cause their own anxiety because they don't have the ability to put the situation in its proper context. Adults need to be cognizant of this tendency and attempt to alleviate children's anxiety before it occurs by carefully explaining the difference between probability and possibility.

In treating anxiety, it is important to identify the negative interpretations and beliefs that result in anxiety. As Antony and Swinson (2000) noted, when a person is anxious and interprets a situation, the prediction is often inaccurate. They identified several types of anxious thinking, such as probability overestimation (a prediction that someone thinks is likely to occur, even though the likelihood is quite low), mind reading (making negative assumptions about what others are thinking, especially as it relates them), personalization (taking on too much responsibility for a negative situation), and "should" statements (incorrect assumptions about how things *should* be).

Ellis (1998) noted that irrational beliefs resulting in anxiety are related to personal inadequacy, awfulizing, "I-can't-stand-it-itis," and other forms of all-or-nothing thinking or overgeneralizing, including the following:

Something bad might happen; it must not happen.

I can't stand being anxious.

I should not feel anxious.

I am a rotten person because I can't cope with my anxiety better.

If something bad happens, it would be awful and terrible, and I couldn't stand it.

The following interventions can be adapted for use with children and adolescents who are experiencing anxiety.

What If?

RATIONALE Young children often experience anxiety about new situations or unfamiliar people or places. Sometimes they imagine the worst. This intervention, based on ideas presented in Nancy Carlson's book (1994), *What If It Never Stops Raining?* helps children reframe negative perceptions that create anxiety.

MATERIALS ▷ What If? Cards (p. 96)

▷ A pen or pencil

▷ A sheet of paper

▷ 2 puppets

PROCEDURE 1. When a young client presents with anxiety, often about typical developmental issues that are firsts (staying overnight with a friend, participating on a sports team, being in a performance such as a spelling bee or dance recital), she can learn different ways of thinking to avoid the "what if" thoughts and awfulizing.

2. After she has discussed some of the things she is anxious about and you have identified her "what if" thinking (What if I get scared when I stay with my friend? What if I strike out in the ball game and everyone laughs? What if I can't remember how to spell the words?), engage her in the What If? game.

3. The game goes like this. You and the client take turns drawing a card and reading the situation. Together you imagine what could happen (positive and negative), and you write these down on the back of the card. Do this for five or six cards, depending on time. For example, if the card reads, "What if there is loud thunder and I get scared?" responses could be "Thunderstorms don't last long," "It's just loud noise," "We could bang on pots and pans and see whether we could make noise louder than the thunder."

4. Next, each of you selects a puppet. Explain to the client that you will draw a card. Your puppet will talk about the situations, and her puppet will try to respond in a way that helps your puppet be

less worried or anxious. For example, you may draw a card that says, "What if my sister forgets to pick me up after school?" (If the client doesn't reply, you could model the first response by the client puppet and prompt on others as needed.) The client's puppet could answer, "Then you would have to call your dad to come and get you." Then draw another card or use the same card and expand on the first response by saying, "But what if my dad can't come?" The client's puppet could answer, "Then you could call your mom and ask her whether you could walk home with me; that would be fun," and so forth. Including some positive reframes is important.

5. After several puppet interactions, discuss what the client learned from this intervention. Focus on the idea of possibilities: Many different things are possible, and there are usually alternative ways of thinking about the situation.

6. Read the story by Carlson (1994), *What If It Never Stops Raining?* Discuss the various things that the boy in the story worried about and how many of these things actually happened. If they did happen, were they as bad as he predicted they would be? Help the client see that this is often what happens with anxiety: Many of the things we worry about don't happen or aren't as bad as we imagine they would be.

7. Invite the client to write her own What If? book to help her deal with her own anxieties.

What If? Cards

What if everyone makes fun of my new hair cut?	What if I my sister forgets to pick me up after school?
What if I lose my lunch money on the way to school?	What if I get lost on the way home from my friend's house?
What if it snows so hard we can't even get outside the next day?	What if the teacher won't let me go to the bathroom when I have to go?
What if I miss a lot of notes when I play in the piano recital?	What if my friend plays with someone else at recess?
What if I forget how to spell the words on my spelling test?	What if . . . (create your own)
What if I get scared in the night?	What if . . . (create your own)

Worry-Wart

RATIONALE Worrying and anxiety are typical reactions as children face developmental challenges associated with peers, school, and competition. In addition, many children grow up in dysfunctional family situations that contribute to anxiety and worry. This intervention helps them learn ways to manage these negative feelings.

MATERIALS
▷ A large sheet of butcher paper

▷ A pen or pencil

▷ A rock that is relatively flat and smooth on top and small enough to fit in a pocket

▷ Markers

PROCEDURE
1. When a client presents with anxiety, discuss the things that worry him. Then have him lie on his back on the sheet of paper on the floor so that you can trace around his body. Next, ask him to think about what he is anxious about and where he feels it—in his tummy, head, and so forth. Then have him write words or draw pictures on the body outline to depict this.

2. Once you have an idea about his worries, ask him to pick two or three of the things that he worries about the most and draw a circle around them on the body outline.

3. With regard to these two or three major worries, ask the client to describe specifically the thoughts he has about these concerns. Write these beside each worry.

4. Next, teach him how to develop rational coping self-statements as a way to address what he worries about. For example, if he is worried that he might perform poorly on his social studies oral report, a rational self-statement could be "I just have to practice it a lot and do my best, but, if I don't, I know that everyone makes mistakes sometimes." Or, if he worries about being called names by an older kid, a rational self-statement could be "When he calls me stupid and stinky, I can just remember that I am pretty smart and

I don't stink, so what he says isn't true." Help the client identify rational coping self-statements for the other key worries he circled and write them beside each worry.

5. Time permitting, work on identifying other coping self-statements for the remaining worries, encouraging him to think what he can say to himself and writing these beside his worries.

6. Next, give him the rock, which can be his worry-wart rock. Invite him to draw something on the rock that would remind him not to worry so much. He can keep the rock in his pocket and touch it when he is anxious, which will remind him that he can think about rational coping self-statements to help him feel better. Also give him the body outline to tape in his room as a reminder of how he can reduce his anxiety.

Wanda the Worrier

RATIONALE Young children often do not have the cognitive ability to look at situations that create anxiety for them from multiple perspectives that could in fact reduce their worry. This intervention is designed to facilitate that development.

MATERIALS
▷ Wanda the Worrier story (p. 101)

▷ A pen or pencil

▷ A sheet of paper

PROCEDURE
1. After discussing the client's worries and anxieties and how they affect her, introduce the Wanda the Worrier story as an intervention that may help her learn more about her worries and what she can do about them.

2. After reading the story, discuss it by asking the following questions:

   What were some of the things that Wanda worried about?

   Do you worry about any of the same things that Wanda worried about? (Ask for examples and write them down in the form of a list.)

   Are there things that Wanda worried about that you don't worry about? (Ask for examples and add them to the list.)

   Do you ever get tummy aches or headaches when you worry too much? Or are there other ways in which the worry affects you?

3. Next ask the client what she thinks Wanda could do to alleviate some of her worries. Are there things she can think about or do so that she wouldn't have to worry so much about everything? Discuss these and brainstorm other ideas as appropriate.

4. Then ask the client to select one of her worries (from the second item in the question list under step 2). Discuss what she has done

to help her with that worry. Then teach her the following irrational thoughts:

> Sometimes worries get worse when people think that the worst could happen. Are there any examples of that in the story or with regard to your own worries?

> Sometimes worries get worse when you think something will always be this way (that is, just because someone teased you once, does that mean he will always tease you?). Are there examples of this in the story or with regard to your own worries?

> Sometimes worries get worse when we assume things, such as nobody will sit by us. Are there examples of this in the story or with regard to your own worries?

5. After discussing the irrational thoughts described in step 4, teach her how to dispute these thoughts by asking herself, "Does everything always turn out like the worst thing possible?" "Just because something happened once, does that mean it will always be like that?" "How does it help to assume that something will be a certain way until I have checked it out?"

6. Ask the client to take several of the worries from the written list and work through them, identifying the irrational thoughts and what she could think to herself to dispute these thoughts.

Wanda the Worrier

Wanda was a worrier. As soon as she got up each morning, she looked out the window and worried about whether it would rain or snow that day. As she started to get dressed, she worried about what she should wear to school. What if she wore her red-and-white striped pants and everyone laughed at her? Or what if she wore her purple pants and kids said they were ugly? She finally decided to wear jeans and a yellow T-shirt, but she worried that she would get cold.

Finally, she went down for breakfast. Her father had made her pancakes, but she worried about getting too full and throwing up, so she ate only a couple of bites, but then she worried about her dad getting mad at her because she hadn't eaten much. She grabbed her coat and backpack and went out the door. She was worried about missing the bus, but as it turned out, she had plenty of time. While she waited, she worried about who she would sit by. What if all the kids her age were sitting together and the only place left for her was by an older kid? What if he made fun of her like someone did one time she had to sit by an older kid?

As it turned out, she did sit by an older kid, but he didn't pay any attention to her. Throughout the bus ride she worried about getting to school late because the bus had to stop at so many stoplights. Then she started worrying about her spelling test and other things at school. Did she practice her words enough so that she could get them all right? Would the math drills be too hard? What if she sang wrong notes during music or couldn't do a good job shooting baskets during gym class? If she missed her shots, would the other kids make fun of her?

By the time she got off the bus, Wanda had worried so much that her tummy ached. Then she worried about throwing up. That would be awful, she thought. Things actually went all right during the morning, and her tummy ache gradually got better. But just before lunch she started to worry again. What if the food was yucky and it made her sick? What if none of her friends wanted to sit by her? What if the lunchroom teacher was mean?

By the time Wanda went to lunch, her head was hurting from all her worrying. But the lunch wasn't too bad, and she did get to sit by her friends. But then she began to worry about who she would play with at recess. She wasn't a very good kickball player, so what if her friends wanted to play that game but didn't want her to be on their team because she wasn't good? Then what would she do?

As Wanda left the lunchroom and headed outside, she then started to worry about the afternoon. What do you think Wanda worried about?

From *More What Works When with Children and Adolescents: A Handbook of Individual Counseling Techniques,* © 2009 by Ann Vernon, Champaign, IL: Research Press (800-519-2707, www.researchpress.com)

Wash Away the Worries

RATIONALE   This concrete intervention helps children learn more about anxiety and identify ways to deal with it.

MATERIALS   ▷ A small bucket of water

▷ A sponge

▷ Another small bucket (empty) to wring the sponge water into

▷ A pen or pencil

▷ A sheet of paper

▷ Envelope containing the letters R, P, T, and S, written on individual slips of paper

PROCEDURE   1. When a client presents with anxiety and worry, explain that when we worry, we often keep things inside and we get bogged down with our thoughts, much like what happens when you soak a sponge in water.

2. To illustrate, hand the client the sponge and ask him to dip it into the water and describe how it feels before and after it has been in the water. Then have him wring out the sponge into the empty bucket and compare how it feels now to how it felt when it was full of water.

3. Next, have the client discuss some of the things that worry him and help him see that rather than keeping them inside like the water in the sponge, it is better to do something to "let go" of some of the worry, similar to wringing out the sponge. Ask him to select a particularly bothersome worry, describe it, and then think about what he could do to lessen the worry—as if he were wringing out the sponge.

4. Help him identify rational coping self-statements (for example, if he is worried about failing a test, a coping self-statement might be that if he studies hard, his chances of passing are much better; he usually gets good grades on tests, so chances are he will again, etc.).

Also help him identify other things that might be helpful. This could be done through brainstorming (recording his ideas on paper) or by having him randomly draw the following alphabet letters out of an envelope: *R, P, T,* or *S.* Ask him:

Can you think of anything to do starting with the letter *R* that would help you deal with your worries? (Examples could be relax, run around, read a book.)

The letter *P?* (Play a game, play with my pet, pray.)

T? (Talk to someone.)

S? (Sing a song, share my feelings.)

5. In closing, ask the client what he learned and which strategies he thinks would be most helpful in his situation.

Anxious About Being Anxious

RATIONALE Although anxiety is not an uncommon emotion for adolescents to experience, they often make themselves more anxious by feeling anxious about their anxiety. This intervention helps them learn more about anxiety and how to reduce the anxiety about being anxious.

MATERIALS ▷ Anxious About Being Anxious Worksheet (p. 106)

▷ A pen or pencil

PROCEDURE 1. When an adolescent presents with anxiety, it is important to ask how she feels about being anxious, because frequently she will be depressed, guilty, or anxious about the anxiety, which can increase the severity of the primary anxiety. Introduce the Anxious About Being Anxious Worksheet to help her see how the cycle of being anxious about being anxious develops and results in other negative emotions.

2. After explaining the connection between beliefs (B) and emotional consequences (C), ask the client to come up with an example of something she is anxious about and identify that as the A (activating event). Then identify the beliefs (B), as well as what she is telling herself to create the anxiety (C, emotional consequence). Then have her do the same for the secondary emotion of feeling anxious or depressed or guilty about being anxious. Discuss her examples.

3. Next, teach the client how to dispute the secondary emotions by disputing the irrational beliefs, such as the following:

I shouldn't feel this way

Disputes

Where is it written that I shouldn't feel this way?

There isn't any law against feeling anxious; it happens to lots of people.

I'd rather not feel this way, but how does it help to put myself down for feeling guilty or depressed about my anxiety?

Why can't I cope with things better?

Disputes

Am I trying to deal with it the best I can?

Aren't I getting professional help so I can deal with it better?

Other people can handle their problems without getting anxious, so why can't I?

Disputes

Where's the proof that others don't get anxious?

What does it say about me if I can't handle my problems without getting anxious and others can? Does it mean I am a bad person?

How does it help me to put myself down because I sometimes get anxious?

4. Work with the client to help her identify disputes to her own secondary emotion.

5. Then help her learn to dispute the beliefs associated with her primary anxiety, explaining that it will be easier to deal with that if she isn't also feeling anxious, guilty, or depressed about being anxious.

6. Encourage the client to keep track of the irrational beliefs related to her anxiety and her primary and secondary emotions, and practice the disputing techniques.

Anxious About Being Anxious Worksheet

Example 1—primary anxiety

A = Taking my driver's license test

B = I will never pass it.

My friends will laugh at me.

I'll be the only kid in high school without a license.

This is terrible.

I'm so stupid.

C = Anxious and depressed

Example 2—secondary anxiety

A = Anxious and depressed

B = I shouldn't feel this way.

What's wrong with me?

Why can't I cope with things better?

Other people can handle their problems without getting anxious, so why can't I?

C = Guilty, depressed

Walk Away, Anxiety

RATIONALE   This intervention teaches adolescents how let go of worry and anxiety.

MATERIALS
- ▷ A sheet of paper
- ▷ A pen or pencil
- ▷ A roll of masking tape
- ▷ 8 to 10 index cards

PROCEDURE
1. When a client presents with anxiety, explore how the anxiety affects him physically, emotionally, and behaviorally. Ask him to share a specific example of a time when his anxiety was high.

2. Explain to him that anxiety is often about *possibility* versus *probability*. In other words, almost anything is possible: He could be riding in a car and be in an accident, he could take a test and fail, and so forth. Ask him to think of other examples of possibilities as they apply to his life—things that he gets anxious about—and write these down.

3. Then discuss the concept of probability, or the likelihood that the things he worries about will occur. For example, if he says that he is worried about playing in his first football game and not doing anything right, explore the likelihood of this happening: Would he actually not do *anything* right? Or might there just be *some* things that he doesn't do right? If he is afraid to ask a girl for a date because it is possible she could turn him down, ask what the probability of this is, based on his previous experiences with asking girls out, and so forth.

4. Next, place a strip of masking tape on the floor. Label one end "highly probable" and the other end "not very probable." Take an example from the client's list and ask him to identify the possibilities—what could happen? Then ask him to take a place on the line that represents the probability of that happening. Place an index card on the line with a short description of the problem.

5. Repeat this procedure for other anxieties on the list. When finished, ask the client to study where the index cards fall on the line, reflecting that some of the things he worried about have higher probabilities of occurring than others, and, if he keeps this in perspective, he might not feel as anxious about everything. Ask what he learned about the possibility of something happening versus the probability and how this strategy might help him walk away from some of his anxiety.

Worry Management

RATIONALE Adolescents can easily become overwhelmed by their worries, and this intervention is a good way to help them put worries in perspective in order to cope more effectively.

MATERIALS ▷ Worry Management Sorting Board (p. 110)

▷ An 8½ × 11-inch sheet of paper, cut into 15 individual strips

▷ A pen or pencil

PROCEDURE 1. When a client describes how worried she is about issues related to peers, performance, family relationships, the future, and so forth, engage her in the following intervention.

2. First, have her use the individual strips of paper, recording one worry per strip.

3. Next, ask her to use the sorting board (Part I, Time Frame) and place each of the worry strips in the category that most accurately describes the worry.

4. After she has finished sorting, discuss what is in each of the categories. Then ask her what she could do to help herself learn to deal with the most immediate worries first so that she doesn't become overwhelmed.

5. Next, have her return to the sorting board and this time place the same strips of worries into the Part II (Degree of Control) categories. When she has finished, discuss what she put in each category and what she can do to deal with the worries that she thinks she has more control over. Also discuss the worries she thinks she doesn't have much control over: What prevents her from having more control? What could she do to gain more control, if possible?

6. Process the activity by asking the client what she learned by doing it and what techniques she can use to better manage her worries.

Worry Management Sorting Board

Directions: Place the individual worry strips in the category that most accurately describes it. Multiple strips can go in each category.

Part I—Time Frame

Immediate Worry (within 24 hours)
Not-So-Immediate Worry (within the week)
Longer-Term Worry (within the next few weeks)
Long-Term Worry (in the next month or longer)

Part II—Degree of Control

Worries I Have Control Over/Can Do Something About
Worries I Don't Have as Much Control Over

Away with Anxiety

RATIONALE This intervention helps adolescents identify irrational beliefs that contribute to anxiety and learn how to dispute them.

MATERIALS ▷ A magnifying glass

▷ Away with Anxiety Worksheet (p. 113)

▷ A pen or pencil

PROCEDURE 1. When a client describes his anxiety, explain that often we make the anxiety worse by imagining the worst, or "magnifying" the problems. Hand him the magnifying glass and ask him to look through it, noting the difference between using it and not using it so that he gets the concrete image firm in his mind. Then ask whether he can think of an example of magnifying a problem (or provide one: Does he ever get anxious before taking an exam, thinking he will surely fail it?). Discuss the concept of catastrophizing, or magnifying the problem, which contributes to anxiety.

2. Give the client the Away with Anxiety Worksheet and ask him to first list things he has worried about in the past few days or weeks. Then ask him to complete the next two columns, which ask him to identify the worse-case scenario and the actual outcome.

3. Review the worksheet and encourage him to reflect on how catastrophizing does or does not contribute to his anxiety. Help him learn how to dispute catastrophizing thoughts by teaching him the following strategies.

   Challenging logically: How logical is it for me to think this way? Does it really make sense?

   Challenging empirically: Where is the evidence that the worst will happen. Does it usually?

   Challenging empirically: Even if the worst happens, where is the evidence that I couldn't stand it?

Challenging functionally: How does it help me to think the worst?

4. Ask him to apply these disputes to the worries he identified on the worksheet and see whether he feels differently after having done so.

5. Discuss with the client how to use these disputes routinely to help keep his anxiety in check.

Away with Anxiety Worksheet

Directions: In column 1, list things you have been anxious or worried about in the past few days or weeks. In column 2, identify the worst-case scenario: What was the worst thing you imagined happening relative to this worry? In column 3, indicate how the worry "turned out," if it is in the past.

Worry or anxiety	Worst-case scenario	Actual outcome
1. Thump x2	dead owl.	Fine
2. Homework	Failing	usually got done to
3. Ronica	bad spinon and	ok he po
4. Sick Cough	Throw up	Nothing to fk
5. Pain in le,le	that gives out	oh running
6.		
7.		
8. reflection Consider: reality – Stats		

From *More What Works When with Children and Adolescents: A Handbook of Individual Counseling Techniques,* © 2009 by Ann Vernon, Champaign, IL: Research Press (800-519-2707, www.researchpress.com)

DEPRESSION

Depression is probably the most recognized internalizing disorder, defined simply as a "feeling of sadness and dejection resulting in an increasingly pessimistic outlook on life" (Carter & Minirth, 1995, p. 7). Although depression encompasses an affective component that involves feelings of low self-worth, it is also a clinical syndrome that includes emotions, thoughts, and behaviors. The emotional component is characterized by despair, guilt, sadness, and irritability. Behaviorally, depressed clients may be tired and lethargic, inactive, socially withdrawn, and unable to derive enjoyment from things that normally give them pleasure. Furthermore, changes in appetite, weight, and sleep patterns may occur. Depressed clients suffer from distorted cognitions that relate to worthlessness and self-deprecation. They may experience difficulty making decisions, be more irritable, and could be preoccupied with death (Merrell, 2001). They also tend to think dichotomously; overgeneralize; and engage in selective abstraction, viewing only the negative aspects of their behavior (Vernon, 2006c).

Christner and Walker (2007) stressed the importance of mediating depression in youth, noting that depressed adolescents have more negative peer relationships, fewer friends, and are generally more unhappy than their nondepressed peers. Depression is connected to problems in other areas of life as well, including school performance and family issues. Depressed adolescents are more at risk for substance abuse and suicide.

Seligman (1995), in noting that depression has reached epidemic proportions among children and adolescents, cited irrational thinking as a major contributor to this problem. He identified the following three cognitive errors associated with depression: permanence, pervasiveness, and personalizing. Seligman explained that children and adolescents who are most at risk for depression believe that the causes of bad events that happen to them are *permanent,* as opposed to temporary. Therefore, they are more likely to think about their failures, rejections, or challenges as *always* this way, or *never* getting better. Depressed children also incorrectly assume that the cause of something negative is generalizable across all situations, or *pervasive,* as opposed to situationally specific. For example, if two students are in a contest and work hard, but neither is selected as the winner, the pervasive thinker would consider himself a total loser who never does anything right. The nonpervasive thinker, on the other hand, would recognize that, although she did not win the contest, it does not mean that she never does anything right. The former view represents a global negative thought pattern that contributes to depression.

Personalizing refers to the concept that when bad things happen, we blame either ourselves or others. Children and adolescents who continually blame themselves for everything feel depressed, guilty, and ashamed. In contrast, children who realistically evaluate each situation do not consistently internalize blame and are not as readily prone to depression.

Merrell (2001) concurred with Seligman that the way in which children think has a strong influence on the development of depression. He identified three models: attributions children make about their world, cognitive distortions, and the self-control model. According to Merrell, if children believe that they are helpless to change events in their life, they may become depressed. If they feel like they have no power to make changes, they see no use in trying. Second, children who have a negative view of themselves, the world, and the future and interpret their experiences in dysfunctional ways may become depressed. Third, the self-control model relates to the concept that depressed children have a maladaptive way of monitoring events in their lives. They pay more attention to immediate as opposed to future consequences of behavior, evaluate themselves unrealistically, pay more attention to negative than to positive events, and criticize themselves. All of these patterns make them more vulnerable to depression.

The following irrational beliefs that contribute to depression relate to a negative, pessimistic view of self and the future and include notions of hopelessness, helplessness, and worthlessness (Wilde, 1996):

I'm no good and will never amount to anything.

No matter what I do, I will never succeed.

Nobody could love me, because I am worthless.

I can't do anything right.

I deserve the rotten treatment I get.

What's the point of going on? I'll never get over this.

I can't change the horrible things that have happened to me, so I'm doomed forever.

There's no way out.

Life sucks now and always will.

The following cognitive-behavioral interventions have proven helpful in working with depressed children and adolescents.

Sad, Sad, Sad

RATIONALE When a young client is sad, it is not uncommon for her to think that she will never feel happy again. Accompanying this feeling of forever is a sense of powerlessness—that she cannot do anything to feel better. Given that many circumstances in children's lives that result in feeling sad are things over which they have little control, it is important to show them that they can exercise some degree of control over sad feelings.

MATERIALS ▷ A box of crayons

▷ Several sheets of paper

PROCEDURE

1. After the client has talked about what she is sad about, ask her to select three crayons from the box that represent her feelings when she is sad. Invite her to use these crayons to draw pictures of all the things she has ever been sad about in the past one or two months, making the picture(s) of her most current sadness larger than the rest and putting a mark beside any of the others that she is still very sad about.

2. Then ask her to think of some things that she used to be sad about but no longer is. Have her select three other crayons to represent her feelings about those things and draw pictures of what she used to be sad about but no longer is.

3. When she has finished drawing, process this intervention by discussing how some sad feelings disappeared or weren't as strong, and how or why this happened. Emphasize how some things we are sad about don't last long, even though we think they will at the time, and that there are things we can do to stop feeling as sad.

4. Take a sheet of paper and draw two heads, one with a very sad face and one with a moderately sad face. Draw a few "thought bubbles" coming out of each head. Then ask the client to choose something she is still very sad about and write it underneath the very sad face. Explain to her that when she is sad, the way she thinks influences how sad she will be. For example, if her dog died, it

would be normal to be very sad, but, if she told herself that she would never be happy again, that her life would always be awful without her dog, and that she didn't ever want to do anything with her friends because her dog was her best friend, she would probably be very sad and stay sad for a long time. As you talk about these thoughts, write them in the bubbles above the very sad face. Then tell her that she could still be quite sad, but, if she told herself different things, she probably wouldn't stay sad as long. Ask her if she knows what she could think, or give her this example to help her: She could think to herself that she will miss her dog for a long time, but eventually she will be happy again because maybe her dog wouldn't want her to stay sad, or that even though it was bad that he died, her whole life isn't awful, or that even though her dog might have been her best friend, he probably would want her to play with her other friends because she might have fun and not be so sad. (It would be preferable to elicit these thoughts from her; if she isn't able to generate the ideas, this example will help her understand the two kinds of things she can say to herself.)

5. Discuss her understanding of the two different kinds of thoughts and ask her to take another problem she is very sad about and identify whether there is anything she can think about that will help her deal with the problem. Work together to draw talking heads and identify the irrational and rational thoughts.

6. As a homework assignment, give her several sheets of talking heads and encourage her to use them whenever she is feeling extremely sad.

If You're Sad and You Know It . . .

RATIONALE   The song associated with this lesson can be a concrete way for children to think about new strategies for dealing with sad feelings. The auditory component is effective in helping them remember the concepts for future reference.

MATERIALS   ▷ 2 puppets

PROCEDURE   1. When a young client presents with sadness, after some discussion about these sad feelings, invite him to join you in singing a song that may help him learn new strategies to deal with his sad feelings.

    2. This song is to the tune of "If You're Happy and You Know It, Clap Your Hands."

If you're sad and you know it, make a face.
If you're sad and you know it, make a face.
If you're sad and you know it, make a face that truly shows it.
If you're sad and you know it, make a face.

If you're sad and you know it, try to smile.
If you're sad and you know it, try to smile.
If you're sad but start to smile, then in a little while,
You can do something else to feel better.

If you're sad but want to be glad, clap your hands.
If you're sad but want to be glad, clap your hands.
If you're sad but want to be glad, then give up feeling bad.
Then smile so we know you're not so sad.

If you're still a little sad, that's not so bad.
If you're still a little sad, that's not so bad.
If you're still a little sad, then start acting like you're glad.
And then before you know it, you're not sad!

3. After singing the song, discuss how the client felt singing it and whether there were any messages in the song that give him some clues about what to do about sad feelings. Throughout the discussion, emphasize that children usually don't like to feel sad, but that there are things they can do so the sad feelings aren't as strong.

4. Ask him to recall a time when he felt sad but no longer feels sad about that issue: What did he do or think to feel less sad?

5. Next, give the client two puppets, asking him to designate one as the puppet who is sad and one as the puppet who knows how to make sad feelings go away. Encourage him to dialogue with the puppets about how to feel better when one is very sad.

6. After the puppet plays, identify the ideas expressed and write them on the back of the song sheet so he can remember what to do the next time he feels sad.

Crying Takes the Sad Out of You

RATIONALE   Most children will identify crying as a common response when sad. This intervention helps them identify what the sad feelings are about and how they can use their tears to "let the sadness out" so they can reduce the intensity of the sadness.

MATERIALS   ▷ A pan of water

▷ Blue food coloring

▷ A sheet of paper

▷ Crayons

PROCEDURE   1. After discussing what the child has been crying about recently, give her a pan of water and a bottle of blue food coloring. Indicate that the food coloring drops are like tears as she squeezes them out of the bottle into the water. Tell her that each time a "tear" drops into the water, she can talk about what the tears represent: What are the sad feelings? Allow her to do this several times, encouraging her to elaborate on the sadness as needed.

2. Next, point out that as the "tears" hit the water, they eventually disappear, and discuss whether her sadness is like that. Are there things that she used to be sad about, but after a while, she stopped being so sad? Talk about how that happens:

   After a while, you may forget about why you were so sad.

   You do something to help you feel less sad.

   Something about a situation improves.

   You change what you think so you are not as sad.

3. Invite the client to give examples of the points in step 2. If she is not able to identify how her thoughts can change, illustrate that concept by using an example such as the following:

Juanita was sad because her best friend was sitting by someone else in the lunchroom. Juanita assumed that her friend didn't like her anymore, and she was very sad. But then she thought to herself that maybe there was another reason her friend didn't sit by her, and that she still liked her. When she considered this possibility, she wasn't as sad.

4. Next, give the client a sheet of paper and the crayons. Ask her to identify something she is sad about and draw a picture of it in the upper half of the paper. Then suggest that she draw several teardrops in the lower half of the paper and write things in the teardrops to help her remember how to deal with her sadness. She can take this paper with her to serve as a reminder of how to help herself when she is very sad.

So Long, Sadness

RATIONALE   Most children feel sad from time to time, but given that their sense of time is immediate, it is easy for them to get discouraged if they aren't able to deal with their feelings effectively. This concrete strategy involves them in generating things they can do to feel better.

MATERIALS   ▷ A sheet of paper

▷ A pen or pencil

PROCEDURE   1. When a client presents with sad or depressed feelings that he doesn't want to have, give him a sheet of paper and ask him to trace his hand. Then, on each finger, have him write what he is sad about.

2. Next, engage him in a short role play where you play the role of the sad child, using one of the issues that the client is sad about. Ask the child to be someone else—a friend, teacher, parent, grandparent, or counselor who will help the "child" deal with the sad feelings.

3. After the role-play scenario, discuss the ideas that were generated for dealing with sad feelings and ask the client to write these ideas between and around the finger that relates to the role-played problems.

4. Repeat this procedure with the other problems he identified, first doing the role play and then writing down the ideas that were generated.

5. Discuss with the client that once he has ideas about what to do with his sad feelings, he can imagine himself waving his "hand" (fingers with problems and solutions): So long/goodbye to sad feelings.

Chapter 3 • Interventions for Internalizing Problems

Am I Depressed?

RATIONALE Although many adolescents experience some degree of depression during their teenage years, they often are unaware that what they are experiencing has a label and that there are common identifiable symptoms. Helping them learn more about their symptoms and engaging them in a self-assessment is a necessary first step.

MATERIALS ▷ Am I Depressed? Checklist (p. 124)

▷ A pen or pencil

▷ A blank sheet of paper

PROCEDURE 1. When a client is referred by parents or teachers who suspect depression, or when she self-refers because she just isn't feeling "right," it is important to inform her about symptoms of depression and engage her in a self-assessment.

2. Share the Am I Depressed? Checklist and invite her to check off symptoms that apply to her, informing her that you will discuss the symptoms together to determine the extent to which she might be depressed and how it affects her.

3. After she has completed the list, review it together, noting the intensity and frequency of the symptoms and discussing how they affect her.

4. Next, ask the client to use the blank sheet of paper to identify what she has tried so far to help her feel less depressed and to rank the degree of effectiveness using a 1 (not very effective) to 5 (helps quite a bit) scale.

5. Review the list and ask her to select two things to try during the following week, sharing with her that in the next session, the two of you will identify other things she can do, including a discussion of medication if the depression is severe.

Am I Depressed? Checklist

Directions: Read each of the symptoms and do your best to identify the frequency and intensity of these feelings using the following rating system.

Circle Y (yes) or N (no) beside each symptom. If you circle **Y**, indicate the frequency and intensity by circling the appropriate letter, as follows:

Frequency: H = hourly, **S** = several times a day, **D** = once a day or less, **W** = 2 or 3 times a week or less

Intensity: L = low (not strong, not much), **M** = (moderate), **H** = high (intense, bad)

Symptom			Frequency				Intensity		
Irritability	Y	N	H	S	D	W	L	M	H
Negativity	Y	N	H	S	D	W	L	M	H
Sleep problems	Y	N	H	S	D	W	L	M	H
Cry easily	Y	N	H	S	D	W	L	M	H
Inability to concentrate	Y	N	H	S	D	W	L	M	H
Appetite change	Y	N	H	S	D	W	L	M	H
Unhappy	Y	N	H	S	D	W	L	M	H
Tired, lethargic	Y	N	H	S	D	W	L	M	H
Hopeless	Y	N	H	S	D	W	L	M	H
Overwhelmed	Y	N	H	S	D	W	L	M	H
Racing thoughts	Y	N	H	S	D	W	L	M	H
Down on self	Y	N	H	S	D	W	L	M	H
Suicidal thought	Y	N	H	S	D	W	L	M	H
Pessimistic	Y	N	H	S	D	W	L	M	H
Loss of interest in usual activities	Y	N	H	S	D	W	L	M	H
Anxious	Y	N	H	S	D	W	L	M	H
Emotionally "dead"	Y	N	H	S	D	W	L	M	H
Bored	Y	N	H	S	D	W	L	M	H
Aches, pains	Y	N	H	S	D	W	L	M	H
No energy	Y	N	H	S	D	W	L	M	H
Indecisive	Y	N	H	S	D	W	L	M	H
Withdrawn	Y	N	H	S	D	W	L	M	H
Isolated	Y	N	H	S	D	W	L	M	H
Want to/stay in bed a lot	Y	N	H	S	D	W	L	M	H
Agitated	Y	N	H	S	D	W	L	M	H
Don't shower or pay attention to appearance	Y	N	H	S	D	W	L	M	H
Excessive guilt/self-blame	Y	N	H	S	D	W	L	M	H

From *More What Works When with Children and Adolescents: A Handbook of Individual Counseling Techniques,* © 2009 by Ann Vernon, Champaign, IL: Research Press (800-519-2707, www.researchpress.com)

Don't Stay Depressed

RATIONALE Given that adolescents live in the "here and now," it is easy for them to become overwhelmed and feel hopeless when they are depressed. Consequently, it is important to empower them so that they have many different strategies for coping more effectively because it is difficult for them to generate ideas when they are down.

MATERIALS ▷ 3 envelopes (one labeled *Think,* one labeled *Do,* one labeled *Who*)

▷ 15 to 20 small index cards

▷ A pen or pencil

PROCEDURE 1. After discussing what the client feels is relevant relative to his depression and he has shared some examples of what he thinks and does when he is depressed, indicate that there are many things that can help alleviate depressed feelings. Explain that these strategies can be divided into different categories: What the client can *think* (things that would help him feel better, ways to correct distorted thinking, etc.), what the client can *do* (activities), and *whom* he can turn to for support.

2. Hand the client the first envelope, labeled *Think,* and encourage him to identify five things he could think about (pleasant thoughts) or how he could challenge distorted thinking (e.g., is everyone against me, or just a few people?). Write these on the index cards. If he cannot think of anything, give a few examples to help stimulate his own ideas. For example, if he gets depressed because he doesn't perform well in sports and therefore thinks everyone will laugh at him when he tries to shoot a basket, challenge his thinking: Has this ever happened to you or others before? If so, did everyone laugh? and so forth. After he has identified different things he can think relative to what he is depressed about, have him put them in the *Think* envelope.

3. Then hand him the second envelope, labeled *Do,* and ask him to think about things he can do to make himself feel better (take a walk, listen to good music, call a friend, etc.). Give him several

---

index cards. Ask him to write things he can do on these cards and put them in the envelope when finished.

4. Finally, give him the third envelope, *Who,* and have him identify on the index cards whom he can contact when he needs support, putting these in the *Who* envelope.

5. Invite discussion and contract with the client to keep the ideas close at hand so that he can have ready access to them when needed. During the next counseling session, review what he tried and how it worked, and encourage him to add ideas to each envelope.

Depression "Tool Box"

RATIONALE   When adolescents are very depressed and may have suicidal ideation, it is difficult for them to remember happier times or believe that they will ever feel better. This intervention is a good "hands-on" reminder of things that make life worth living.

MATERIALS   ▷ A "tool box" (a cardboard box with a lid, such as a shoe box)

▷ Brightly colored paper

▷ Glue

▷ Scissors

▷ Colored markers

▷ A sheet of paper

▷ A pen or pencil

▷ Artifacts (see procedure, step 5)

PROCEDURE   1. After talking to the adolescent about her depression and accompanying feelings of hopelessness, invite her to make a depression tool box that she can open each time she feels very depressed. Inside the box she will put things to help her remember good things in her life.

2. Invite her to decorate the box, using the paper, markers, glue, and scissors to make designs that will cheer her up.

3. As she is working on the box, ask her to think about reasons she has to live and things that cheer her up when she is depressed. Write these ideas down for her on a sheet of paper.

4. After she has finished decorating her box, continue to discuss positives in her life—things worth living for—and add those to her list.

5. Then invite her to take the box and the list home and find an artifact or a symbol for each of the ideas she generated. For example, if she has a special relationship with her grandmother and that is one of her reasons to live, she could find something that reminds

her of her grandmother: a picture, a poem, a song, or any other object that symbolizes this special relationship. Encourage her to do this for each reason she identified on her list.

6. Invite her to use her tool box on a regular basis when she is down; reviewing the contents will help her refocus on meaningful things in her life.

Spin Away the Blues

RATIONALE   Helping adolescents identify what to do when they are getting depressed helps them realize that they don't have to be powerless over these overwhelming feelings. This concrete intervention reminds them of what they can do to feel less depressed.

MATERIALS   ▷ Two tagboard circles in bright colors; one 8 inches in diameter and the other 16; each circle should each be divided into eight even pie shapes

▷ One brass fastener

▷ A pen or pencil

PROCEDURE   1. When an adolescent client presents with depression and seems at a loss about what to do about it, invite him to take the two tagboard circles and put the smaller one on top of the larger one, fastening them together with the brass fastener.

2. Next, have him think about how he feels or acts when he is depressed and write these in the pie-shaped spaces (one per space) on the inside circle. Encourage the client to identify six to eight descriptions, such as "always tired," "irritable," "just want to sleep," "don't feel like doing anything," and so forth.

3. Then, on the pie-shaped space on the outside circle, have him write things he can do to make himself feel better when he experiences those feelings or behaviors associated with depression: things such as dressing in something he feels good in, getting some exercise, calling a supportive friend, and so forth. Help him generate ideas in a brainstorming format, as needed.

4. Have him spin the circle so that ideas about what to do line up with the feelings or behaviors. For example, if he identified feeling tired on the inside circle, after spinning, it might land on an idea such as getting exercise. This intervention should provide him with several ideas to help himself.

STRESS

According to the dictionary, stress is defined as mental, emotional, or physical tension. Stress results in wear and tear on the body and has many other detrimental effects. Although it is typical to associate stress with adults, some would question whether children and adolescents are prone to this condition. In fact, we have begun to look more seriously at childhood stress, for a variety of reasons. First, as noted in chapter 1, children have to contend with the normal stressors associated with growing up, which for some can be difficult. Second, children today live a complex, rapidly changing society. They are bombarded with choices, ranging from 50 types of cereal in the supermarket, to hundreds of games at the video arcade, to choices about roles to assume in adulthood—roles that used to be clearly defined but now are more ambiguous. Thanks (or no thanks) to the media and the Internet, children and adolescents are exposed to massive amounts of information, making them more aware of issues that may discourage them about their future or make them feel vulnerable, unsafe, and skeptical. In addition, many facets of life that were once considered "off limits" are now very real with the flip of the remote or a flick of the mouse, which may result in anxiety and confusion if they are not developmentally prepared for what they see and hear.

Perhaps more important is the fact that children and adolescents often have little or no control over the decisions that significant adults in their lives make, but that are nevertheless stressful. Some of these situational factors are those that even their parents have little control over, such as losing a job during tough economic times, developing a disability or serious illness, and so forth. Thus, in addition to typical developmental stressors, it is increasingly common for children and adolescents to have to deal with situational factors that can be stressful, such as moving, changing schools, losing a family member or close friend, living in a dysfunctional family where substance abuse and violence create anxiety and uncertainty, or living in poverty.

Although we often associate stress with physical symptoms such as tension in the body, exhaustion, and changes in eating and sleeping, stress is also an emotional condition that is experienced when life's circumstances are overwhelming and coping methods are inadequate. This is of particular concern with children and adolescents whose coping ability is significantly impacted by their developmental capabilities—their ability to think clearly and rationally, put problems in perspective, and generate alternatives and consider consequences.

From a cognitive perspective, stress is an internalizing disorder because it is not an external event that creates stress, but how it is perceived—stress is "in the eye of the beholder." That is to say, what is stressful for one person may not be for another. Dealing with stress from a cognitive perspective by increasing children's rational internal dialogue helps decrease the negative effects of stress. Children can learn that thinking irrationally about the stressor (the activating event—A—in the REBT framework) results in varying degrees of unhealthy emotions (depression, anxiety, irritability, moodiness), unproductive behaviors (acting out, difficulty getting along with others, self-criticism, complaining, lying, stealing, abusing substances), and physical effects such as sleep disturbance, changes in appetite, bed-wetting, exhaustion, and headaches and stomach aches or other illnesses.

Children who think rationally about the stressors they encounter throughout life will be more likely to exhibit characteristics associated with effective coping. They will be more self-accepting and resourceful, have an array of coping mechanisms and a sense of control, be able to tolerate frustration and delay gratification, be more flexible, express feelings in healthy ways, and not overreact to stressful events. The following interventions have proven useful in helping children and adolescents with stress management.

Where Is My Stress?

RATIONALE   Many younger children experience stress related to family situations, performance, peer relationships, or overscheduling. Often they react behaviorally or experience physical symptoms because they are unable to express their feelings emotionally. It is important to help them understand where and how they experience stress so that they can begin to deal with it more effectively.

MATERIALS   ▷ Large sheet of butcher paper or poster paper

▷ Crayons or markers

PROCEDURE   1. When a client expresses or appears to be experiencing signs of stress, explain that stress is something that we feel in our bodies and our minds when we have too much to do or have problems that we cannot handle. Share some examples: getting stomach aches when things aren't going well in her family, getting headaches if she has too many things to do, or yelling at people when she feels tense and under pressure to perform well.

2. Invite the client to lie down. Indicate that you will be making an outline of her body. When this is completed, have her sit up and give her crayons or markers.

3. Ask her to think about a recent situation in which she felt stressed—perhaps it was studying for a test, worrying about something in the family or with friends, or having too many things to do. Invite her to draw a picture (on the body outline) of this situation in relation to where she felt it in her body. For example, she may feel stress in her tummy, her head, her neck, or other body parts.

4. When she has finished, discuss the pictures and invite her to elaborate more about where she experiences it in her body or how she expresses the stress.

5. Next, point to the head on the body outline and explain to the client that she can reduce her stress if she thinks differently. For example, if she is stressed about doing well on a test, she can think,

"I will do my best, and, if I don't do well, it doesn't mean I'm dumb and stupid or a bad kid." Help the client generate other rational coping self-statements she can use to help reduce her stress about this situation and write these inside the head on the body outline.

6. Then ask her to think of another situation in which she felt stressed, and have her draw a picture of it relative to where she experiences it in her body. After talking more about this stressful event, ask her whether there are things she can do with her body that will help reduce her stress. Have her draw a picture of these suggestions (or write them) on the various body parts (for example, she may draw a picture of running because the activity may help her feel less stressed).

7. Invite the client to keep the body outline as a way of remembering how she can deal with stress more effectively.

Stop Stressing

RATIONALE Teaching children at a young age to identify and manage stress helps reduce more serious effects of stress as they get older. Simple concrete strategies will help them remember stress-management techniques.

MATERIALS ▷ An 8 × 10 sheet of cardboard or tagboard

▷ Crayons or markers

PROCEDURE 1. When a client has issues with stress, invite him to discuss the stressful situations and describe what strategies he has tried to reduce the stress.

2. Referring to the previous intervention about where and how his body experiences stress, explain that we can reduce the effects of stress if we can stop and think situations through.

3. Give the client the sheet of tagboard and ask him to draw a large picture of a stop sign, using the crayons or markers to color it, writing the letters *S, T, O,* and *P* in the middle of the sign.

4. Ask the client to "stop" and think about what he can do to reduce stress that starts with the letters on the sign. For example, he could sleep (*S*) more so that he is better prepared to deal with problems, talk (*T*) about what is bothering him, ask others (*O*) what they have tried, or take a break and play (*P*). Invite the client to think of other strategies and write all of these around the stop sign. Give him the sign as a visual reminder of what he can do to help himself.

Stress Busters

RATIONALE   Knowing a variety of stress management strategies can empower children to deal proactively with stress, as opposed to letting it get them down.

MATERIALS   ▷ An old (flat) bedsheet or a comparable-sized sheet of durable plastic, divided into 20 squares, randomly colored in 5 different colors (red, green, blue, yellow, purple) for the Stress Buster Board.

▷ 5 sets (4 cards each) of Stress Buster Cards (p. 137); these should be color coded (you can use colored stick-on dots, or just mark them with colored markers) so that they match the 5 colors on the sheet.

▷ Another set of 20 Directions Cards (p. 138); these should be coded with a colored X on the card that corresponds with the first direction (i.e., the first card would be green, the second would be blue, the third would be yellow, etc., for a total of four cards per color). Place these in a paper bag or box.

PROCEDURE   1. When a client experiences physical, emotional, or behavioral reactions to stress, discuss her reactions and what is stressful for her.

2. Then invite her to play a game that will help her learn new ways to handle stress.

3. Put the Stress Buster Board on the floor and put the color-coded Stress Buster Cards in five piles beside the board.

4. Instruct the client to select a Directions Card from the paper bag or box and follow the instructions on the card. For example, the card may read "left foot yellow, right hand purple," in which case the client places her left foot on a yellow space on the Stress Busters Board and her right hand on a purple space. Then, you draw a card from the yellow pile of Stress Buster Cards because yellow is the first color on the Directions card. Read the Stress Buster Card out loud and discuss with the client whether this is an intervention she has tried or could try as a way to alleviate her

stress. Make sure to discuss this in enough detail so that she clearly understands the concept.

5. Continue the game in this manner, discussing the various strategies the client can use to help her deal more effectively with her stress.

Stress Buster Cards

Get exercise every day.	Do something fun every day.
Get more sleep.	Keep a journal or diary.
Take a break.	Drink lots of water.
Break big tasks into smaller tasks.	Talk out your problems or worries.
Eat healthy foods.	Watch funny movies that make you laugh.
Stop eating junk food.	Practice relaxation exercises.
Laugh.	Ask for help when you need it.
Take deep breaths.	Don't let others get you down.
Think different thoughts.	Don't try to do too many things at once.
Think positive thoughts.	Do your best, even if it isn't perfect.

From *More What Works When with Children and Adolescents: A Handbook of Individual Counseling Techniques,* © 2009 by Ann Vernon, Champaign, IL: Research Press (800-519-2707, www.researchpress.com)

Directions Cards

Right foot green, left foot red	Left foot yellow, right hand purple
Left hand blue, right foot yellow	Right knee purple, right hand blue
Left foot yellow, right hand blue	Left foot blue, left elbow red
Right elbow purple, left foot green	Right elbow red, left foot green
Left foot blue, right foot purple	Right foot green, left hand yellow
Right hand red, left knee green	Left toes yellow, right toes purple
Left toes yellow, left hand red	Right foot purple, left knee blue
Right foot red, right hand green	Left fingers blue, right fingers red
Left toes purple, right knee green	Right palm red, right foot green
Right hand green, left foot red	Left palm green, right foot purple

Take a Deep Breath and Relax

RATIONALE   Children may not be able to identify strategies to help them reduce bodily tension when they are under stress. This guided relaxation exercise is something they can easily learn to do to help them deal with future tension.

MATERIALS
- ▷ A CD of relaxing (ocean sounds, etc.) music
- ▷ A large, thick rubber band
- ▷ A big balloon (not blown up)
- ▷ A 6-inch piece of elastic
- ▷ A small rubber ball
- ▷ Take a Deep Breath and Relax Script (p. 141)

PROCEDURE
1. When a client is stressed or feeling tense, invite him to participate in the following relaxation intervention.

2. Explain that when we are uptight about things, it is helpful to do things to relax our bodies. Invite the client to lie down on the floor and get comfortable. At this point start playing the relaxing music at a low volume.

3. Next, provide the following instructions:

    With the client lying down on the floor, show him the balloon and ask him to close his eyes and relax, imagining that he is blowing up that balloon by slowing pumping air into it.

    Then, when the client feels like the balloon is full of air, tell him to take a big deep breath and hold it for several seconds, and then let it out slowly. Do that again . . . and again.

    Now ask your client to scrunch up his toes up as tight as he can and slowly count to ten. On the count of ten, he should take a big deep breath and let his toes relax.

Now show the client the rubber band and ask him to pretend that his legs are a giant rubber band and that he is going to stretch the rubber band (his legs) as tight as he can.

Tell him to hold his legs still and count to ten slowly—then, at the count of ten, he should take a deep breath and pretend that he is letting go of the rubber band so that all the tension is gone.

Next, give the client the piece of elastic and have him stretch it. Ask him to imagine that his arms are like the elastic—he is going to stretch them and hold them tight. He is to count slowly to ten, take a big breath, and imagine that he is letting go of the elastic so that it snaps back into a relaxed state.

Finally, give the client the rubber ball and ask him to clench it in one of his hands, holding his breath and holding the ball tightly as he slowly counts to ten. At the count of ten, he should release the ball as he breathes out slowly.

4. After the relaxation exercise, ask the client to describe what that experience was like for him and discuss how he can do this on his own to help reduce his stress when he experiences tension in his body.

5. Give him the balloon, rubber band, piece of elastic, rubber ball, and a copy of the relaxation script so that he can continue to practice relaxation.

Take a Deep Breath and Relax Script

Lie down on the floor. To begin, close your eyes and relax, visualizing a balloon that hasn't been blown up. Now imagine that you are blowing up that balloon by slowly pumping air into it. Then when it "feels" like it is full of air, take a big, deep breath and hold it for several seconds, and then let it out very slowly. Do that again . . . and again.

Now scrunch up your toes as tight as you can and slowly count to 10. On the count of 10, take a big, deep breath and slowly let your toes relax.

Now visualize or hold the rubber band and pretend that your legs are a giant rubber band and that you are going to stretch the rubber band (your legs) as tight as you can. Hold your legs very still and count to 10 very slowly—then at the count of 10, take a deep breath and pretend that you are letting go of the rubber band so that all the tension is gone.

Next, visualize or hold the piece of elastic and imagine stretching it tight. Pretend that your arms are like the elastic . . . you are going to stretch them and hold them very tight. Slowly count to 10, take a big breath, and imagine letting go of the elastic so that it snaps back into a relaxed state.

Finally, visualize the rubber ball and imagine that you are clenching it in one of your hands as you hold your breath, squeeze the ball tightly, and count to 10. At the count of 10, release the ball as you breathe out slowly.

Is It Stress?

RATIONALE   Many adolescents find it difficult to juggle school, extracurricular activities, work, and their family and social lives. Although they may not label it as stress, it is not uncommon for them to experience physical as well as emotional effects. Helping them learn to identify these symptoms is the first step in alleviating stress.

MATERIALS   ▷ Is It Stress? Survey (p. 143)

▷ A pen or pencil

▷ A sheet of paper

PROCEDURE   1. When a client presents with stress-related symptoms but doesn't identify them as such, offer a simple explanation such as the following:

> Stress is frequently described as "wear and tear on the body." It is an emotional condition that occurs when things in your life seem overwhelming and you can't figure out how to cope with them.

Invite the client to reflect on this definition and discuss how it may relate to what she is experiencing.

2. Next, give her the survey to complete, indicating that it might help her learn more about stress and the symptoms associated with it.

3. When she has completed the survey, encourage her to share her results or ask questions about things she may not be clear about.

4. Next, give the client a sheet of paper and have her make a list of all her current stressors, rank ordering them, with number 1 being the most stressful. Ask her to reflect on which of the items on the survey describe how she reacts to these current stressors.

5. Discuss with the client what she is currently doing to try to alleviate the stress associated with her most stressful events and to brainstorm other things she might try in order to reduce this stress.

Is It Stress? Survey

Directions: Respond to the following questions by putting a check mark in the column next to each item that best describes you.

	A lot like me	Somewhat like me	Not like me
1. I have lots of things to juggle in my life (school; work; extracurricular activities such as sports, music or drama; religious commitments; friends and family).	☑	☐	☐
2. I often feel like I can't manage everything that I have to or want to do.	☑	☐	☐
3. When I have lots going on, I often feel overwhelmed.	☐	☑	☐
4. When I have lots of things to juggle, I have trouble falling asleep.	☐	☐	☐
5. When I have lots of things to juggle, I am more irritable.	☐	☑	☐
6. When I have lots of commitments and things that need to be done at the same time, I experience tension in my body—tight muscles, headaches, etc.	☐	☑	☐
7. When I have too much on my plate, it is as if I am paralyzed and can't accomplish anything.	☐	☐	☑
8. When I have lots of things going on, I am more forgetful.	☐	☑	☐
9. When I have too much to juggle, I am more likely to get sick.	☐	☑	☐
10. When I have lots of commitments and things I have to do at the same time, it seems like things are worse than they really are—that I will never get things done or be able to meet my obligations.	☐	☑	☐
11. If I feel like I am having trouble juggling everything, I am more anxious.	☐	☑	☐
12. Sometimes I feel like I just can't cope with everything.	☐	☐	☑

Am I Stressed Out?

RATIONALE Although adolescents experience stress, they are often unaware of all the symptoms associated with it. This intervention increases awareness about stress-related symptoms and helps adolescents identify effective ways to reduce their stress in order to prevent more serious negative effects.

MATERIALS ▷ Am I Stressed Out? Checklist (p. 146)

▷ A pen or pencil

PROCEDURE 1. When a client presents with stress-related symptoms, explain that there are many different responses to stress. Invite him to learn more about them by completing a short checklist.

2. After he has completed the checklist, invite him to discuss which symptoms are most problematic for him; encourage him to elaborate more about the stressors.

3. Next, discuss how stress can be managed more effectively by changing the way we think. Illustrate this by giving an example. Suppose he has a major paper due in one of his classes in two days and he hasn't even started it. Explain that this is what happened (the event). Then ask how he would feel if this were a true scenario, indicating that those feelings would be his emotional response. Also ask him how he might respond behaviorally, referring to the checklist he just completed: Would he lose sleep? Be more irritable? Avoid doing anything by watching more television? etc.

4. Next, ask him to identify his thoughts when he is in situations like this. In the case of a paper due, does he think he'll never be able to get it done on time, and, if that is the case, that his teacher will think he is incompetent or lazy? Would he think that it would be the end of the world if he didn't get it done on time? Work with him to identify other thoughts that contribute to being stressed about an event such as this.

5. Explain that one of the things he can do to reduce stress is to replace the thoughts that stress him out, which are often irrational,

with more sensible thinking. For example, he can think to himself:

> Just because I don't meet a deadline, how does that prove that I'm incompetent and inefficient?

> How does stressing out about it help me accomplish what needs to be done?

> What's the worst that could happen if I try my best to finish it but can't meet the deadline?

6. Discuss the process of disputing erroneous beliefs and replacing them with more reasonable, rational responses. For example, he could say things to himself such as "The worst thing that would happen is that my teacher might flunk me in the class, but that is unlikely," or "I'd like to meet the deadline, but, if I don't, it doesn't mean I am incompetent." After disputing the irrational beliefs, he can replace them with more rational thoughts, such as "I'd really prefer to get the work done by the deadline, and I will do the best I can," and so forth.

7. Work with the client to identify other rational responses to irrational beliefs he might have about current issues that are creating stress in his life.

Am I Stressed Out? Checklist

Directions: Reflect on the degree to which each of these symptoms may or may not relate to what you are experiencing. Put a check mark in the appropriate column.

	A lot	A little	None
1. Moodiness	❏	❏	❏
2. Prone to accidents	❏	❏	❏
3. Pounding heart	❏	❏	❏
4. Anxiety, extreme worry	❏	❏	❏
5. Tics, trembling, grinding teeth	❏	❏	❏
6. Easily startled	❏	❏	❏
7. Explosive crying or increase in crying episodes	❏	❏	❏
8. Decline in achievement	❏	❏	❏
9. Loss of interest in school	❏	❏	❏
10. Compulsive cleanliness	❏	❏	❏
11. Chronic complaining	❏	❏	❏
12. Compulsive hair pulling, nail biting	❏	❏	❏
13. Aggressive behavior (verbal, physical, defiance, destructiveness)	❏	❏	❏
14. Listlessness, loss of interest in things	❏	❏	❏
15. Change in eating habits	❏	❏	❏
16. Alcohol, drug use	❏	❏	❏
17. Lying, stealing	❏	❏	❏
18. Difficulty getting along with others	❏	❏	❏
18. Exhaustion (too much overscheduling)	❏	❏	❏
19. Increase in risk-taking behavior (fast driving, etc.)	❏	❏	❏
20. Withdrawal, social isolation, excessive TV watching	❏	❏	❏
21. Sexual acting out	❏	❏	❏
22. Excessive self-criticism	❏	❏	❏

From *More What Works When with Children and Adolescents: A Handbook of Individual Counseling Techniques,* © 2009 by Ann Vernon, Champaign, IL: Research Press (800-519-2707, www.researchpress.com)

Away with Stress

RATIONALE   Because adolescents can become easily overwhelmed and consequently overgeneralize and awfulize about things they find stressful, it is important to help them develop an array of coping skills that they can employ when they are experiencing stress-related symptoms.

MATERIALS
- ▷ Away with Stress Worksheet (p. 148)
- ▷ A pen or pencil

PROCEDURE

1. When a client presents with stress-related symptoms, discuss in more detail which symptoms are the most problematic and ask her to identify what she has done in the past to deal with her stress.

2. Then give her the Away with Stress Worksheet and explain that stress management can include things she can do physically, mentally, or emotionally, as identified on the worksheet.

3. Discuss the suggestions on the worksheet, then ask her to generate other suggestions in each category.

4. As a homework assignment, ask the client to select one thing she would like to try first to help reduce her stress. Give her the completed worksheet as a reminder of other things she can do.

Away with Stress Worksheet

Directions: Identify things you could do in each of the three areas to manage stress. Write them in the spaces provided.

Things to do physically to manage stress

1. Exercise or do other physical things such as jog or play basketball.

2. Eat healthy foods.

3. _____

4. _____

5. _____

6. _____

Things do to mentally to manage stress

1. Minimize the stress by deciding what is essential to do and what isn't.

2. Ask myself, "What's the worst that could happen if I can't do everything or please everyone?"

3. _____

4. _____

5. _____

6. _____

Things to do emotionally to manage stress

1. Watch funny movies or read humorous jokes or stories—laugh!

2. Keep a journal or a diary and record my feelings.

3. _____

4. _____

5. _____

6. _____

From *More What Works When with Children and Adolescents: A Handbook of Individual Counseling Techniques,* © 2009 by Ann Vernon, Champaign, IL: Research Press (800-519-2707, www.researchpress.com)

De-Stressing Your Stress

RATIONALE   Stress is in the "eye of the beholder," and it is important for clients to understand how their perceptions influence the degree of stress they experience. This intervention equips adolescents with tools they can use throughout their lifetime to deal more effectively with stress.

MATERIALS   ▷ De-Stressing Your Stress Worksheet (p. 151)

▷ Cognitive Distortions Contributing to Stress handout (p. 152)

▷ A pen or pencil

PROCEDURE   1. When a client presents with stress, have him describe exactly what is stressful to him about one particular event and verbally rate his degree of stress on a scale of 1 (low) to 10 (high). Then ask him to speculate about the following: If he took a poll of all the students in his class or all the kids in his neighborhood, would they all perceive this event as stressful and, if so, would they all rate their degree of stress exactly as he did? If his response is affirmative and he still believes that everyone would experience this as stressful as he would, ask him whether he thinks everyone in his city or state would rate it as stressful as he did, making the point that stress is in the "eye of the beholder."

2. Next, give him the De-Stressing Your Stress Worksheet and ask him to complete it. After he has completed the worksheet, discuss his examples, ratings, and thoughts. Help him see that what he thinks about the stressor contributes to his level of stress. For example, if he perceived competing in a swim meet as stressful, his thoughts might be that it would be terrible if he didn't do well, that others would think less of him if he didn't win, or that his parents would be upset if he wasn't the best.

3. Then show him that another peer could experience the same event but not be as stressed about it by asking him what that peer might be thinking that wouldn't make this so stressful for her: that it would be disappointing but not devastating if she didn't perform well; that maybe others would think less of her, but maybe not;

and that her parents might hope that she does well, but they might not be that upset if she didn't. Work with him to identify alternative thoughts so that he clearly understands the concept.

4. Share the Cognitive Distortions Contributing to Stress handout (based generally on Merrell, 2001) with the client. After explaining the concepts, ask the client to identify those that he thinks contribute to his stress about the events he identified on the worksheet. Discuss with him how to change his thinking by referring to the example with the peer.

5. Ask the client to take several items on his list and identify alternative thoughts that would reduce his level of stress.

De-Stressing Your Stress Worksheet

Directions: First, make a list of what is stressful for you. Next, rank each on a scale of 1 (low stress) to 10 (high stress). Finally, identify at least one thought that you have about each of the stressors that may contribute to the stress.

Stressor	Rating	Thoughts
1.		
2.		
3.		
4.		
5.		
6.		
7.		
8.		

Cognitive Distortions Contributing to Stress

Tunnel vision

Seeing only what fits now and ignoring all other aspects (friends who usually call you and hang out with you didn't ask you to go to the movies last night, so you think they are not your friends now).

Overgeneralization

Drawing a general conclusion based on one incident (concluding that you will fail the test just because last time you didn't do very well).

Arbitrary inference

Drawing a conclusion that either is contrary to the data or is not supported by evidence (your mother is asking you to do these chores just because she wants to irritate you).

Selective abstraction

Focusing on a detail taken out of context and ignoring other aspects of the situation; arriving at erroneous conclusions (the teacher deducted 50 points from your research paper, and you don't think that was fair because you worked hard on it and did a good job; however, you selectively forgot that the paper was turned in late).

Magnification/minimization

Over- or underemphasizing either the entire or selected aspects of the situation (magnifying is blowing an event out of proportion and thinking it is absolutely catastrophic; minimizing is failing to look at consequences, such as thinking it's not a big deal if you flunk an important test or get picked up for shoplifting).

Personalization

Inappropriately relating external events to oneself without an obvious basis for making that connection (your mother came home from work earlier than usual; you assume she came home early to check on you because she doesn't trust you).

Mind reading

Assuming you know what the other person is thinking (thinking that the teacher doesn't like you because he doesn't call on you).

Polarized (dichotomous) thinking

All or nothing (thinking you're popular or not, or that you're dumb or smart)

Dark glasses

Thinking only about the negative and focusing on the bad aspects of a situation (this job is too hard; you will never be successful).

Fortune-telling

Making predictions about the future, without evidence.

From *More What Works When with Children and Adolescents: A Handbook of Individual Counseling Techniques,* © 2009 by Ann Vernon, Champaign, IL: Research Press (800-519-2707, www.researchpress.com)

GRIEF

Grief, which results from loss and transitions, endings and beginnings, is a normal and natural reaction. However, as James and Friedman (1998) pointed out, society holds some myths about children and grief, including the notion that children don't grieve. In fact, according to Fiorini and Mullen (2006), children do experience grief and loss profoundly, even though their understanding of it is different than that of adults.

Although we typically associate grief with loss due to death, the reality is that there are multiple kinds of losses that affect children and adolescents. In addition to grief related to the death of parents, pets, and other family members, children and adolescents may experience grief whenever there is any change or disruption in their lives, such as when parents divorce or remarry, when their best friend moves, when they break up with a boyfriend or girlfriend, or when they aren't selected for an award or a scholarship. There is grief associated with developmental changes: puberty and its accompanying physical changes, or being old enough to realize that Santa Claus doesn't exist. Children may grieve over family life-cycle changes such as the birth of a new baby or a sibling leaving home to go to college. Certainly there is grief associated with traumatic events such as abuse. Even happy events such as graduating from high school or moving to a new house might result in feelings of grief and loss.

Fiorini and Mullen (2006) identified four tasks that children work through in mourning a loss: understanding, grieving, commemorating, and moving on. These authors stressed that the degree of understanding is impacted by a child's developmental level. Children in the preoperational stage of development have difficulty understanding the concept of loss, and, due to their egocentricity, think that they could have done something to prevent it. In the concrete operational stage, they are more capable of some abstract thinking but may draw erroneous conclusions about the loss or change. As they move into formal operational thinking, adolescents are more capable of thinking abstractly and are better able to comprehend the nature of the loss. However, because the rate at which adolescents develop formal operational thinking varies so much, it is important to carefully assess their cognitive abilities in order to help them work through their grief more effectively.

Grief affects children emotionally, behaviorally, and physically. Typical feelings associated with grief include anger, anxiety, sadness and depression, fear, confusion, helplessness, hopelessness, guilt, and insecurity. Children may internalize their grief or lack the ability to verbally express their feelings. Consequently, they act them out through tantrums or regressive behaviors. Adolescents may act out through aggressive or risk-taking behaviors. In addition, grieving children often have physical symptoms: sleep disturbances, somatic complaints, stomach aches and headaches, or changes in eating habits (Fiorini & Mullen, 2006).

Traditionally, grief therapy has focused on the emotional dimension, with a heavy emphasis on catharsis to help alleviate the intensity of the emotions (Malkinson, 2007). However, this focus failed to consider the importance of cognitions, which, according to Malkinson, can be a mediator between adverse life events and emotional distress. From an REBT perspective, grief is a normal and healthy reaction to a negative life event. Thus, when there is a significant loss, children will most likely experience a variety of strong negative emotions as well as behavioral consequences, which is normal. REBT therapists acknowledge these feelings but move beyond catharsis. They help children think more rationally—looking at the facts instead of making assumptions, putting the loss in perspective and not catastrophizing, and helping them build resiliency by learning what they can and can't control. This process is ultimately healing, and, depending on the nature of the loss, the intensity of the strong negative emotions is reduced over time, some more quickly than others.

The following interventions can be used to help children and adolescents deal with grief.

It's Good to Grieve

RATIONALE Losing a pet is often one of the first losses children experience. Adults may make the mistake of immediately replacing the pet with another, thinking that this will help them get over the loss. In fact, this is not advisable because children may develop the misconception that what is lost is replaceable, which is usually not the case. This intervention teaches children that it's good to grieve so they can eventually move on.

MATERIALS
▷ Several sheets of blank paper

▷ A pen or pencil

▷ Crayons or markers

▷ 2 sheets of construction paper to make a book cover

PROCEDURE
1. When a child has lost a pet, one of the most important messages we can give her is that it is important to grieve the loss before we can move on.

2. Engage her in a mutual story-telling process, where you supply the prompts and serve as the secretary to write the story. Begin by telling the client this:

> I am so sorry that your pet died. I remember how hard it was for me when my dogs died, but it helped if I talked about it and shared some of my memories with others. So, if you are willing, I'd like you to tell me a story about your pet. I will suggest some topics and you can tell me what you would like to say about them. I will write down what you share, and we can make a book about your pet.

Assuming that the child agrees, use the following starters in the story so that it reads like a short book.

Title (have client suggest it)

My pet's name was _____. We named her that

because _____. My pet was about

the size of _____, and she was _____ (color).

We got my pet at _____. Some of the things

I remember about my pet when she was little are _____

_____.

Her favorite toy was _____. Her

favorite food was _____.

Some of the funniest things I remember about my pet are

_____.

If my pet was naughty, she would _____

_____.

Some of the things I liked to do with my pet were _____

_____.

What made my pet happy was _____

_____.

The reason my pet died was because _____

_____. She was _____ years old.

When she died, I felt _____.

What I will remember most about my pet is _____

_____.

3. After she has finished with her story, invite the client to make a book cover using construction paper and crayons and illustrate the book by drawing pictures on the blank paper and attaching them to the end of the story.

4. Encourage the client to read her book and share it with others because it will help her talk about her memories of her pet and how she feels about losing it.

Memory Mobile

RATIONALE Grieving is a natural process, but adults sometimes don't like to see children in pain and may consciously or unconsciously convey the message that children shouldn't think about their loss or talk about their grief. This is counterproductive. Instead, children should be encouraged to share memories associated with their loss so that they don't repress their feelings.

MATERIALS
▷ A coat hanger

▷ 10 or more pieces of string, cut in varying lengths

▷ 10 to 15 3×3 squares, cut from different colors of construction paper, each with a small hole in the top to attach a string

▷ A pen or marker

PROCEDURE
1. When a child presents with any type of loss, invite him to make a memory mobile.

2. First, invite him to talk some about his memories relative to the loss—the person, pet, object, transition, and so forth. Then give him the squares of paper and either serve as the recorder or ask him to write a memory associated with his loss (one memory per square). As he is completing this task, encourage him to verbalize his thoughts and feelings.

3. Next, attach a string through the hole on each square. Ask the client to tie each square on the hanger to make a mobile. He can hang it in his room until he wants to take it down because he is ready to move on.

Getting Through Grief

RATIONALE   Although it may seem like a minor distinction, getting *through* grief is not the same as getting *over* grief. Getting *through* grief implies a "working through" process in which children express their emotions, commemorate the loss, and then move on by learning new ways to function without denying or minimizing the loss.

MATERIALS   ▷ A pen or pencil

▷ 4 envelopes; one labeled *Feelings,* one labeled *Thoughts,* one labeled *Behaviors,* and one labeled *Things That Will Help.* Each envelope should contain 8 to 10 blank strips of paper

PROCEDURE   1. When a client presents with loss issues, suggest to her that the two of you work on a strategy that might help her get through her grief.

2. First, give her the envelope marked *Feelings.* Invite her to take out a strip of paper and write a word on it that describes how she feels about this loss (you may need to be the recorder, depending on the age of the child). Encourage her to talk about the feeling. Then ask her to identify other emotions, writing each on separate strips.

3. Second, give her the envelope marked *Thoughts* and repeat the previously described procedure, but this time ask her to identify thoughts she has about this loss, such as "It's terrible," "I'll never get over it," "It's not fair," and so forth. You may need to provide some guidance by asking her to talk more about the loss and probing for what she is thinking.

4. Next, give her the envelope marked *Behaviors* and repeat the previously described procedure, but this time ask her to identify how she is behaving as a result of this loss. For example, having bad dreams, crying a lot, throwing tantrums, and so forth. Sharing some typical behavioral reactions such as "Some kids cry, stay in their room by themselves, get real quiet, wet the bed, or throw tantrums" might be necessary to help her describe what she does.

5. After the feelings, thoughts, and behaviors have been identified and discussed, give her the last envelope (*Things That Will Help*) and help her identify things she can think or do to help her work through her loss, perhaps offering suggestions such as writing a letter to the loss, planting some flowers as a way to remember someone or something, and keeping a diary.

How to Heal

RATIONALE   Young children who are in the preoperational or concrete operational stage of thinking need guidance in identifying strategies that help them heal. This intervention can facilitate that process.

MATERIALS   ▷ 12 bandages

▷ 12 strips of paper cut into the shape of a bandage, but larger than a bandage (big enough for the sentence starter and a response). On each strip, write one of the following sentence starters:

When I feel sad, I can . . .

When I feel sad, I can . . .

When I feel mad, I can . . .

When I feel mad, I can . . .

It helps me feel better if I . . .

It helps me feel better if I . . .

When I feel confused, I can . . .

When I think that this is too hard, I can tell myself . . .

When I feel scared, I can . . .

If I have bad dreams, I can . . .

If I think that it's my fault, I can tell myself . . .

If I think that things will always seem terrible, I can tell myself . . .

▷ A pen or pencil

PROCEDURE   1. When a client presents with a loss issue and has had adequate time to share his thoughts and feelings, introduce the intervention at the appropriate time.

2. First, give the child one of the bandages, explaining that when we fall down and hurt ourselves, we often put a bandage on it to help it heal. Indicate that the purpose of this activity is to identify ways to help him heal from the loss he has described.

3. Next, ask him to take the bandage and apply it to one of the strips of paper (the side without the writing). Then ask him to turn the paper over, read the sentence starter, and write a response that will help him heal.

4. Continue with the rest of the bandages. Discuss which ideas he thinks will be most helpful and allow him to take the bandages with him as a reminder of what he can do to help with the healing process.

Living with Loss

RATIONALE Many of the losses adolescents deal with are invisible or intangible, such as loss of personal power or health, or are in the form of non-events—something that was reasonable to expect would happen but didn't, such as not being selected for an honor society even though the student met the criteria. Because these are not necessarily recognizable events, adolescents may not be able to readily identify or articulate feelings about such losses, but it is important for adolescents to understand how the losses affect them so that they can work through them. This intervention is designed to support them in this endeavor.

MATERIALS ▷ A sheet of paper

▷ A pen or pencil

PROCEDURE 1. To help an adolescent who presents with depression or other emotional upset that could be related to loss, explore the concept of intangible or non-event losses by explaining the following to her:

> Although you may not have experienced a major or primary loss, your depression may be related to an intangible loss, such as losing your reputation after classmates spread rumors about you; or to a non-event, such as not getting an honor you expected because you were highly qualified, or losing your dream of going to a prestigious university because you didn't score as well on your entrance exams as you needed to. These types of losses are often silently mourned because people may be unaware of the loss or it isn't the type of loss that is recognized or dealt with in a more public way, such as when someone dies. For this reason, it may be harder to cope with these losses due to lack of support.

2. After discussing this concept with her, help her identify other possible examples, such as losing a sense of safety if her car was broken into, losing respect and trust if she discovered that her mother

or father was having an affair, or losing her sense of identity if she could no longer be a cheerleader because she had broken her leg.

3. Next, give her a sheet of paper and ask her to draw a line across it and designate a time frame (i.e., August 2007 on one end to August 2008 on the other end, or whatever period is relevant for her). Invite her to think about her life over that time period and designate any major losses by making a large dot on the line and then writing these losses beside the line according to when during that time period they occurred. Ask her to do the same for non-event or intangible losses.

4. When she has finished, invite her to draw arrows above or below the line from each of the losses and write any feelings she has associated with these losses.

5. Explore these feelings more in depth and discuss the possibility of writing a letter to one or more of the intangible or non-event losses, explaining how the loss has impacted her life and what she wished could have been different.

Loss After Loss After Loss

RATIONALE
A primary loss is accompanied by secondary losses that may not be readily recognized by adolescents. For example, parental divorce may be the primary loss, while secondary losses might include having to move out of the neighborhood or community, not having as much money, having to change schools and peer groups, and so forth. Adolescents need to be able to identify and grieve these secondary losses as well as the primary loss.

MATERIALS
▷ 1 or 2 sheets of paper cut into 10 to 12 strips, 2 inches wide

▷ A pen or pencil

▷ A stapler

▷ Loss After Loss Worksheet (p. 166)

PROCEDURE
1. When a client presents with grief issues over a loss, explore the nature of the loss with him and invite him to talk about his thoughts and feelings related to this situation.

2. As he talks about the primary loss, listen for secondary losses as well. Explain to him that secondary losses, which involve transitions and changes and other sorts of loss, usually accompany a primary loss but are sometimes not as readily identified. To help him identify these for himself, give him the strips of paper and a pen. Ask him to write down the major/primary loss on one strip and then, on subsequent strips (one loss per strip), write down other losses that relate to the primary loss, as well as a feeling associated with each loss. Staple these strips together to make a paper chain, starting with the primary loss and followed by the secondary losses in order of significance to him.

3. As he identifies the secondary losses, invite him to discuss these and how they have affected his life, emphasizing how they interact with and affect each other, as illustrated by the paper chain.

4. Next, help the client identify what coping strategies he is using to deal with these losses. Then, give him the Loss After Loss Worksheet and help him generate additional coping strategies.

Loss After Loss Worksheet

Directions: Using the examples given in each category, identify as many other alternative coping strategies as possible in each category.

Behavioral/physical

1. Exercise.

2. _____

3. _____

4. _____

5. _____

Emotional

1. Write a story about these losses.

2. _____

3. _____

4. _____

5. _____

Cognitive/thinking

1. Stop thinking that I will never be able to work through this.

2. _____

3. _____

4. _____

5. _____

Heal Your Heart

RATIONALE

A romantic break-up is often a major loss for adolescents, resulting in anger, depression, hopelessness, and self-downing. During times of loss such as this, it is difficult for them to think rationally, which can easily compound the problem. This intervention teaches adolescents how to reduce the intensity of the negative emotions, which are often accompanied by self-defeating behaviors, by practicing rational thinking.

MATERIALS

▷ A large cut-out of a heart, made out of pink or red construction paper

▷ A pen or pencil

▷ Heal Your Heart handout (p. 169)

PROCEDURE

1. When a client presents with issues related to relationship loss, invite her to talk about how the loss occurred. Then give her the heart cut-out and ask her to write all the feelings she has that are associated with this loss, rating their intensity on a scale of 1 (low) to 10 (high).

2. Next, ask her to turn the heart cut-out over and write down the negative thoughts she has that are associated with this loss, such as "This is so unfair," "I'll never get over it," "I can't stand this," and so forth.

3. Without minimizing her loss, explain that, while intense negative feelings are common with respect to a loss of a romantic relationship, those feelings are generally intensified if she thinks that this is the end of the world, that she will never get over it, that she can't stand it, and so forth. Help her see the connection between how she feels and what she thinks by asking her whether she has had a friend whose romantic relationship has ended and whether this friend felt exactly the same way she did. If she says no, you can make the point that because it is a similar event, it is their thinking that creates the difference. For instance, her friend might have realized that she could stand the pain of the break-up,

that eventually she would heal, and that life goes on. Contrast that to someone else who might think that this is the worst thing that could ever happen to her, that no one will love her again, and that she is a total loser.

4. Give the client the Heal Your Heart handout and ask her to read the examples of irrational beliefs, checking the ones that apply to her situation and adding others, if necessary. Then help her understand the irrational belief patterns by pointing out the overgeneralizing (i.e., "I'll never be happy again," "I'll never be able to trust anyone again," "I'll never get through this."). Ask her whether she knows others who have gone through something like this, as painful as it may be, but who have eventually gotten through it, were happy again, and learned to trust. Help her recognize the self-downing ("It's all my fault," "I must be a loser," "I'm a fool," and so forth) by asking her for evidence that she is a loser just because this relationship ended, or how could it be all her fault when relationships involve two people.

5. Once she understands the concept of disputing, ask her to go back to the thoughts she wrote on her heart and identify more rational thoughts for each of the beliefs that contributed to her intense negative emotions, writing these on the heart underneath the irrational belief.

6. Help the client understand that, while romantic relationship break-ups can be painful, healing can occur and is facilitated by rational thinking.

Heal Your Heart

Directions: Read through this list and put a check mark next to each one that is applicable to your situation.

❏ I'll never get through this—it's too painful.

❏ I'll never have a relationship as good as this one was.

❏ It's all my fault that this relationship ended.

❏ I must be a loser because I got rejected.

❏ I'll never be happy again.

❏ I'll never be able to trust another person in a romantic relationship.

❏ I can't ever do anything right.

❏ Others will know something is wrong with me because this relationship ended.

❏ Life isn't worth living if I can't be in this relationship.

❏ I was such a fool for not realizing that the relationship was going bad.

❏ There must have been something I could have done to keep this from happening.

❏ I never want to be in another relationship.

❏ There's nothing good about my life now.

❏ All men (or women) are jerks.

❏ It's not fair that this happened.

❏ Add your own: _____

❏ Add your own: _____

Beginnings and Endings

RATIONALE   Grief is a normal reaction to any type of loss—the conflicting feelings that adolescents experience when there is an end or change in something that is familiar. Adolescents experience a lot of these endings as they go through puberty, graduate from high school, terminate or change relationships, or experience something more major like the death of a friend or relative. This intervention helps them learn about a variety of coping strategies to help them recover from losses they experience.

MATERIALS   ▷ Beginnings and Endings handout (p. 171)

▷ A pen or pencil

PROCEDURE   1. When an adolescent presents with grief issues related to endings, beginnings, and changes, ask him to discuss the one that is most disturbing to him and have him identify what he wishes had been different about that situation. For example, if his best friend committed suicide, his wish might be that if he had been more aware of how depressed and suicidal his friend was, he could have tried to prevent the suicide. Or, if he is about to graduate from high school and is grieving the loss of the part of his life that will soon be over, he might wish that he could stay in school another year.

2. Do the same for any other losses he wants to discuss, if appropriate.

3. Next, share the handout of the things that keep people stuck in their grief and ask him to check off any that apply to him. Discuss why with him in more detail, exploring why these things are not helpful in working through losses.

4. Then, help him identify cognitive ways to get unstuck, such as thinking that it's okay to express his feelings about his loss, that it's good to talk about it, and that he doesn't have to be brave.

5. Work with him to identify other rational thoughts that could help him get unstuck and other things he can do to help deal more effectively with his grief.

Beginnings and Endings

Directions: Read this list of things that keep people stuck in their grief. Put a check mark next to each one that applies to you.

❑ Saying "I'm fine" when that really isn't the case.

❑ Putting up a good front so that you will have others' approval.

❑ "Replacing" a loss by getting another pet, another relationship, and so forth before you have worked through the loss.

❑ Being brave or strong, especially in front of others.

❑ Clinging to the negative and not letting go of the anger.

❑ Thinking that you will never feel better again.

❑ Not thinking about it—repressing your feelings.

❑ Not thinking about it—distracting yourself so that you don't deal with the grief.

❑ Add your own: _____

❑ Add your own: _____

CHAPTER 4

Interventions for Externalizing Problems

As we know only too well, aggression and violence have become major problems among youth. In fact, according to Lochman, Powell, Boxmeyer, Deming, and Young (2007), "Within our youth population, behavioral patterns involving aggression, acting-out, and other generally disruptive behavior patterns represent the highest referral rates for mental health services" (p. 333).

The repercussions of aggression include serious consequences such as school shootings, bomb threats, and assaults in the classroom, as well as bullying, which is a pervasive social problem that negatively affects the entire school (Frey, Herschstein, Snell, Edstrom, MacKenzie, & Broderick, 2005). However, the majority of serious violent crimes involving youth between the ages of 12 and 18 do not occur in schools, according to Riley and McDaniel (2000). Therefore, in addition to concern about school violence, it is important to direct attention to general violence prevention focusing on conflict resolution and anger management. Furthermore, because aggression during childhood is often a precursor for delinquency, school dropout, and violence, as well as serious antisocial behavior later in life, early intervention is critical (Lochman et al., 2007).

Although youth violence was previously conceptualized as isolated reactions of temper, it is now considered a potential developmental issue in which situational factors, societal influences, personality characteristics, and biology all play a role. Lochman et al. (2007) contended that family environment and poor parenting practices may contribute to aggressive behavior. This becomes more complex in that the more oppositional children become, the more negative reactions they receive from parents, teachers, and peers. Consequently, their bonds with those potential sources of support may decrease, which may make them more susceptible to anxiety, depression, and deviant peer influence, as well as early onset substance abuse (Lochman et al., 2007).

Fryxell and Smith (2000) noted that, although violence is a complex issue with multiple causes, one important variable is a high degree of anger and hostility, which is often a precursor to acting out and aggressive behavior. High levels of anger and hostility are also associated with poor academic performance and a wide range of social and behavioral problems in and out of school (McWhirter & Burrow-Sanchez, 2009).

DiGiuseppe and Kelter (2006) stressed that, although anger and aggression often coexist, it is important to distinguish between anger and aggression. Anger is an emotion, whereas aggression is physical or verbal behavior that may result in harm to a person or object. Aggressive children are typically diagnosed as having oppositional defiant disorder (ODD) or conduct disorder (CD), which is more severe because societal norms are violated.

Because of the interrelatedness of problems that stem from anger and aggression, it is clear that we need to increase our efforts to help children and adolescents deal more adaptively with their emotional and behavioral reactions. We should also help them learn to deal more effectively with low tolerance to frustration, which often leads to anger. In addition, internalized problems such as anxiety and depression, which aggressive children and adolescents are more susceptible to (Lochman et al., 2007), can be externalized as self-defeating behaviors such as eating disorders, self-injury, suicidal actions, and substance abuse. Because it is much more difficult to intervene when problems reach that level, it is imperative to do everything possible to prevent these serious problems from developing.

In this chapter, four externalizing disorders are addressed: low frustration tolerance, anger, acting out (including self-defeating behaviors), and bullying. Specific interventions for children and adolescents are identified.

LOW FRUSTRATION TOLERANCE

Frustration, defined as a "natural, primary, affective response to a perceived barrier" (Knaus, 2006, p. 134), is part of life. Some children and adolescents, however, become frustrated more easily than others and are therefore more likely to blame others, rationalize, or make excuses, according to Knaus. Central to the REBT theoretical foundation is the concept of low frustration tolerance (LFT), which is the demand that life's conditions be exactly the way you want them to be, and, if they aren't, it is intolerable and unbearable.

In today's fast-paced, technological society, it appears that low frustration tolerance is on the rise. Fast food and instant messages pave the way to immediate gratification, which reinforces the demand that you shouldn't have to wait for anything or experience frustration in the process. Well-meaning parents, who don't want to see their children experience discomfort or frustration, rescue them—robbing them of the opportunity to work through frustrating experiences on their own, which they will undoubtedly encounter repeatedly throughout life. They inadvertently may teach their children that throwing a temper tantrum in the supermarket is a good way to get what they want because the parents themselves cannot tolerate the frustration of having the child beg and whine for a treat. These same children grow up to be demanding adolescents who can cajole their parents into doing their homework if it's too hard or manipulate them in various other ways to make their life less frustrating and more comfortable. Parents who intervene too quickly to protect their children from frustration are, in fact, doing them a great deal of harm. These children learn to avoid difficult tasks, give up easily, and develop a demanding "I don't have to do this" attitude.

Knaus (2006) explained that, although everyone experiences low frustration tolerance to some degree, it becomes maladaptive when it interferes with personal and social goals. In children and adolescents, LFT manifests itself in various ways, through whining and complaining, shirking responsibility, procrastinating, arguing, and cheating or doing poorly on homework because they think they can't stand to put forth the effort. Knaus (2006) warned that low frustration typically increases as children get older and continues into adulthood. The consequences of LFT become increasingly more serious, impacting job performance and social relationships, as well as self-discipline.

According to Bernard (2004), irrational beliefs such as the following can contribute significantly to low frustration tolerance:

I can't stand it.

It's too hard/it's too boring.

I shouldn't have to work this hard.

I can't take it.

It's unbearable.

Given that low frustration tolerance has significant negative implications, it is important begin teaching children, at a young age, how to tolerate the frustration and discomfort that are part of life. The following interventions are designed to help young clients develop higher frustration tolerance.

I Can Stand It

RATIONALE Children with LFT are often referred by parents and teachers because they give up easily, throw tantrums in class, or procrastinate because they think the task is too hard. These behavior patterns, if reinforced, create multiple problems throughout life. This intervention is designed to help children learn more about LFT and how to change the way they think in order to develop higher frustration tolerance.

MATERIALS
▷ A sheet of paper

▷ A pen or pencil

▷ 2 puppets

PROCEDURE
1. When a child is referred for LFT issues, sing the following songs to her to help her distinguish between low and high frustration tolerance. The songs are to the tune of "Where Is Thumpkin?"

   I can't stand it.
   I can't stand it.
   No, I can't; no, I can't.
   This is just too boring.
   I just feel like snoring.
   I can't do it.
   I can't do it.

   ***

   I can stand it.
   I can stand it.
   Yes, I can; yes, I can.
   I don't have to like it.
   I don't need to fuss about it.
   I can stand it.
   I can stand it.

2. After singing the songs to the child, invite her to sing them, too, then discuss the differences between these songs. Help her see that, in the first song, the child thought she couldn't stand it because the work was too boring, and, in the second, she realized

that she didn't have to like it but she could stand it. Discuss other things that the client thinks might be too frustrating, such as something being too hard, taking too much time, and so forth, eliciting as many of the client's personal frustrations as possible.

3. Next, introduce the puppets and encourage the client to carry on a conversation between them, with one being the "I can't stand it" puppet and the other being the "I can stand it" puppet. Ask the client to think of a situation in her life that she feels like she can't stand or that is frustrating or uncomfortable and talk to the other puppet about this. The "I can stand it" puppet can explain to the other one why she *can* stand it.

4. After some dialogue, further discuss the differences between these two attitudes. Then invite the client to write her own "I can stand it" song to help her remember that she *can* stand things she doesn't like or that are hard or uncomfortable.

Red Light or Green Light?

RATIONALE   Elementary-aged children are constantly learning new skills: how to read, tie their shoes, tell time, count, or play sports. For some children, these new challenges can be more frustrating than they are for others. Teaching clients who struggle with frustration how to overcome it will result in healthier lifelong learning habits.

MATERIALS
- A sheet of paper
- A pen or pencil
- A shoelace and a shoe without a lace
- A jacket or sweater (with buttons) approximately the size of the client
- Red Light/Green Light cut-outs, pasted to tongue depressors (see procedure, step 5)
- Poster board for Green Light poster (see procedure, step 6)

PROCEDURE

1. When a client is referred for problems related to frustration tolerance, invite him to share a recent example of when he was frustrated. As he talks, make a list of the words he uses to describe the frustration, such as "It's too hard," "It's boring," "I can't do it," "I can't learn it," "I don't understand it," "I want to do it my way," and so forth. If the client isn't able to verbalize his thoughts, you may need to tell him what some children think—then share the typical examples in the previous sentence.

2. After getting a sense of the things that frustrate him, invite him to participate in a short experiment. First, take the shoe and the shoelace and ask him to lace the shoe before you can count to ten. This is usually difficult to do; after the time is up, ask him to verbalize how he felt about not being able to do it.

3. Next, give him the sweater or jacket and ask him to put it on backward and button it. As he is doing this, ask him what is going through his mind—is he thinking that this is too hard, that he can't do it, or what?

4. After these two short experiments, talk with the client about the fact that sometimes when children are doing something in a short time period, or doing something that requires coordination or extra effort because it isn't something they typically do (such as put a sweater on backward and button it), they might get frustrated, just like he probably did when he was doing the experiments. Explain that children act different ways when they get frustrated, which he will learn more about as he plays Red Light/Green Light.

5. To play the game, give him the two traffic light cut-outs, pasted on tongue depressors, one colored in with red and the other with green. Explain that the red light indicates behaviors that would not help him accomplish a frustrating task and the green light is for a behavior that would help him develop tolerance for completing the task. Tell him that as you read from a list of behaviors, he should hold up the red light or the green light, based on how he thinks the behavior would help him or not help him complete a task. As you read, allow time for the client to hold up the red or green light and discuss why he thinks the behavior would or would not help him complete the task and develop higher tolerance for frustration. (Put a check mark next to each of the green light behaviors he correctly identifies so that you can write those on the Green Light poster; see procedure, step 6).

Red Light/Green Light behaviors

Throws down the pencil and tears up the paper when the work is too hard.

Just keeps trying to do the work.

Peeks at a classmate's paper and writes down the same answer.

Asks the teacher for help.

Throws a fit and refuses to do anything.

Hurries through the work and doesn't care whether it's right.

Whines until his mom says she will help him.

Yells to the teacher that he can't do it.

Takes a breaks, then finishes the task.

Keeps thinking to himself, "I can do it if I just keep trying."

6. To conclude, ask him to identify any other green light behaviors he can think of. Write his suggestions on the Green Light poster, along with the green light behaviors he identified in step 5. Give him the poster as a reminder of how he can increase his tolerance to frustration.

Fighting Frustration

RATIONALE   Helping young children learn how to fight frustration results in improved performance in various areas of their lives. This intervention introduces the concept of "fighting" frustration as a useful metaphor to facilitate acquisition of the concept.

MATERIALS   ▷ Fighting Frustration story (p. 182)

▷ A pen or pencil

PROCEDURE   1. When a client presents with or is referred for problems resulting from frustration, invite her to listen to a story about Frances, who fought off her frustration.

2. After reading the story, discuss with the client what Frances was frustrated about, as well as how she felt, thought, and behaved. Ask her to evaluate Frances's behavior: Did she think it was a good way to behave? Has she ever been in situations like this, and did she feel, think, and behave in a similar fashion? Invite discussion about her issues with frustration.

3. Next, ask the client to write an ending to the story, thinking about what advice she might give Frances about how to deal with her frustration. Make a copy of the story, and have her write her advice on the back of the page.

4. After she has read her ending to you, discuss her ideas, then engage her in a role play where you act like Frances and the client helps you deal with your frustration by using the advice she would give Frances.

5. Discuss any additional ideas she may have, and let her keep the story as a way of helping her identify strategies for fighting frustration.

Fighting Frustration

Frances was always frustrated. It seemed like whenever she tried to do something, it was just too hard. For example, she wanted to learn to roller skate, but she kept falling down. Her brother told her to just get back up and try again, so she did . . . but she fell again. Frances felt stupid because when she saw her friends skating around the block, she thought, "If they can do it, why can't I? This just isn't fair." So, although she was in a bad mood, she thought she would give it one more try, and, if she couldn't do it, she was giving up. Her brother told her that learning something new takes time, but Frances kept telling him that it shouldn't be this hard . . . it was too much trouble to keep on trying. After she fell down for the third time, she quit but felt sad as she watched her friends skate past her house, looking like they were having fun.

The next day at school, Frances had a new list of spelling words. Her teacher told her that she would have a test on them tomorrow, and she let the students work in pairs to memorize the words. After the first word, Frances just threw down the paper and said, "I'll never learn how to spell these words. They're just too hard. I give up." Her partner told Frances that she shouldn't give up because they were brand new words and it would take some time to learn them, but Frances wouldn't listen. She just sat in her seat and sulked. She didn't study the words, and when she took the test, she got a bad score and had to stay in for recess. This made her all the more frustrated because she couldn't do what she liked best, which was to play during recess.

When Frances got home, her older sister told her that she had to clean her room before dinner or she wouldn't be able to watch her favorite television show later. This made Frances mad. She stomped out of the kitchen, mumbling that it wasn't fair that she had to clean her room in order to watch her favorite show. Nevertheless, she dragged herself up the stairs and walked into her room. It was a mess. There were toys all over the floor, clothes all over the bed, and books everywhere. She didn't know where to start, so she just sat down and started crying.

It seemed to Frances that no matter what she did, it was too hard and too frustrating. She thought, "I shouldn't have to work so hard to learn something, should I? Is it fair that I am punished for not doing things, like studying my spelling words? Why should I have to pick up my room when it is too messy to know where to start? Why should I have to do things I don't like to do?" All the time she was thinking these thoughts, she got madder and madder. She felt like fighting . . . with her brother for telling her to keep on trying to learn to skate, with her teacher for making her stay in for recess, and with her sister for insisting that she clean her messy room or she couldn't watch her favorite show. "It's just not fair; it's just too frustrating," she thought to herself.

If you were Frances, what would you do to deal with these problems? How would you fight your frustrations?

From *More What Works When with Children and Adolescents: A Handbook of Individual Counseling Techniques,* © 2009 by Ann Vernon, Champaign, IL: Research Press (800-519-2707, www.researchpress.com)

I Think I Can

RATIONALE Developing higher frustration tolerance is a skill that can be taught. This intervention is one that children can readily recall and employ when they need extra help in working through frustrating experiences.

MATERIALS
▷ I Think I Can story (pp. 184–185), adapted from *The Little Engine That Could* by Wally Piper (1986), and the I Think I Can song (p. 186)

▷ A sheet of paper

▷ A pen or pencil

PROCEDURE
1. When a client presents with low frustration tolerance issues, read him the I Think I Can story and discuss what happened: What did Tim think and do that helped him overcome his uncomfortable feelings about being in the water?

2. Invite the client to relate the story to his own issues with frustration tolerance or discomfort. Was there anything in the story that would help him?

3. Share the I Think I Can song (sung to the tune of "Twinkle, Twinkle, Little Star") with the client to help him remember the "I think I can" concept. Then work with him to write his own song.

I Think I Can

Once upon a time there was a boy named Tim who wanted to swim. All his friends were just like fish, splashing around in the water, and Tim felt very embarrassed because he couldn't even make himself get in the water. You see, even though Tim knew how to swim, he couldn't even stand to get in the pool if the water was too cold, and he definitely couldn't put his head in the water. That was just too yucky, with water getting in his eyes and nose. But because his little brother and sister loved to swim, his grandma took them all to the pool all the time. So, day after day, as he watched his brother and sister and his friends having lots of fun, Tim felt worse and worse and just stayed in the shallow end of the pool so he didn't have to get his head wet, or on the side of the pool if the water was too cold.

One day Tim decided he had had enough. He was going to swim, no matter what it took. He thought long and hard about what he needed to do, and he finally figured out that he could first practice putting his head under water and getting used to that. He went into the bathroom, filled the tub with water, and stepped in. Taking a deep breath, he held his nose and slowly lowered his head, all the time thinking to himself, "I think I can, I think I can." He counted to ten before he lifted his head out of the water.

"Whew! That wasn't too bad," Tim thought. "I think I'll try it again." This time he counted to 15, and it wasn't that bad at all. Feeling quite proud of himself, Tim got out of the tub, let the water drain out, then filled it with very cold water. He really didn't want to get in, so he just sat on the side of the tub for a few minutes with his feet in the water, thinking that maybe if he did this a little at a time it wouldn't be so bad. At first Tim didn't think he could stand it because the water was so cold, but then he remembered that he didn't want to sit beside the pool all summer when his friends were having fun swimming, so he counted to ten, took a deep breath, and thought, "I think I can, I think I can," as he quickly lowered himself into the tub. At first he shivered so hard that he thought his arms and legs would shake off, but then he gradually got used to it and it wasn't so bad.

Tim forced himself to stay in the tub for quite a while, and, by the time he got out, he didn't feel cold at all. He felt proud of himself that he had been able to put his head in the water and stay in when it was cold. Now it was time for the big challenge—to repeat this in the swimming pool. All the way to the pool he kept thinking to himself, "I think I can, I think I can."

But when he got to the pool, he had second thoughts. He really wondered whether he could stand it if the water was too cold or if he got water in his eyes or nose. He thought it might be intolerable if other kids splashed him. Maybe he should just wait until tomorrow when the water might be warmer. With that in mind, he settled himself on his towel and felt some relief.

But after a few minutes, he started to think about his accomplishments that morning. He hadn't really liked it, but he had been able to keep his head under water. He also remembered that even though the water was cold at first, he had gotten used to it and it hadn't been so bad after all. Taking a deep breath, he thought, "I think I can, I think I can," as he jumped into the water.

I Think I Can

(To the tune of "Twinkle, Twinkle, Little Star")

When I try to learn something new, sometimes I just sit and stew.
It's too hard, it's too tough.
I don't want to work hard enough.
I can't stand to do hard things—it's just easier to laugh and sing.
But if I don't push myself,
I'll miss out on lots of stuff.
So I need to toughen up.
Thinking that I will, I can.
If I try it won't be so hard.
Then I'll be able to play in the yard.

It's Frustrating to Be Frustrated

RATIONALE Low frustration tolerance can result in many bad habits that can persist throughout life. Teaching adolescents to identify and deal with LFT will facilitate their accomplishment of more challenging tasks.

MATERIALS ▷ A list of difficult words that you think the client cannot spell and/or define, such as *conundrum* (a problem with no satisfactory solution), *copacetic* (excellent, superb), *tellurian* (inhabiting the earth), *testaceous* (having a shell-like covering), *fuliginous* (sooty), *moke* (donkey), and *panophobia* (fear of everything)

▷ A pen or pencil

▷ A sheet of paper

▷ A children's puzzle

▷ A blindfold

▷ Frustration Chart (p. 189)

PROCEDURE 1. When a client presents with issues related to frustration tolerance, such as procrastination, anger, avoidance, or daydreaming, invite her to participate in two short exercises. First, give her the pencil and paper and ask her to spell and define the words that you will read to her (identified in the Materials section). To make this activity more frustrating, give her only ten seconds per word. When she has completed the task, ask how she felt while doing it, eliciting the word *frustration,* which is how a person feels when a goal is thwarted.

2. Next, blindfold her, then give her the puzzle and ask her to put it together. As she does this, ask her to describe how she feels. After several minutes, take the blindfold off and allow her to complete the puzzle, comparing how much less frustrating it was when she was not blindfolded.

3. After exploring more about how she felt during these activities, ask her to identify examples in her own life that evoke similar feelings. Invite her to discuss these in more detail, helping her clarify behavioral reactions as well as other emotional responses related to these examples.

4. Ask the client to turn the spelling word sheet over and write several examples of how she can more effectively deal with frustration. Invite her to share her ideas, and brainstorm others with her, which might include breaking tasks into smaller tasks; accepting the idea that some things are naturally frustrating, especially when they are new or difficult tasks; staying calm; and watching how others handle frustrating tasks without engaging in negative behaviors.

5. Encourage her to employ the strategies she identified and to keep the Frustration Chart to note her progress.

Frustration Chart

Directions: Complete this chart each day, identifying the frustrating event, the level of frustration (1 = low, 5 = high), what you did to constructively deal with it, and how well the strategy worked (1 = not well, 5 = very well).

Event	Frustration level	What I did	How it worked
1.			
2.			
3.			
4.			
5.			
6.			
7.			
8.			
9.			
10.			

From *More What Works When with Children and Adolescents: A Handbook of Individual Counseling Techniques,* © 2009 by Ann Vernon, Champaign, IL: Research Press (800-519-2707, www.researchpress.com)

Talk Yourself Out of It

RATIONALE   Low frustration tolerance language simply reinforces the tendency to give up rather than work through things or avoid discomfort rather than realize that it is usually tolerable. This intervention helps adolescents change their LFT language and employ rational coping statements to deal with frustration.

MATERIALS   ▷ Talk Yourself Out of It Checklist (p. 192)

▷ A pen or pencil

▷ Several index cards

PROCEDURE   1. When an adolescent experiences low frustration tolerance, give him the Talk Yourself Out of It Checklist and ask him to check off any of the phrases that he thinks or uses when he is frustrated or experiences discomfort.

2. Review the list with him, asking him to give specific examples of when he uses these phrases.

3. Next, teach him how to dispute these phrases by asking questions such as

Is it a fact that you *really* can't stand it, or is that just what you think or say?

Is it actually unbearable or intolerable? If it was, would you have gotten through the situation?

Where's the evidence that you really *cannot* take it?

Is it possible to go through life and never experience anything hard, frustrating, or uncomfortable? How realistic is that?

What law states that you should never have to work so hard?

Is it possible to go through life without being frustrated some of the time?

4. After he understands the disputing process, ask him to select a frustrating situation and explain it to you. Then you assume the role of the irrational person, exaggerating the frustration and the

discomfort of the situation he described. His role is to use examples such as those identified in step 3 and dispute your irrational beliefs.

5. After the role play, process what occurred, asking him whether the disputing helped put the situation in better perspective. Encourage him to use this process when he encounters frustration or discomfort in the future.

6. Teach him to use rational coping statements. Give him several index cards and have him write statements that will help him deal with frustration, such as "I can stand this even if it is hard" and "It might take time, but I can eventually do it."

Talk Yourself Out of It Checklist

Directions: Think about situations in which you feel frustrated or experience discomfort. Check off the phrases that apply to you under those circumstances.

- ❏ I can't stand it.
- ❏ It's intolerable.
- ❏ It's unbearable.
- ❏ I can't take this.
- ❏ I can't do it.
- ❏ I won't do it.
- ❏ It's overwhelming.
- ❏ It's terrible.
- ❏ It's too frustrating.
- ❏ It's too hard.
- ❏ It's too confusing.
- ❏ It's too time consuming.
- ❏ I shouldn't have to work so hard.
- ❏ This is too difficult.
- ❏ This is too uncomfortable.
- ❏ I shouldn't have to put up with this.
- ❏ Add your own: _____
- ❏ Add your own: _____

From *More What Works When with Children and Adolescents: A Handbook of Individual Counseling Techniques,* © 2009 by Ann Vernon, Champaign, IL: Research Press (800-519-2707, www.researchpress.com)

Deal with It

RATIONALE   Low frustration tolerance can lead to avoidance of long-term challenges, which can negatively impact an adolescent's life in numerous ways. This intervention helps clients learn to deal with frustration more constructively.

MATERIALS   ▷ Deal with It Worksheet (p. 194)

▷ A pen or pencil

PROCEDURE   1. When an adolescent client presents with frustration tolerance issues, present her with the Deal with It Worksheet, asking her to identify the behaviors she experiences when she is frustrated.

2. Next, have her rate the level of helpfulness of each of the behaviors, then ask her to identify consequences of the behavioral reactions—for example, if she procrastinates, how might that affect her grades or her privileges, and so forth.

3. After she has completed the worksheet, invite her to share the information she identified, and encourage her to discuss her frustration tolerance behaviors in more detail, with an emphasis on the positive or negative consequences.

4. Next, help the client identify irrational beliefs that typically result in some of the negative behaviors, such as "I shouldn't have to do this; it's too hard," "I should be able to do fun things, not this," I will never get this done, so why start?" "This is so overwhelming—I just can't deal with it."

5. Once irrational beliefs have been identified, ask the client to think of more rational beliefs that would help her avoid the negative behaviors, such as "There's no proof I will never get this done, but I won't know unless I start," or "I can deal with it even if it is overwhelming—I just have to take it a step at a time." Work with the client to identify other rational beliefs.

6. Encourage her to practice rational thinking by rewarding herself each time she completes a frustrating task in a constructive manner.

Deal with It Worksheet

Directions: Place a check mark beside each of the behaviors that you typically use when encountering a frustrating task or difficult situation. Next, evaluate how helpful these behaviors are (1 = not very, 5 = very), and identify the consequences.

When I have to do something that is too hard, too challenging, too uncomfortable, or too inconvenient, I . . .

Behavior	How helpful	Consequences
❏ Procrastinate	_____	_____
❏ Daydream	_____	_____
❏ Just do it	_____	_____
❏ Copy others' work	_____	_____
❏ Argue about it	_____	_____
❏ Blame others	_____	_____
❏ Get disruptive	_____	_____
❏ Break it into small tasks	_____	_____
❏ Reward myself when finished	_____	_____
❏ Get others to do it for me	_____	_____
❏ Make excuses	_____	_____
❏ Whine and complain	_____	_____
❏ Suck it up and get busy	_____	_____
Add your own:	_____	_____
❏ _____	_____	_____
❏ _____	_____	_____

From *More What Works When with Children and Adolescents: A Handbook of Individual Counseling Techniques,* © 2009 by Ann Vernon, Champaign, IL: Research Press (800-519-2707, www.researchpress.com)

Is It Worth It?

RATIONALE Developing higher frustration tolerance is a skill that must be practiced and reinforced in order for the positive habits to replace the negative. This intervention introduces adolescents to a procedure that they can use in real-life situations.

MATERIALS ▷ Is It Worth It? Scenarios (p. 196)

▷ A pen or pencil

PROCEDURE 1. When a client has issues with frustration tolerance, discuss his frustrations. Then give him the Is It Worth It? scenarios and ask him to identify the irrational beliefs that promote the low frustration tolerance behavior by underlining them.

2. After discussing these irrational beliefs, ask him to evaluate the decisions the character in the scenarios made, which for the most part involve giving in to his low frustration tolerance. Ask him to think of possible ways to challenge this unproductive thinking, referring to previous interventions that addressed the concept of disputing and rational coping statements.

3. Next, ask what prevents him from applying the more rational thoughts that would result in higher frustration tolerance and help him develop strategies that will facilitate their application. For example, if he says that it is just easier to maintain his old habits, ask him how those habits are helping him in the long run. If he thinks that everything has to be easy or enjoyable, ask how he thinks he will get through life if he can't tolerate frustration or discomfort. Work with him until he can get past these barriers.

4. To help reinforce the new way of thinking, ask him to write a letter to himself, explaining what he can do the next time he encounters frustration.

Is It Worth It? Scenarios

1. You have a semester test in your most difficult subject. Your grades in this class are pretty bad, so you think there's no point in studying for the test because it won't matter anyway.

2. You want to go out for track, but when you find out how many laps you would have to run every day just to warm up, you decide it would be too much hassle. Because you don't want to have to do that and practice, too, you don't try out.

3. You have been saving money to buy a car by doing odd jobs for your grandparents, who let you do the jobs whenever you wanted to. The problem is that you haven't made much money, and you really want a car, so you are thinking about getting a job. You start calling around to places that are hiring, but you don't want any of the jobs because you would have to get up too early, work on weekends, or do things that you don't like to do, like clean restrooms. You decide that's it's too hard to work, so you'll just have to wait to buy a car, even though you want one pretty badly.

4. You have a part-time job mowing lawns or delivering papers. The only problem is that you have to get up early in the morning, and you absolutely can't stand that, so despite the fact that you want the money, you quit the job after a week because it is too unbearable.

5. Your parents inform you that in order to go out on the weekends, you need to do chores around the house, like clean your room, mow the lawn, and sweep the garage. You hate doing these things, and you don't think it's fair that they make you work when, after all, you are just a kid. You whine and complain and wait until the last minute to get things done.

6. You really want to go to a concert by one of your all-time favorite bands. The ticket is pretty pricey, but your parents said they would help you out with it if you would wash their cars for the next three weeks and paint the fence. You hate both of these jobs, so you are still thinking whether it is worth it to go to all this discomfort in order to go to the concert.

ANGER

The term *anger* can be used to describe a range of emotional reactions, some of which are appropriate and healthy, such as irritation, disappointment, displeasure, and annoyance. These manifestations of anger are moderate in intensity, motivate clients to change, are consistent with reality, and do not interfere with the ability to achieve goals. At the other extreme are unhealthy angry reactions, such as rage, hate, bitterness, contempt, and hostility. These reactions are based on demanding, blaming, and condemning. They interfere with the ability to achieve goals because they result in a great deal of emotional turmoil, often lead to negative retaliatory behaviors, and are almost always self-defeating (Wilde, 1996). In most cases, these angry and hostile reactions exacerbate already difficult situations.

Although we repeatedly hear declarations such as "He made me mad," anger is in the eye of the beholder, according to REBT theory. A stressful or frustrating event does not *cause* people to be angry any more than other people *make* them mad. Rather, it is each individual's perception that results in a particular emotional reaction, because two people can experience the same situation and react differently. Anger is associated with a demand, and it is experienced when we escalate our desires or wishes into absolutes: "I really want that car. Therefore, I *must* have it." If a person merely *wanted* the car, he would be naturally disappointed if he didn't get it. But when he escalates the preference into a demand, he is angry when he doesn't get what he thinks he *must* have (DiGiuseppe & Kelter, 2006).

Anger often results when children feel that their personal space has been violated, their rights have been threatened, or they have been treated unfairly. An element of low frustration tolerance ("I can't stand this") is often present. Because of their limited cognitive abilities, young people often assume that others are intentionally attacking them in some way, when this often is not the case. Furthermore, their egocentric nature contributes to their belief that others should act in accordance with *their* rules, rights, and reasons.

Anger can be directed at the world, at oneself, or at others. Young people who are angry at the world tend to demand that life give them what they want and that everything be fair and just. Adolescents in particular are very idealistic and often have rigid ideas about how the world must be and how they must be treated. Children who are angry with themselves believe they shouldn't have acted the way they did and therefore are bad, or no good. Anger at oneself can lead to feelings of depression and guilt. When children are angry at others, they think their rights have been violated in some way or that others haven't followed their rules. Their anger stems from their belief that others shouldn't have treated them in this manner—it is awful, they can't stand it, and the wrongdoers deserve to be punished.

Unfortunately, far too many children in today's society are growing up in situations in which they have been severely mistreated or have had their rights violated because of aggressive treatment on the part of others. Of course, this abuse is wrong and should not occur—but it has occurred. Therefore, young clients need to consider whether their anger helps them deal constructively with a situation such as mistreatment, something over which they have little or no control.

Because anger can so easily lead to oppositional behavior, verbal and physical aggression, and other forms of acting out, it is important to help young clients identify the irrational beliefs that cause their anger and teach them how to reduce the intensity of their anger through effective disputing. Examples of challenges to anger-related irrational beliefs include the following: "Where is it written that you should always get what you want, that the world must be fair, and that you always have to have your way?" "How is your anger helping you?" and "How is your anger hurting you?"

Functional disputes, illustrated by the latter two questions, are particularly useful in helping youngsters manage their anger because they may be reluctant to give up their feelings of anger, believing that these angry feelings are justified. Anger often empowers them, and so they consequently feel "righteous" and strong in their convictions. Therefore, it is important to elicit both the advantages and the disadvantages of anger and its associated behaviors. By doing so, the therapist can help young clients realize that when they are angry, they often act against their own best interests by yelling at, hitting, or opposing others who have power over them. Results typically include punishments such as being grounded, getting suspended from school and team sports, and getting hurt physically in altercations with peers. It is essential to show them that, by getting angry, they are likely to lose self-control and give their power away. Thus, anger actually makes them weak, as opposed to strong.

Because children and adolescents usually do not like the idea of giving others control, this realization of empowerment is often a strong motivating factor in encouraging them to work on anger management. It is equally important to teach children that they may not be able to control many aspects of their lives, but what they *can* control are their emotional and behavioral reactions to activating events; these controlled reactions constructively empower them. Finally, it is essential to show children how anger clouds their judgment, as well as their decision-making and problem-solving abilities, and puts them in a "feeling fog."

Irrational beliefs that are associated with anger include the following:

I must have what I want.

The world should be fair.

I must have things go my way.

Other people must treat me the way I want them to, and when they don't, they deserve to be punished.

The following interventions can help children and adolescents identify the demands that result in anger and learn how to manage their anger-related emotions more effectively.

Anger Antenna

RATIONALE Children need to know what triggers their anger so they can learn how to deal with it before it gets out of control. This activity, which involves a concrete way of remembering concepts presented in the lesson, can engage children in thinking more about this issue.

MATERIALS
▷ A sheet of paper

▷ Several pipe cleaners

▷ Glue

▷ Crayons and a pencil

PROCEDURE
1. When a client has anger issues, engage her in a discussion about what an antenna is—something that acts as a signal. Elicit examples, such as antennas on top of high buildings that signal airplanes from coming too close. Explain that people sometimes need an antenna to help them know when their anger is getting out of control, and, if they use their antenna, they can learn how to better handle this emotion.

2. Give the client several pipe cleaners, crayons, glue, and a sheet of paper. Ask her to make an antenna and glue it in the middle of the paper.

3. Once this has been completed, engage the client in a discussion about what she is aware of when she first starts to get angry. For example, does she notice any change in her breathing? Are her hands sweaty? Does she raise her voice or clench her fists? As she thinks of examples, have her write them on the left side of the antenna.

4. Next, discuss the fact that, although these are signals that she is getting angry, she also can do something to decrease her anger. Together, brainstorm ideas, such as taking deep breaths, thinking of something funny as a distraction, or counting to ten. Ask her to write these ideas on the right side of the antenna.

5. Finally, engage the client in an imagery exercise. First, have her recall a time when she was very angry and have her visualize the event so that she can feel that anger. Then, ask her to visualize herself using one of the ideas she generated to help her de-escalate the anger, staying with that image until she feels her anger decrease.

6. Process the visualization and give her the sheet with the antenna as a way to remember the other strategies she can employ the next time she feels angry.

Anger In? Anger Out?

RATIONALE Children often receive mixed messages about what to do with their anger—let it out or hold it in? Role modeling from home also influences their decisions about what to do. This activity is designed to help children learn more about expressing anger.

MATERIALS ▷ An envelope

▷ Several strips of paper

▷ A pen or pencil

▷ A tape recorder and a blank tape

PROCEDURE 1. When a client presents with anger issues, engage him in a discussion about what he typically does when he is angry: Does he keep it in or let it out? If he keeps it in, discuss the consequences of doing that. For example, does he continue to feel angry, or can he forget about it? Does he have any physical discomfort such as headaches or stomach aches? Does he feel distracted because he is holding onto anger? As he talks about the consequences, write them on the slips of paper (one per slip) and put them inside the envelope.

2. If he lets his anger out instead of keeping it in, discuss the consequences of this approach: Does he feel better or worse after letting it out? Does letting the anger out result in others getting angry back? Does letting it out get rid of it or just keep reminding him about what he is angry about? Write his responses on one side of the outside of the envelope.

3. After discussing which approach the client usually takes, discuss the consequences of the opposite approach and record them on strips to place inside the envelope or write them on the outside of the envelope (the blank side) to give him a visual of the consequences of both options.

4. Engage the client in a discussion about both approaches: What are the advantages and disadvantages of keeping anger in or letting it out? If he lets it out, are there better ways to do it than others?

5. Finally, place an empty chair in front of the client and have him pretend that his best friend is sitting in the chair. Instruct your client to discuss the advantages and disadvantages of letting his anger out and the advantages and disadvantages of keeping it in. As he does this, tape record his responses.

6. After he has completed the empty chair exercise, play the tape recording and discuss what he learned about these approaches and how he might handle his anger as a result.

Angry Annabelle

RATIONALE   It is important to help young children identify their own ways to deal with anger so that they can make independent decisions, especially if older role models find anger acceptable and encourage them to express it in a manner that might be unproductive. Working with the client on the unfinished Angry Annabelle story can serve as a stimulus for good discussion about alternative ways to deal with angry feelings.

MATERIALS   ▷ Angry Annabelle story (p. 205)

▷ A pen or pencil

PROCEDURE   1. When a young client is referred for problems with anger or presents with this issue, read the Angry Annabelle story together and invite the client to verbally respond as you fill in the blanks.

2. Throughout the story, stop to process the client's responses, encouraging elaboration and personalization. For example, if the client says she doesn't know what Annabelle would be angry about, ask her what she gets angry about.

3. After the story is finished, contract with the client to try one strategy to deal with her anger.

Angry Annabelle

Annabelle attends Andersonville Elementary School. Lately she has been getting into trouble with her teacher because she is always angry. When Annabelle gets angry she _____.

When the teacher asks her what she was so angry about, she says

_____.

When her teacher asks Annabelle why she gets so angry, she replies

_____.

When the teacher asks Annabelle whether she thinks her anger helps her deal with her problems, she says _____.

When the teacher asks Annabelle whether she always expresses her anger in the same way and, if not, what else does she do, Annabelle replies _____.

The teacher asks Annabelle to make a list of all the things she does when she gets angry and to put a plus or a minus beside each one (a positive or negative way of handling the anger). Annabelle came up with the following list:

1. _____   2. _____

3. _____   4. _____

When the teacher asks Annabelle which of the ideas on the list are the ones she thinks might work best for her the next time she gets angry, she says _____.

The teacher then asks her which of the ideas might not work very well or would have negative consequences. Some of those negative consequences could be _____.

Then the teacher asks which idea she would most like to try the next time she gets angry, and Annabelle says _____.

From *More What Works When with Children and Adolescents: A Handbook of Individual Counseling Techniques,* © 2009 by Ann Vernon, Champaign, IL: Research Press (800-519-2707, www.researchpress.com)

Adios, Anger

RATIONALE Anger is the root of many problems that affect relationships at home and at school. Helping children identify ways to let go of anger is advantageous both in the present and future. This activity actively engages the client in thinking about how to deal with anger.

MATERIALS
▷ A sheet of paper

▷ A pen or pencil

▷ A hopscotch board that can be drawn with a marker on an old bed-sheet or flannel-backed plastic tablecloth

PROCEDURE
1. After discussing what the client is angry about in some detail, explore the consequences of hanging onto the anger versus letting it go. Assuming that he wants to let it go, engage him in the following activity.

2. First, have him make a list of what he is angry about. If it is just one issue, there may be various aspects to it, so have him list those as well.

3. Next, lay out the hopscotch board and explain that you will read what he is angry about, one issue at a time. After you read the issue, the client should think about what he could do to say "adios/goodbye" to his anger, then hop to the next space (for example, he could journal about his anger, pretend that he is a balloon and little by little let go of the anger, or run around the block to let his angry energy out). Write the ideas at the bottom of his list so that he will have a visual reminder of things he can do with his anger.

4. Continue with this activity until the client reaches the end of the board and can say "Adios, anger!"

5. Discuss what he learned and which ideas seem most feasible to try.

Expressing Your Anger

RATIONALE When an adolescent presents with anger issues, it is often difficult to help her diffuse the anger because it can be intense. Letting her vent can be cathartic, but, at the same time, repeatedly talking about the anger keeps it "alive" and refuels it. This intervention is designed to help the client decrease anger and learn how to express angry feelings toward others assertively and with less intensity.

MATERIALS
▷ 12 to 15 index cards

▷ A pen or pencil

▷ A sheet of paper

▷ 12 to 15 envelopes

PROCEDURE
1. When a client presents with anger issues, first discuss them with her. Then give her a sheet of paper and suggest that she make a list of everything about the incident(s) that she is angry about. When the list is complete, ask her to rank order her list, with 10 representing awfully angry to 1 being least angry. Then instruct her to write these issues, along with their ranking, on separate index cards and put each in a separate envelope with the ranking on the outside of the envelope.

2. Discuss the rankings with the client, noting how many are high (7 to 10 range), medium (4 to 6 range), and low. Ask her to reflect on the difference between the issues she rated high and low. For example, are certain thoughts reflected in the high-intensity items, such as "She shouldn't betray me," "I can't stand it when people are dishonest," and "Friends should be loyal"? Are these thoughts different in the low-intensity items, such as "I wish she wouldn't act this way," "I don't like the way she is treating me," and so forth? Encourage discussion about this.

3. Next, invite her to take the high-intensity envelopes and, on the index cards contained inside, have her write down the specific thoughts that contributed to the anger relative to the incident

written on the card. When she is finished, invite her to discuss these thoughts with you so that you can help her see the difference between those that contribute to more-intense and to less-intense anger.

4. Explain to the client that one of the best ways to reduce the intensity of anger is to ask yourself questions such as "How does it help me or the relationship/situation to be this angry?" "Even though I think she shouldn't treat me this way, can I control her?" "Is there a law that says she shouldn't treat me like this?" Work on different beliefs related to her issue(s) so that she clearly understands the disputing process.

5. Explain to the client that once she has disputed the problematic beliefs that contribute to the intense anger so that she is less angry, she may still want to say something to the other person. In doing so, she cannot expect to change the person's behavior, but she can express how she feels. Discuss with her the differences between assertion and aggression, stressing that it is always preferable to send assertive messages that state how you feel and explain the effect on you of the other person's behavior or the particulars of the situation. Tell the client that when a person is assertive, her voice tone isn't angry, and she doesn't use harsh words—the goal is to increase understanding while expressing the anger in a helpful way. Contrast this to aggression, which is an attack on the other person, using "you" language that sounds accusatory. The goal of an aggressive message is to vent your feelings without considering those of the other person or how it will impact the relationship.

6. Engage the client in a role play, using a situation involving a person she wants to confront. First ask her to be aggressive toward you, as you play the role of the person she wants to confront, then be assertive. It may be necessary for you to model both assertive and aggressive responses so that she clearly understands the differences between these two types of responses.

7. After several behavioral rehearsals, ask the client which type of response she thinks will be most helpful for her in dealing with anger in relationships.

Angry Attitudes

RATIONALE   This intervention helps adolescents understand more about angry attitudes and how they affect themselves as well as others.

MATERIALS   ▷ Angry Attitudes Scenarios (p. 210), cut apart and placed in an envelope

▷ A pen or pencil

PROCEDURE   1. When a client presents with an angry attitude, which is often reported by others but denied by the client, ask him whether he knows anyone with an "angry attitude" and discuss what the word *attitude* means—your disposition toward something, or how you react to things. Encourage discussion about how one's attitude often affects the ways others react to him; for example, there are people who have negative attitudes about everything and aren't pleasant to be around, people who have cynical attitudes and are sometimes difficult to relate to, and people who have positive attitudes and are enjoyable to be with.

2. Next, ask the client how he thinks a person with an angry attitude typically acts toward others. For example, how does a person with an angry attitude get along in sports or in work settings, or how does a person with an angry attitude get along with his friends? After some discussion, invite the client to draw the scenarios out of an envelope, and have him write a response to each scenario on the back.

3. When the client is finished, discuss his responses. Ask him whether he ever has a problem with an angry attitude and, if so, did he learn anything from thinking about these scenarios that might help him deal with his angry attitude? If he denies having an angry attitude, simply ask whether he enjoys being around others who have one and what he learned from talking about angry attitudes.

Angry Attitudes Scenarios

You are applying for a job mowing lawns. With an angry attitude, how might you respond to the question "Are you dependable?" What might happen as a result of your response?

During a basketball game, the referee makes a call that you don't agree with. With an angry attitude, what might you do or say? What might happen as a result of your words or actions?

Your parents say that you can't go out with your friends. With an angry attitude, what might you do or say? What might be the outcome?

You find out that several of your friends went to the movie and didn't include you. With an angry attitude, what might you do or say to them, and how might that affect the friendship?

You studied hard for a test but got a bad grade anyway. With an angry attitude, how might you react when you get the test back? What might happen as a result of your reactions?

You recently got a job mowing lawns for the neighbor. One day he tells you that you didn't trim thoroughly enough. With an angry attitude, how might you respond, and what might be the result?

Your parents leave for a few hours and tell you to have all your chores completed by the time they return. With an angry attitude, how might you react to this, and what might they do in return?

You and your lab partner were talking in science while the teacher was explaining another task to complete. Because you didn't hear the directions, you turn around to ask the person behind you. The teacher tells you to stop talking and to sit in the back of the classroom. With an angry attitude, how might you respond, and what might the teacher do in return?

You are selling concessions at the ball game and it is very busy. Two people are taking forever to decide what to order. You are getting impatient. What might you say to them if you had an angry attitude? What repercussions might there be?

From *More What Works When with Children and Adolescents: A Handbook of Individual Counseling Techniques,* © 2009 by Ann Vernon, Champaign, IL: Research Press (800-519-2707, www.researchpress.com)

Anger Is . . .

RATIONALE   Adolescents are often overwhelmed by their anger but unable to express how it controls them or affects them. This intervention is designed to facilitate their expression of their anger so they can learn better ways of dealing with it.

MATERIALS   ▷ Anger Is Inside You poem (p. 212)

PROCEDURE   1. When an adolescent client presents with anger but can't really describe how it is affecting her, give the client a copy of the Anger Is Inside You poem, written by an adolescent female, then use it as a springboard for reflection and discussion.

2. After the client reads the poem, ask her to reflect on it and describe what it meant to her: Could she identify with anything in particular? How is her anger like or unlike that of the teen who wrote the poem? Does she think that her anger controls her, and, if so, in what ways? In her situation, who is "winning" the battle—she, or her anger?

3. Next, invite your client to write her own "Anger Is" poem, or she could write a song describing it or draw a picture and add words that describe her anger.

4. Finally, ask her to think of one thing she can do to keep her anger from "winning," if that is her goal. If it is not the goal, ask her to identify reasons for letting it win the battle and determine whether the anger will help her.

Anger Is Inside You

Anger is inside you.
It burns you up, like the gates of hell.
It controls you, fills you up.
Anger is red.
It is hot, like the sun.
It is powerful, like money.
Anger takes hold.
It grabs your arms and legs.
It breaks you down.
Anger is a bright flash.
It is the emotional battle you're trying to win.
You against anger—who's keeping score?

Anger—Any Advantages?

RATIONALE When an adolescent client presents with anger, it is often difficult for him to see any disadvantages because anger often is equated with power (real or perceived) and serves as a defense mechanism against hurt. Many adults will try to talk an adolescent out of being angry and point out the negative consequences, but it is important for the adolescent to arrive at his own conclusions.

MATERIALS ▷ Anger Advantages Worksheet (p. 214)

▷ A pen or pencil

PROCEDURE 1. After discussing with the client how he is currently experiencing his anger and what he is angry about, give him a copy of the Anger Advantages Worksheet and invite him to complete it.

2. After he completes the task, engage the client in a discussion about his responses on the worksheet: Was he surprised by any of his ratings? Which questions were the most difficult to respond to? What did he learn about his anger?

3. Next, invite discussion about the open-ended questions relative to the advantages and disadvantages of anger. Challenge any misconceptions, such as anger helps resolve problems: Does it help preserve relationships? Encourage rational problem solving? Have positive, long-term consequences? Because adolescents have a tendency to think in the "here and now," try to help him see the bigger picture through logical and empirical challenges: How realistic is it to think that getting angry will help you keep a job? Where is the evidence that getting angry helps solve problems in a productive manner?

4. Finally, discuss what he can do if he wants to control his anger, and brainstorm alternatives he can try.

Anger Advantages Worksheet

Directions: Read the following statements and circle the number that best applies to you on a scale of 1 (never) to 5 (always).

When I get angry, I feel powerful and in control	1	2	3	4	5
When I get angry, I get my way	1	2	3	4	5
When I get angry, I am embarrassed about my actions	1	2	3	4	5
When I get angry, I feel good	1	2	3	4	5
I think my anger helps me deal with issues	1	2	3	4	5
When I get angry, I like how others react to me	1	2	3	4	5
I think my anger can quickly get out of control	1	2	3	4	5
I think I have good ways to deal with my anger	1	2	3	4	5
I would like to stop getting so angry	1	2	3	4	5
Getting angry is a productive way to resolve problems	1	2	3	4	5

Complete the following:

Five advantages of being angry:

1. _____
2. _____
3. _____
4. _____
5. _____

Five disadvantages of being angry:

1. _____
2. _____
3. _____
4. _____
5. _____

If I don't want my anger to get out of control, I can do the following:

1. _____
2. _____
3. _____
4. _____
5. _____

ACTING OUT

Anger and frustration often lead to various forms of acting out, such as temper tantrums; impulsive behavior; yelling and screaming; hitting, kicking, and punching; bullying and fighting; stealing; destroying property; or engaging in more serious acts of violence and aggression. Low self-worth may contribute to acting-out problems such as bullying, in which the bully irrationally thinks that the only way to feel approved of or worthwhile is to be the toughest kid in the neighborhood. Children who steal may feel worthless because they don't get enough love or approval and may try to compensate for their feelings of inferiority by taking what they want in order to feel better (Bernard & Joyce, 1984). Some children act out as a way to control others or their environment, having learned that parents may give in and let them have their way in order to avoid their own discomfort. Children may also behave badly because they lack socialization skills or behavioral self-control.

Underlying most forms of aggression is demandingness (DiGiuseppe & Kelter, 2006): I must have my way and others should give me what I want—if they don't, I'll figure out a way to get it. It is common to hear children say they "can't help how they act" because they fail to see the connection between how they think, feel, and act. It is also not surprising, given their tendency to think in the here and now, that children don't consider the possible negative consequences of their behavior—because of their faulty thinking, youngsters may assume they won't get caught or that it's not a big deal even if they do get caught.

It is important to distinguish between acting out and more serious oppositional defiant and conduct disorders. These more serious disorders evince a persistent pattern of conduct that violates the basic rights of others or major age-appropriate social norms. Children with these disorders might respond better to behavioral interventions than to cognitive interventions (DiGiuseppe & Kelter, 2006).

Irrational beliefs that accompany aggression or acting out include the following:

I must have my way, and, if I don't, I can't stand it.

Others must be punished if they violate me in any way.

If I don't get what I need or want from others, I'll get it myself.

Although we typically think of acting out as impulsive behavior, tantrums, failure to comply, and various forms of aggression, there are other forms of acting out that may not be as typical but are serious and self-defeating: eating disorders, self-injury, and addictive behavior. Clearly these self-defeating behaviors coexist with other internalizing disorders such as anxiety and depression, as well as with externalizing disorders such as lying, stealing, and other forms of acting out (Chernicoff & Fazelbhoy, 2007).

Self-injurious behavior is defined as "any behavior causing damage to the self that is used as a paradoxical coping tool" (Jones, 2007, p. 367), such as cutting, burning, scratching, neglect of self-care, and other dangerous or risky activities. Self-injurers are usually not suicidal; in fact, they hurt themselves to relieve their pain or to let others know how badly they feel in order to prevent escalation to suicide, according to Jones. Self-injury results in immediate gratification and release from pain, and it therefore can be addictive. Goals of therapy include helping the client learn what functions their behavior serves, what thoughts trigger their emotional responses, and how to replace their self-defeating behaviors with healthier coping skills.

Substance abuse continues to be a pervasive problem and is a major concern because of the serious long- and short-term negative consequences on physical, emotional, social, and academic development, according to Chernicoff and Fazelbhoy (2007). These authors also indicated that suicide is strongly linked with binge drinking, which adds further complications. Low frustration tolerance, or the inability to withstand discomfort, is a major contributor to substance abuse in that abusers want to escape from pain; numbing themselves with alcohol or drugs seems to be a viable way to achieve that purpose.

Distorted cognitions relating to self-worth and identity may influence an adolescent to act out in order to express herself as a separate individual who is capable of doing grown-up things, as Chernicoff and Fazelbhoy (2007) noted. Goals of treatment include identifying and clarifying distorted cognitions and developing higher frustration tolerance, as well as dealing with internalizing disorders such as depression or externalizing disorders such as anger.

Another serious problem that has become prevalent for adolescents, females in particular, is eating disorders. Although multiple factors, such as family relationships, low self-esteem, puberty, peer relationships, and the influence of the media, contribute to the onset and maintenance of the disorder (Bloomgarden, Mennuti, Conti, & Weller, 2007), dysfunctional beliefs also factor in. As Beck (1995) noted, dysfunctional thinking patterns help develop as well as maintain eating disorders, especially cognitions related to self-worth. Treatment must target identification and disputation of distorted beliefs about body image, control, and self-worth, with the goal of helping clients see the connections among their thoughts, feelings, and self-defeating behaviors in order to develop healthier responses.

The following interventions can be adapted, as necessary, to help children and adolescents develop more control over acting-out and self-defeating behaviors.

How Do I Act?

RATIONALE   Helping young children become more aware of their behavior is the first step in changing negative patterns. This intervention is especially geared to children whose impulsive behavior is problematic.

MATERIALS   ▷ A bowl of popped popcorn or an unopened package of popcorn that can be popped while you and the client are working

▷ A jar of molasses and a bowl

▷ A glass of water and an empty glass

▷ How Do I Act? story (p. 220)

▷ When I Want to Run Around song (pp. 221)

PROCEDURE   1. In talking with your client about her behavior, it is helpful to use concrete objects to facilitate her awareness. Introduce this intervention by asking whether she knows what molasses is, then ask her to pour a small amount into the bowl. As she pours, ask her to reflect on whether it pours quickly or slowly. Next, have her do the same with a glass of water, pouring it from one glass to another. Is it fast or slow? Finally, show her the bowl of popped popcorn (or pop it in the session, which is much more effective). Ask her to describe what popcorn sounds like and looks like when it is popping, eliciting the idea that it is random, starts off slow, then builds up until it is popping up all over and hard to control.

2. Next, ask her to think about how one of her siblings or one of her classmates acts—is their behavior more like molasses (they move slowly, talk slowly, do things as if they were in slow motion), water (they move fast, talk fast, and do everything rapidly), or popcorn (they are impulsive, popping from one place to the next; it's hard to get them settled down)? After she has identified these characteristics in others, ask her to describe her behavior. If she is inaccurate, you can share that others, such as her teacher or her parents, sees her in a different way.

3. Next, read her the How Do I Act? story.

4. After reading the story, discuss how Irma's behavior worked for or against her, then ask the client to think of other ideas that might help Irma stay in one place. Then ask her which of these ideas she thinks could work best for her when her behavior is like "popcorn."

5. Teach the client the When I Want to Run Around song, which might help her remember to control her behavior. It's sung to the tune of "Twinkle, Twinkle, Little Star."

6. After singing the song and discussing the concepts, invite the client to make up her own song. Give her a copy of the song and the one she composes as reminders of how to control her impulsive behavior.

How Do I Act?

Irma, who was 8 years old, was very impulsive. She didn't know what this big word meant, but her father told her that she was just like popcorn . . . she kept popping up all over, and it was hard for her to control her behavior. She guessed that he was right, because whenever she sat down to read a book, she was up out of her seat in a minute, running to another room to ask her brother something or peeking in to see what her parents were watching on television. She hated it when they had to remind her to go back to her room to read or when they yelled at her because she didn't do what they asked her to.

At school she also got into trouble because she was always out of her seat, roaming around the room. The other kids, as well as her teacher, repeatedly told her to take her seat. It was hard for her to sit still—it was much more fun to wander around and talk to her friends, especially when her schoolwork was hard or boring. But, unfortunately, the teacher didn't see it her way; consequently, Irma often had to stay in for recess to finish her work.

Irma was really tired of having her parents and teacher—and even her older brother and some of her classmates—tell her to settle down. Especially when they said it in a mean voice, which made Irma feel bad. One day, after her mother had asked her many times to stay focused and do her homework, Irma told her mother that she must be a really bad kid because everyone was always picking on her. Irma's mother reassured her that she wasn't a bad kid, but that her behavior could use some improvement. She asked Irma whether she had any ideas about how she could do that. Irma just looked discouraged and shook her head no.

Her mother thought that maybe it would help if Irma pretended that she had glue on her bottom and couldn't get out of the chair . . . Irma laughed at that one. Then Irma said that maybe it would help if she pretended that she was tied to the chair and couldn't move. Her mother agreed that that was a good idea, too. Irma couldn't think of anything else she could try. Can you?

From *More What Works When with Children and Adolescents: A Handbook of Individual Counseling Techniques,* © 2009 by Ann Vernon, Champaign, IL: Research Press (800-519-2707, www.researchpress.com)

When I Want to Run Around
(To the tune of "Twinkle, Twinkle, Little Star")

When I want to run around,
I should remember that they frown.
They don't want to yell at me,
They just want me to agree
That it's best if I behave,
So I need to learn some ways.

One thing that I think I can do
Is to pretend I stick like glue,
Then I can't be up and about,
Then I won't be tempted to shout.
If I can remember what to do,
I think I will be as happy as you.

Stop or Go Behavior

RATIONALE   Using this intervention can help children learn to distinguish between positive and negative behaviors.

MATERIALS

▷ A game board (from the appendix or one of your own design; if you construct your own game board, you should depict a road with 20 spaces, along which the client advances his car)

▷ A small toy car, such as a Matchbox car

▷ A sheet of paper

▷ A pen or pencil

▷ Stop or Go Cards (pp. 224–225)

PROCEDURE

1. When a client presents with behavioral problems, engage him in this intervention that helps him recognize the difference between positive and negative behaviors.

2. To play the game, invite your client to take the car and place it on the space labeled "start." Explain to him that this game requires him to identify negative behaviors that should be stopped and positive behaviors that he can continue to use.

3. To begin, ask the client to draw a Stop or Go Card from the pile and read it. If he thinks that this is a positive ("go") behavior, he moves his car one space ahead and discards his card. If he thinks that the card he drew is a negative ("stop") behavior, he moves back one space and puts that card in a separate discard pile.

4. If, after all the cards have been drawn, the client is not at the end of the road, he can take the cards from the "stop" behavior discard pile, suggest a better behavior, and advance a space.

5. Continue until the client reaches the end of the road. Debrief by asking what he learned about "stop" and "go" behaviors, which ones he uses most often, and which ones he would like to use.

6. Have the client select three "go" behaviors he would like to work on and make a specific plan outlining how he will do this. Ask him

to draw a picture of a car on a sheet of paper and write his plan on the car to serve as a reminder of positive behaviors he wants to work on.

Stop or Go Cards

A classmate makes a face at you, so you punch him.	Your locker mate leaves his stuff on your side, so you throw it onto the floor.
The teacher quietly asks you to stay in your seat. You stick your tongue out at her.	In music class, someone makes fun of the way you sing. You hit her with your book.
Your father reminds you to do your chores, and you do them right away.	Your little brother, who shares a room with you, keeps talking to you while you are trying to get to sleep. You scream at him to shut up.
You are playing flag football. When the coach takes you and a couple of other players out and puts others in, you get mad and yell at the coach.	You are playing in the park and see someone take a ball from a much younger girl. You walk over to the boy and tell him that you saw him do that and that you think he should give it back to her.
You are walking home from school, and a kid from another class teases you about your backpack. You just ignore him and keep on walking.	You are in gym class and everyone is shooting baskets. Your friend keeps trying to shoot but can never make a basket. You tell him that it's good that he tried and that some-day he'll be better.

You are in the supermarket with your dad. He refuses to let you have a snack, so you throw yourself on the floor and have a fit.	The teacher tells the class that they have to stay in for recess because they were too rowdy. You don't think it is fair. You get really mad and kick the chair.
You and a friend are riding your bikes home from school when you see some younger kids ahead of you. You don't like these kids and you really want to beat them up, but you don't.	In science class, the girl in the row ahead of you keeps turning around and staring at you. You can't stand her. You tell her in a quiet voice that you are working and would she please stop bothering you.
You and your brother are watching television. He flicks the channel to a show you don't like, but instead of getting mad at him, you just go and find something else to do.	Yesterday on the way home from school, a kid in your class kept trying to steal your backpack. Today you put your chewing gum on his chair.
One of your classmates calls you a name. You know it's not what you are, so you just ignore her.	You don't think it is fair that your brother, who is a year younger, gets to stay up as late as you do to watch a special television show. You are mad, but you don't make a big deal about it.
Your dad tells you that you can't have a treat until you finish your vegetables. You hate vegetables, so you spit out what's in your mouth and tell him you aren't going to eat them.	At school, your math partner keeps peeking at your paper. It really makes you mad, but you just tell him that he should do his own work.
You really want to stay overnight at your friend's house but your parents won't let you. You scream and throw a tantrum and tell them that they are the meanest parents on the block.	On the way to school, two older kids start picking on you and your friend. You just keep walking and do your best to ignore them.

What's the Consequence?

RATIONALE Understanding the connection between how they act and the consequences of those actions is an important skill for children. This intervention emphasizes how to anticipate consequences in order to avoid negative repercussions.

MATERIALS ▷ A set of 8 index cards containing the following words (one word per card): *hunt, find, listen, learn, trip, fall, eat, grow*

▷ A crystal ball (a ball covered with crinkled-up aluminum foil)

PROCEDURE 1. When you are counseling a young client who has difficulty anticipating consequences of her behavior, randomly place the index cards face down on a table. Ask her to pick them up, one at a time, and decide what words can be paired because one action would logically result in another.

2. Discuss the concept of logical consequences: being able to anticipate what can happen based on an action. For example, if you forget to study for a spelling test, you might get a bad grade. Or if you act out in class, you probably will be scolded by the teacher. Ask the client to identify other examples of consequences.

3. Next, hand the client the "crystal ball" and tell her that if she looks into this ball, she should be able to predict consequences of her actions. Tell her that you will read some actions to her and she should "look into the ball" and tell you what she thinks the consequences will be. Read examples such as the following:

    You forget to take the medicine for your really bad tummy ache.

    You have a test tomorrow, and you forget to take your book home to study for it.

    You really want the candy bar at the store, but your mother refuses to buy it for you, so you sneak it into your coat pocket.

On the playground, you push one of your classmates down when he tries to intercept your ball.

Your parents have to work late. They called and told you to stay in the house and not have anyone over. One of your friends calls and asks whether she can come over to play, and you say yes.

Instead of going right out to the bus stop in the morning, you keep watching television.

You are walking home from a friend's house for the first time. Your older sister had showed you where to turn, but you weren't paying attention.

After school you are supposed to go straight home, but instead you go to the playground and stay for a long time

4. After she has finished identifying possible consequences, discuss how to apply the crystal ball in her own life. What does she need to do in order to anticipate consequences?

5. Next, ask the client to write two short stories: one about a character who doesn't think ahead and anticipate consequences, and another who does.

6. Invite her to read her stories, then ask her to describe the consequences in each.

7. Finally, ask her to identify a behavior she would like to work on and use her "crystal ball" (which she may keep) to anticipate consequences.

Me and My Actions

RATIONALE
Young children often lack behavioral self-awareness; consequently, it can be challenging to help them change their behavior. This intervention is designed to increase self-awareness, a first step in modifying behavior.

MATERIALS
▷ 3 small, plastic buckets, such as those used at the beach; label one bucket *Like Me,* one *Not Like Me,* and the third *Sometimes Like Me*

▷ Another plastic bucket containing 20 plastic or real golf balls

▷ Me and My Actions Cards (p. 230); you can adapt the cards or create new ones to address specific client behaviors

PROCEDURE
1. Engage your client in the following intervention to help him gain awareness of his behavior. First, explain that he gets to play a game that helps him learn more about his behavior. Show him the three plastic buckets and the golf balls, which are in the fourth bucket.

2. Place the three buckets about 2 or 3 feet in front of the client (adjust accordingly, depending on the age or motor skills of the client), with at least a foot of space between each bucket. Then give him the bucket of balls. Explain that you will be reading some action cards describing different kinds of behavior. As he listens, he needs to decide whether each behavior is like him, not like him, or sometimes like him, and toss a ball into the bucket that best describes that behavior in relation to himself.

3. Continue until all action cards have been read. Then, ask the client to count the balls in each bucket and discuss the results. Engage him in a discussion about how he feels about these designations and whether there are balls in any of the buckets that he would like to have in a different bucket.

4. Explore the changes he would like to make in more detail, asking what prevents him from behaving differently. Have him identify two or three changes in particular he wants to make, and work through the advantages and disadvantages of engaging in these behaviors: the specific ones he wants to change, strategies he has

tried in the past and how they worked, and something he can do now to make a change.

5. If the client did not put any of the negative balls in the "like me" bucket, and you know that not to be the case, gently confront him about this, explaining that bad behaviors don't make him a bad kid. Also help him see that he is in control of his behavior and that there are people who can help him make changes if he chooses to do so.

Me and My Actions Cards

I always listen when the teacher is talking.	I am polite.
I interrupt others.	I am sneaky.
I grab things out of others' hands.	I don't argue.
I stay in my seat when told to.	I do things to help out, even without being asked.
I argue with teachers and my parents when they tell me to do something I don't want to do.	I throw tantrums.
I think before acting.	I do nice things for others.
I blurt things out.	I say nice things about others.
I follow the rules.	I tell lies or spread rumors about others.
I pick on others.	I am mean to others.
I start fights.	I kick and bite.

From *More What Works When with Children and Adolescents: A Handbook of Individual Counseling Techniques,* © 2009 by Ann Vernon, Champaign, IL: Research Press (800-519-2707, www.researchpress.com)

What's a Consequence?

RATIONALE   For a variety of reasons, many adolescents are unaware of or seemingly immune to the reality of consequences. Adults in their lives may be reluctant to impose consequences because it is easier to ignore negative behaviors than to make young people accountable. In addition, adolescents believe that they are invincible and that bad things may happen to others but not to them. Because behaviors that they engage in may be risky and have the potential for severe short- and long-term consequences, helping adolescents understand more about the concept of consequences is critical.

MATERIALS   ▷ What's a Consequence? Sorting Board (p. 233)

   ▷ What's a Consequence? Cards (pp. 234–235) and 4 envelopes, with each category of card in a separate envelope labeled accordingly: *Drinking alcohol (DA), Anorexia (A), Doing drugs (DD),* and *Skipping school (SS).*

   ▷ A pen or pencil

   ▷ Several blank cards for additional consequences

PROCEDURE   1. When an adolescent presents with issues related to the choices she is making, it is likely that she will not be as concerned about her behavior as others are. Assuming that she will try to minimize the problem and the consequences, engage her in the following intervention. (If you are aware of what her issues are, substitute that topic for one of the topics identified in this intervention.)

   2. Inform the client that all adolescents make multiple choices daily; some decisions are wise and some are unwise. Invite her to give you an example of each, preferably based on her own behavior. If she is resistant, you can ask her for examples of others' wise and unwise behaviors.

   3. Discuss with her what she thinks makes the behaviors wise or unwise, emphasizing the notion of consequences—what happens as a result of an action.

---

4. Next, give her the What's a Consequence? Sorting Board and the four envelopes of cards. Invite her to select one of the envelopes and sort the consequences of the identified behavior into the designated categories, based on what she perceives to be the degree of severity. When she has finished, debrief by asking her how she decided on the severity of the consequences, whether the positives of the behaviors outweigh the negatives, and whether other consequences should be added (if so, she can write them on the blank cards and add them to a category on the sorting board).

5. Empty the sorting board and ask the client to select another envelope of cards, following the same procedure in step 4.

6. Continue in this fashion with the other two topics. Discuss in more depth what the concept of consequences means, emphasizing the lifelong impact of some choices.

7. Encourage the client to identify what might help her think about consequences of her own behavioral choices.

What's a Consequence? Sorting Board

Directions: Take each envelope, one at a time, and read the slips inside that describe various consequences of the identified behavior. Sort these, according to your perception of severity, into the following categories.

Positive Consequence	Minor Negative Consequence	More Significant Negative Consequence
Serious Negative Consequence	**Very Serious Negative Consequence**	**Life-Altering Negative Consequence**

What's a Consequence? Cards

Drinking alcohol

Wake up with a hangover (DA)	Get caught for underage drinking (DA)	Spend a lot of money (DA)
Puke all over (DA)	Get caught for possession (DA)	Act foolish (DA)
Spend time in jail (DA)	Get picked up for OMVI (operating a motor vehicle while intoxicated) (DA)	Feel less anxious because I'm drinking (DA)
Get license suspended (DA)	Have a lot of fun (DA)	Numbs me from my pain (DA)
Drive drunk and have an accident (DA)	Bond with my friends (DA)	Feel like I'm part of the crowd (DA)

Anorexia

More isolated—can't be with friends because it might involve eating (A)	Others praise me because I've lost weight (A)	Can't stop obsessing about food (A)
Obsessed with exercising (A)	Hospitalized because weight is dangerously low (A)	Can't stop obsessing about weight (A)
Feel faint or pass out (A)	Don't look fat (A)	Anxious at mealtimes (A)
Feel more in control (A)	Lose ability to concentrate because of undernourishment (A)	Electrolytes out of balance—in danger of heart attack or death (A)
Others try to make me eat more (A)	Tired all the time (A)	Lose ability to have children because my normal development is disrupted (A)

From *More What Works When with Children and Adolescents: A Handbook of Individual Counseling Techniques,* © 2009 by Ann Vernon, Champaign, IL: Research Press (800-519-2707, www.researchpress.com)

Doing drugs

Feels great to be high (DD)	Numbs me from my pain (DD)	Helps me relax (DD)
Costs a lot of money (DD)	Helps me feel mellow (DD)	Stop going to school (DD)
Steal to have money to buy drugs (DD)	Get picked up for possession or dealing (DD)	Get sent for treatment (DD)
Deal drugs (DD)	Others like me because I can help them get drugs or alcohol (DD)	Obsessed with getting drugs—can't focus on anything else (DD)
Get addicted; can't stop (DD)	Lose my job because I show up high (DD)	Others I sell to get addicted (DD)

Skipping school

Get to sleep in (SS)	Get far behind in work (SS)	Get kicked out (SS)
Get hassled by parents (SS)	Get grounded by parents (SS)	Can't get a good job (SS)
Get hassled by principal and teachers (SS)	Get bad grades (SS)	Have no money (SS)
Get to hang out with friends (SS)	Get suspended from school (SS)	Get kicked out of the house (SS)
No pressure (SS)	Get sent to alternative school (SS)	Don't have to do boring work (SS)

I Am What I Eat

RATIONALE Anorexia and bulimia are serious problems that affect a growing number of adolescents. These disorders can easily get out of hand and become major problems to contend with. This intervention was developed to help adolescents find alternative ways of dealing with their need to feel in control, because the more they try to control what they eat, the more out of control they actually become. This behavior can be addictive and difficult to stop.

MATERIALS ▷ I Am What I Eat story (p. 238)

▷ A pen or pencil

PROCEDURE
1. When an adolescent is referred or self-refers for problems relating to an eating disorder, he may be resistant about talking about the issue. Invite him to read the I Am What I Eat story.

2. After he has finished reading the story, invite him to reflect on it by addressing questions at the end (in writing, if he is reluctant to state them verbally). Discuss his responses, encouraging him to look at whether the eating disorder gives him control or whether it is an illusion of control.

3. Help him identify thoughts that prevent him from giving up the disorder, such as "I must be in control; if I eat normally I'll get fat, which proves that I am not in control," "Nothing bad will happen if I control my eating," "I'll feel better if I don't eat," and "My life will be better and I'll be happier if I don't eat." Discuss whether these beliefs apply to him, and ask whether he can identify other ones.

4. Work with him to dispute these beliefs by referring to the story, if necessary: Where is the evidence that bad things won't happen if you continue restricting and/or purging? Where is the evidence you are happier if you don't eat . . . are you happy now (most adolescents aren't, because depression is prevalent with eating disorders)? How will your life be better if you don't eat . . . is ending up in a treatment facility your idea of a better life?

5. Encourage the client to think of other ways that he can feel in control than by restricting or purging; contract with him to try one of these alternatives.

I Am What I Eat

Chris, age 16, felt like things in his life couldn't get much worse. His dad had a serious drinking problem that the entire family chose to deny, but even so, it made everyone in the house tense. Because his father couldn't be depended on to bring in much income, his mother had to work two jobs, as did his older brother. Chris would get so angry at his dad that it took all he had to not just go off on him all the time. When he wasn't able to control his anger, he'd get aggressive toward his dad, yelling at him about what a loser he was and how he was ruining their family. This just seemed to make things worse. His dad would then verbally attack everyone in the household, which made Chris feel terrible because he had been the one to first attack his father, who then counterattacked.

Matters only got worse, with his mom in denial and his brothers and sisters doing whatever they could to keep things on an even keel. Even so, his dad's drinking got even worse and Chris and his dad got into more fights, which put the family in more upheaval. His mother pleaded with him to just let it go, but Chris wasn't sure how to do that.

It all happened very gradually, but once Chris realized that his anger and aggression was only making things worse for his family, he shut down. He still felt intense anger, but he turned it inward. He became increasingly depressed and withdrawn, and he lost his appetite. He started to avoid dinner, which was always an uncomfortable time, and just stayed in his room. He began losing weight. As weeks went on, he ate less and less, becoming more obsessed with what he ate. He cut out all junk food, meat, and desserts. He allowed himself to eat very low-calorie foods only. He continued to lose weight, and he began to like the feeling of control it gave him.

It became much more difficult to be around his friends because they always wanted to go out for pizza or burgers, two things on his "do not eat" list. If he did allow himself to eat because he felt pressured, he'd purge and feel better. By doing this, he was able to eat if he was in a situation in which he had to, but he knew how to get rid of it. He also started exercising a lot, to the point that he get upset if anything interfered with his running and weight lifting.

Chris continued to reduce his eating and increase his exercise to give him a feeling of control. What he didn't realize is that his situation was getting much worse. He began falling asleep in class because he wasn't eating enough to get energy. He was more depressed. One of his teachers confronted him about what was going on; he denied that he had a problem, but the teacher contacted his mother, who took him to a doctor. The doctor was alarmed because of the excessive weight loss and told Chris he needed to start eating. Easier said than done—by this time, it simply wasn't an option for Chris. He was afraid of giving up his sense of control and he could not force himself to eat like he used to. Things continued to deteriorate until he had to be admitted for inpatient treatment because medical personnel were afraid he could die.

Questions

How effectively did Chris achieve his goal of being in control by developing an eating disorder?

What thoughts prevented him from giving up the obsession with losing weight?

What does he need to do to win his battle?

I'm Hurting

RATIONALE Adolescents who are hurting often engage in self-injury as a way of expressing or acting out their pain. Early intervention may prevent them from escalating that behavior into even more serious forms of self-abuse.

MATERIALS
▷ A sheet of paper

▷ A pen or pencil

▷ "I'm Hurting" Disputing Form (p. 242)

PROCEDURE
1. When a client presents with or is referred for problems related to self-injury, it is important to remember that, although cutting or other forms of self-injury are usually not suicide attempts, it is a signal that the client is hurting and finds relief in this self-defeating way of expressing her pain.

2. Encourage the client to show you her scars and talk about what she feels when she hurts herself—the relief, the catharsis, the shame, the confusion, the anxiety, and so forth. Ask her to imagine that her scars are talking and invite her to verbalize (or write, if that is more comfortable for her) what they would be saying if they could talk.

3. Process her responses, focusing on the themes of hopelessness, depression, anxiety, and self-depreciation. Listen for themes such as awfulizing and overgeneralizing that she will never be without hurt and pain.

4. Next, engage the client in an imagery exercise in which you ask her to close her eyes and imagine her pain being so strong that she wants relief by cutting. Ask her to stay in touch with that feeling and visualize the scars and others' reactions to them. Then ask her once again to visualize the pain and the scars, but this time, ask her to focus on staying calm, letting the scars "fade away," and feeling her pain go away.

5. Debrief the imagery exercise, focusing on how cutting brings temporary relief—but lasting relief comes from thinking differently about the things in her life.

6. Invite her to give you one example of something that is painful for her. Help her identify irrational beliefs that may be connected with anxiety or depression: "I'll never get better," "There's something wrong with me/I'm bad," "Nothing in my life is good," "No one cares about me," and so forth. Help her dispute these beliefs: "Where is the evidence you will not get better?" "You may be depressed and anxious, but how does that mean you are a bad person?" "Is it true that *nothing* in your life is good?" "Is it true that *nobody* cares about you?"

7. Give your client a "I'm Hurting" Disputing Form to use in place of cutting when she needs to get her hurt out. Encourage her to use this document as a way to achieve long-lasting results rather than temporary relief from cutting or other forms of self-injury. Help her identify more positive ways to relieve her pain and contract with her to do one thing.

"I'm Hurting" Disputing Form

Directions: Each time you feel the need to self-injure, use this form to record your thoughts and feelings. Substitute the form for the self-injury to help you feel better.

Triggering event:
Self-Defeating Thoughts:
Feelings:
Thoughts That Are More Helpful:

Triggering event:
Self-Defeating Thoughts:
Feelings:
Thoughts That Are More Helpful:

Triggering event:
Self-Defeating Thoughts:
Feelings:
Thoughts That Are More Helpful:

Pay the Price?

RATIONALE Adolescents are often unable or unwilling to identify long-term consequences of acting-out behaviors. This is especially true with substance abuse, which can have a significant impact, both short-term and long-term. This concrete intervention can be effective in helping them think more seriously about the impact of their behavior.

MATERIALS
▷ 2 sheets of poster paper

▷ Magazines, or a digital or disposable camera

▷ Scissors

▷ Glue

▷ A marker

PROCEDURE
1. When an adolescent presents in counseling with substance abuse issues but is unwilling to stop drinking or using drugs, engage him in the following intervention.

2. Suggest that it probably is too difficult or unpleasant to stop, and ask him to tell you about the positives of his addictive behavior. Don't dispute what he says, because that will lead to further resistance.

3. Rather than ask him to identify any negative outcomes of his behavior, ask him to reflect on what his life will be like in one year if he continues as he is now. Invite him to take pictures that he thinks will represent his life, giving him a few suggestions: Will he have a good job if addictive behavior interferes with holding down a job? Will he graduate from high school, or will his drinking and drugs affect his attendance and performance in significant ways? If he spends a lot of money on his substances, what will his living conditions be?

4. Ask him to paste the pictures he takes or the ones he finds in magazines on one of the sheets of poster paper.

5. Next, invite him to take pictures of what he would like his life to be in five years. He should paste those on the other sheet of poster paper.

6. Discuss the posters, comparing what he wants his life to be like with what it may be like if he continues abusing substances. If he is completely unrealistic about this, you may need to gently confront him; for example, ask him how realistic it is for him to have a nice house, a good job, and a super car if he can't graduate from high school because his addictive behavior has affected his grades and attendance. Continue in this manner until he has more clarity about the possible consequences of his choices.

7. Help the client identify irrational beliefs that contribute to substance abusers' desire to continue, such as "It's too hard to stop," "I deserve to have pleasure in my life," "Life is easier when I'm high or drunk . . . I don't have to face my problems," and so forth. Work with him to dispute his beliefs: "It may be hard, but have you ever done anything difficult before and survived?" "Are there other ways to get pleasure than developing an addiction?" "Where is the evidence life is easier? "Aren't you just creating another problem for yourself—one that, in fact, isn't easy to get rid of?" Ask him to identify his specific irrational beliefs and possible disputes to them.

8. Invite the client to review his poster and think about your discussion. Ask him to reflect on what he has learned. Ask him to identify a goal he would like to work on with regard to his substance issues.

BULLYING

Bullying, which is using physical power and psychological intimidation to dominate and hurt others physically, emotionally, or socially (Frey et al., 2005), has reached an alarming level. In fact, McAdams and Schmidt (2007) reported that nearly half of all students will experience bullying in some form. Most bullying occurs in schools (Kasen, Berenson, Cohen & Johnson, 2004); because it is such a pervasive problem, interventions directed at countering the negative effects that impact the learning environment of a school should be considered high priority.

According to Whitted and Dupper (2005), bullying is considered a prevalent form of low-level violence that takes several different forms. It can be direct, such as verbal and physical aggression, or indirect, such as threats, name calling, insults, and teasing. Indirect bullying may be harder to detect, but it is as damaging as direct bullying. Another type of bullying is relational, which is often perceived as less harmful, but, in truth, is serious. Relational bullying includes social exclusion, spreading rumors, and withholding friendship (Bauman & Del Rio, 2006). In addition, there is racial bullying, which includes racial slurs, offensive gestures, and mockery of the victim's culture, as well as sexual bullying, which involves obscene jokes, spreading rumors that are sexual in nature, grabbing private parts, or forcing someone into unwanted sexual behavior (Whitted & Dupper, 2005). Boys and girls are equally likely to be victims of bullying (Siris & Osterman, 2004), and, although both boys and girls engage in bullying, girls tend to use more indirect methods.

Bullying affects students socially, psychologically, emotionally, and academically (Carney, 2008; McAdams & Schmidt, 2007), resulting in serious problems and significant emotional distress that can have long-lasting effects, not only for the victim but also for the bully. Examples of the harmful effects of bullying include poor psychosocial adjustment, low self-esteem, academic and school attendance problems, increased risk for depression, suicide ideation or attempts, and anxiety (Bauman & Del Rio, 2006). Furthermore, bullies are more susceptible to antisocial, delinquent, and criminal behavior, are less likely to complete school, are more likely to abuse substances (Ando, Asakura, & Simons-Morton, 2005), and are more prone to criminal behavior after leaving school (McAdams & Schmidt, 2007). Even bystanders experience negative effects of bullying, performing poorly in the classroom because they are anxious about being the next victim or feeling guilty because they were too afraid to intervene.

Ando et al. (2005) noted that adolescents who bully others are aggressive, hostile, and uncooperative; dislike school; and lack a sense of justice and sympathy. Victims are insecure, lonely, unhappy, and have more physical and mental problems. They may be quiet and withdrawn, and some victims also become bullies themselves.

There is no doubt that bullying emanates from anger and hostility, fueled by irrational beliefs related to entitlement, self-righteousness, and demandingness. Bullies believe they should have their way; that intimidation and power are the best ways to get what they want; and that other people should treat them exactly as they want to be treated, and, if it doesn't happen, others deserve to be punished.

Unfortunately, bullying is often overlooked or ignored, which only perpetuates the problem. To interrupt the cycle, schoolwide interventions are essential. In addition, bullies may benefit from individual counseling that addresses the irrational beliefs associated with anger and aggression; the counseling should include concrete behavioral strategies and problem-solving skills. Counseling for victims may focus on identifying where teasing crosses the line and becomes bullying, developing assertive skills, and dealing with some of the internalizing disorders that result from externalized behavior on the part of others.

The following interventions address various aspects of bullying.

What's Bullying?

RATIONALE   When a child presents with physical/somatic symptoms, poor school performance or attendance, or anxiety, it is important to consider whether the child is being bullied. This intervention helps children learn more about what bullying is and how to handle it.

MATERIALS   ▷ 3 puppets (one, such as a moose, that is aggressive; one, such as a fox, that is passive; and one, such as a squirrel, that is a relational bully)

PROCEDURE   1. When a child presents with issues that could be related to bullying, introduce her to the three puppets, explaining that the moose is big and mean and loud. The fox is sly and cunning, watching the moose bully others and even helping him a little to get his approval. The squirrel chatters all the time, spreading rumors and telling lies about other animals in the forest. Tell the client that you will be reading a short story about each puppet and that you would like for her to act out the story with the puppets.

2. Hand her the puppets and read her the following story:

> Once upon a time there was a moose that was very fierce, strong, and loud. When he walked in the woods he bellowed at the other animals to frighten them away. He would push them around and threaten to stomp on them with his hooves. All the other animals were very frightened of him. They tried to run away whenever they saw him, but sometimes they couldn't run fast enough—and the moose would grab them and hurt them.

> One day as he was stomping through the woods he saw a baby deer. He kicked the deer and bellowed at him. The fox was sitting nearby. He didn't do anything to help the deer, but just before the moose wandered off, the fox went over and bit the deer because he wanted

the moose to think he was strong. Then he scampered away after the moose.

A few days later the fox saw the squirrel in the forest. The squirrel was busy chattering to any animal who would listen about how none of the animals should play with the chipmunk because she was just a stupid little thing who only made trouble for others. The squirrel told the animals that the chipmunk stole food and that anyone who played with her would get beat up. One by one the other animals scampered away and the chipmunk was all by herself.

3. After reading the story and having the client act it out with puppets, discuss the three different ways that the animals acted:

    Were any of the animals bullies? If so, what were the bullying behaviors?

    Which one of the animals was the meanest, in your opinion?

    How do you think the other animals (not the moose, fox, or squirrel) felt when the moose, fox, and squirrel were in the forest?

4. Next, invite the client to make up a puppet play with these puppets that includes ways to deal with the bullying.

Take Charge

RATIONALE Bullying occurs every day in many classrooms and playgrounds throughout the world, so it is critical that children know how to take charge and learn how to deal more effectively with bullying. This intervention was developed to equip children with more skills to combat the negative effects of this serious problem.

MATERIALS ▷ Take Charge Worksheet (p. 250)

▷ A sheet of paper

▷ A pen or pencil

PROCEDURE 1. When a child presents with concerns related to bullying, ask him to make a list of what he has done to try to deal with it, rating each strategy on a scale of 1 (didn't work well) to 5 (worked pretty well).

2. Next, give him the Take Charge Worksheet. Ask him to read it and underline the strategies the children in each scenario used, rating on the 1-to-5 scale how well he thinks these strategies worked.

3. After he has completed the worksheet, discuss his responses and how he rated them. Together, explore the advantages and disadvantages of the various strategies, emphasizing that sometimes the victim actually encourages the bully to continue the bullying behavior by letting the bully know how upset he is or by lashing out in anger. Help him see how these behaviors reinforce the bully by making him or her feel more powerful.

4. Brainstorm with the client other solutions he can think of that would be better ways to handle bullying. Then engage him in a role play in which you play the role of the bully, teasing him about being a wimp and a sissy. Have the child respond. Debrief this activity by asking the client how well he thought this strategy worked.

5. Continue with brief role plays where the bully pushes and threatens the victim, and mocks him or excludes him from participating in a game. Process these role plays by focusing on how the victim might have felt.

Take Charge Worksheet

Directions: Read each of the scenarios and underline what the victim of bullying did. Circle how well you think it worked on a scale of 1 (didn't work well) to 5 (worked pretty well).

Scenario 1

John is a bully. He picks on Sara, who is in his science class, by calling her names, like "fat pig" and "stupid girl." Every time he does this, Sara just turns her head and focuses on her science project.

How well do you think what Sara did worked?   1   2   3   4   5

Scenario 2

Delia bullies Damon by pushing him, kicking him, and calling him "Damon the Dork" in front of his best buddies. Damon gets so angry that he pushes Delia back and hits her.

How well do you think what Damon did worked?   1   2   3   4   5

Scenario 3

Tony bullies Tina by threatening to beat her up after school. He loves it when he sees her cowering in the hallway, crying. He hangs around a while, laughing at her and calling her "Chicken Little" and "sissy pants" until he sees a teacher at the other end of the hall. He leaves, but says he'll "get her" tomorrow. As he walks away, Tina is still crying.

How well do you think what Tina did worked?   1   2   3   4   5

Scenario 4

Julia is a bully. She picks on Serita by putting nasty notes that are full of rumors in her desk. Serita doesn't even read the notes . . . she just tears them up.

How well do you think what Serita did worked?   1   2   3   4   5

Scenario 5

Kira is having a party but isn't going to invite Kathy. She takes her invitations to school and hands them out to everyone in the class. When she comes to Kathy's desk, she holds out an invitation, then quickly takes it back, saying that she's too ugly to be invited. She laughs when Kathy runs out of the classroom in tears.

How well do you think what Kathy did worked?   1   2   3   4   5

Scenario 6

Thomas bullies Tony by telling all the other kids who are playing baseball not to let Tony play. They all ignore Tony, who keeps asking whether he can play. Thomas yells at him to go away, saying "sissies can't play." Tony runs off in tears.

How well do you think what Tony did worked?   1   2   3   4   5

From *More What Works When with Children and Adolescents: A Handbook of Individual Counseling Techniques,* © 2009 by Ann Vernon, Champaign, IL: Research Press (800-519-2707, www.researchpress.com)

Is It What You Think It Is?

RATIONALE

Bullies typically have different thoughts or perceptions than others do about events; these thoughts can trigger their bullying behavior and make it seem justified. This intervention is designed to help them identify misperceptions about events and mistaken beliefs about the rewards of bullying.

MATERIALS

▷ Is It What You Think It Is? Worksheet (p. 253)

▷ First I'll Check Out All the Facts song (pp. 254)

▷ A pen or pencil

▷ 2 chairs placed across from each other

PROCEDURE

1. When a child is referred because she has been identified as demonstrating bullying behaviors, explain to her that sometimes the reason children bully others is because in their minds, the other person did something to start it (this explanation may make the client less defensive). Ask her to sit in one of the chairs and verbally describe a situation in which this has happened to her.

2. After she has described the event and her perception of it, ask her to switch chairs and see whether she can describe the same situation from the other person's point of view. When she has finished, discuss the differences between the two "sides" of the story.

3. Next, give her the worksheet and ask her to complete it. Discuss her responses, emphasizing how it is often easy to make assumptions about things, and these assumptions can cause bad feelings. For example, if the client assumes that Tinika had her foot out on purpose, as in the fourth example on the worksheet, she might be angry and want to do something to Tinika, but, if she assumes it was just an accident, she might not be as mad or want to do something to hurt Tinika. Work with the client until she understands how a change in thinking can cause a change in feeling and behavior, so if she doesn't assume the negative, she might not be as easily provoked into bullying.

---

4. Finally, teach your client to check out her assumptions that might result in wanting to bully others by remembering the First I'll Check Out All the Facts song (sung to the tune of "Yankee Doodle").

5. Invite her to sing the song with you and ask her whether it will help her remember anything about bullying. Give her a copy to take with her.

Is It What You Think It Is? Worksheet

Directions: Read each of the following situations and write down how you would feel, what you would do, and what you think the person in each situation meant by his or her behavior.

1. **Antonio comes up behind you and taps you on the back.**

   If this happened to you, how would you feel?

   What would you do?

   What do you think Antonio means by tapping you on the back?

   Is there another way of looking at this? What else could it mean?

2. **When you ask Cassandra whether you can borrow her pencil, she doesn't answer.**

   If this happened to you, how would you feel?

   What would you do?

   What do you think Cassandra means by not answering you?

   Is there another way of looking at this? What else could it mean?

3. **On the playground when you are playing kickball, another kid runs right into you.**

   If this happened to you, how would you feel?

   What would you do?

   What do you think it means when the other player runs into you?

   Is there another way of looking at this? What else could it mean?

4. **As you are walking back to your desk, you trip over Tinika's foot because you didn't see it in the aisle.**

   If this happened to you, how would you feel?

   What would you do?

   What do you think Tinika meant by putting her foot in the aisle?

   Is there another way of looking at this? What else could it mean?

5. **When you walk up to the lunch table where Jonelle is sitting, she ignores you.**

   If this happened to you, how would you feel?

   What would you do?

   What do you think it means when Jonelle ignores you?

   If there another way of looking at this? What else could it mean?

From *More What Works When with Children and Adolescents: A Handbook of Individual Counseling Techniques,* © 2009 by Ann Vernon, Champaign, IL: Research Press (800-519-2707, www.researchpress.com)

First I'll Check Out All the Facts

(To the tune of "Yankee Doodle")

First I'll check out all the facts.
Then I'll check my assumptions.
If they're false I won't get mad,
And then I'll not be a bully.

Bullying can make me feel so strong,
But they say it can be wrong.
I don't know quite what to do,
Because sometimes I like it, too.

Maybe now I've learned something new,
And this is what I have to do.
Check out the facts before I act.
And then I'll know what I should do.

Calling All Bullies

RATIONALE
Although most bullies like the feelings of empowerment that come from hurting and intimidating others, it may be helpful for them to examine the pros and cons of bullying and consider alternative ways of behaving.

MATERIALS
▷ 2 sheets of poster or drawing paper

▷ Crayons or markers

PROCEDURE
1. When a client presents with problems concerning his bullying behavior, ask him to imagine that he is a member of the Bullying Club, and the club is trying to recruit new members.

2. Have the client make a poster that he thinks would convince his classmates to join the club: What are the advantages? Why should they be bullies?

3. After he has completed this poster, tell him that there is also an Anti-Bullying Club, which wants to steal members from the Bullying Club.

4. Have him imagine what arguments these anti-bullying club members would use to convince others to join their group instead of the Bullying Club. Ask him to make a poster for the Anti-Bullying Club.

5. Ask the client to share what he put on both posters, engaging in a discussion about the difference between the two clubs, including what he perceives to be the advantages and disadvantages of belonging to each club, as well as the consequences.

6. Next, ask the client to imagine that several members of the Bullying Club have decided that there were too many negative consequences of belonging to that club. They want to identify non-bullying things they can do when they feel like they have been provoked, or are justified in bullying others, or just like to do it to feel strong and important. Ask the client to think what he could do to "unlearn" some of his bullying behaviors and what other

approaches he might try. Write these ideas on the back of the Anti-Bullying Club poster. Let him keep it as a reminder of how to overcome bullying if he chooses to "belong" to the Anti-Bullying Club.

Bullying Can Be . . .

RATIONALE When an adolescent presents with problems related to anxiety, physical/somatic symptoms, poor school performance, or school avoidance, it is important to find out whether she is being bullied. This intervention helps adolescents learn more about what bullying is and how to deal with it.

MATERIALS
- ▷ A roll of masking tape
- ▷ A pair of scissors
- ▷ A pen or pencil
- ▷ 15 to 20 blank index cards

PROCEDURE

1. If a client is referred for symptoms that may be a result of bullying or is upset about being mistreated by peers, explore her concerns in more depth.

2. Next, cut off a long strip of masking tape and tape it to the floor to represent a continuum. Designate one end *Very Serious* and the other end *Not as Serious.* Then ask the client to think about what bullying behaviors she has experienced or witnessed and write each of them on separate index cards. Continue in this manner, asking her for other examples of bullying behaviors.

3. When she has identified as many behaviors as she can think of, it may be necessary to brainstorm other forms of bullying, such as being threatened, intimidated, teased, or rejected; receiving nasty notes; being kicked, hit, or shoved; or being beaten or slapped.

4. After these behaviors have been identified, ask the client to read them and place each on the continuum from *Very Serious* to *Not as Serious,* discussing her criteria for placement. As she is sorting, encourage her to share any experiences she has had with any of these behaviors.

5. After she has finished with the continuum, discuss the fact that there are three types of bullying: physical, verbal, and relational,

---

which includes spreading nasty rumors about the victim, excluding the victim, threatening not to be friends unless the victim does something that the bully wants, and telling lies about the victim. Discuss these forms of bullying and ask her which type she has experienced most often and how it affected her.

6. Next, have her take each of the index cards and identify one thing she can do to deal with this type of bullying. Brainstorm other ideas with her as appropriate.

E Is for Empowerment

RATIONALE   This is an intervention for young adolescents that helps them identify ways to empower themselves against bullies.

MATERIALS   ▷ E Is for Empowerment Strategies (p. 261)

▷ A pen or pencil

PROCEDURE   1. When an adolescent presents with issues related to victimization, ask him to share examples of when others have bullied him, as well as how he felt and what he did.

2. Help him understand that even though bullying isn't right and shouldn't happen, it does. Therefore, it is important to empower him with skills to deal with it.

3. Read the following scenario to him:

> It was just turning dark when Andrew and Alex left the library and were walking home. They hadn't gotten far when Andrew noticed two older boys coming up close behind them. He recognized one of them as being in his sister's class, so he didn't think much about it. Pretty soon one of the older boys started walking faster and kept stepping on Alex's heels. Alex turned around and asked him to please stop, but the older boy laughed and just kept on doing it. Then the other boy did the same thing to Andrew. Andrew and Alex started to walk faster, but the older boys did, too. Andrew and Alex were worried because they were still quite a way from home, and they were in an area that was pretty deserted. When they passed an empty field, one of the older boys kicked Alex in the shin, knocking him over and grabbing Alex's backpack and emptying it on the ground.
>
> By this time Alex and Andrew were really scared, and they kept saying, "Stop this . . . just let us go home." The older boys just stood by and laughed as Alex picked

up the books and papers and quickly stuffed them in his backpack. Andrew and Alex started to run as the boys shouted, "You'd better run faster because we're going to catch you and beat you up." As Andrew glanced back, he saw that the boys were getting closer and closer. Just then they reached the end of the road and turned into their street. They saw Andrew's father standing in the driveway, and they yelled for help. As he started walking toward them, the older boys ran off.

4. Discuss the scenario, asking him in particular to identify how Andrew and Alex dealt with the bullying, whether he thinks they handled it effectively, and whether the boys did anything that might have reinforced the bullying and given the bullies a sense of power and control.

5. Finally, introduce the E Is for Empowerment Strategies and ask the client to complete it. Discuss his examples and brainstorm other options.

E Is for Empowerment Strategies

Directions: Read each of the following strategies that can be used to deal with bullying. Then identify an example of each strategy, based on a personal experience of when you have tried it or an example that you think could work.

1. Do something that the bully doesn't expect, such as something to distract him or her or behaving differently than you usually do. For example, you could . . .

2. Be verbally assertive but not aggressive. In other words, convey your rights by saying things like "Stop treating me like this" as opposed to "You'd better stop treating me like this or I'll . . . " For example, you could say . . .

3. Physically stand up for yourself by showing that you feel confident. For example, you could . . .

4. Don't let the bully know that he or she is getting to you. Don't react in a way that makes the bully feel more powerful. For example, instead of cowering or crying, you could . . .

From *More What Works When with Children and Adolescents: A Handbook of Individual Counseling Techniques,* © 2009 by Ann Vernon, Champaign, IL: Research Press (800-519-2707, www.researchpress.com)

How Will You Handle It?

RATIONALE   One of the factors that perpetuates the cycle of bullying is a passive victim. This can be especially true with relational bullying. This intervention helps the victim learn more about the assertive option as a possible solution.

MATERIALS   ▷ How Will You Handle It? Worksheet (p. 264–265)

▷ A pen or pencil

PROCEDURE   1. When an adolescent presents as a victim of relational bullying, engage her in this intervention that can empower her and reduce victimization. First, make sure she is clear about what relational bullying is: when the bully spreads false rumors about a victim, tells lies, manipulates others so that they exclude the victim from their friendship group, or says or does things that embarrass the victim. Invite her to share her own experiences and how she felt.

2. Next, explain that, although bullying isn't good and others shouldn't do it, it is an unfortunate reality. However, there are things she can do to lessen the hurtful impact. Read the following example to her:

> Sasha was sitting in the lunchroom with her friends. DeAndra came over to the table and started talking in a loud voice about how Sasha had flunked the history test, which only proved how stupid she was. Sasha hadn't failed the test, but she was so embarrassed and upset by what DeAndra was saying that she just got up and left the table in tears.

3. Explore what it means to be assertive: Standing up for your own rights without being aggressive. Typically you state what the other person's behavior is and make a request for it to stop. For example, "Please stop saying that about me because it isn't true." Explain that you do not say it in an aggressive manner, such as "You'd better stop saying these things about me" because that only encourages the bully to be more aggressive. Also explain that being assertive does not mean that you are not just passively

accepting the bullying, which would be to say nothing, show how upset you are, and escape, as the girl in the scenario did. Ask the client whether she is able to be assertive when things like this happen to her, and, if not, why. Deal with her mistaken belief that if she is assertive it will only make things worse: Does she have evidence of this? Point out that bullies often stop when the victim stands up to them.

4. Give the client the How Will You Handle It? Worksheet and ask her to complete it.

5. When she has finished, discuss how being assertive may be an effective skill in dealing with relational bullying.

How Will You Handle It? Worksheet

1. As you reach your locker, another girl comes up and uses her body to block you from getting into it.

    If you were assertive, what would you do or say? _____

    _____

    If you were aggressive, what would you do or say? _____

    _____

    If you were passive, what would you do or say? _____

    _____

2. You intercept a note that was passed down the aisle and read by several classmates. The note is about you and contains many false statements.

    If you were assertive, what would you do or say? _____

    _____

    If you were aggressive, what would you do or say? _____

    _____

    If you were passive, what would you do or say? _____

    _____

3. You and a friend are sitting outside the school building waiting for the lunch period to end. Another girl comes up to the two of you and starts telling your friend how she shouldn't hang around with you because your parents are drug addicts and your brother is in jail.

    If you were assertive, what would you do or say? _____

    _____

    If you were aggressive, what would you do or say? _____

    _____

    If you were passive, what would you do or say? _____

    _____

From *More What Works When with Children and Adolescents: A Handbook of Individual Counseling Techniques,* © 2009 by Ann Vernon, Champaign, IL: Research Press (800-519-2707, www.researchpress.com)

4. **You and a group of friends are standing in the hallway talking about what you are going to do on Saturday. Two other girls come up and listen in, then as soon as you are in class before the teacher arrives, they yell out to the entire class what you and your group had been planning to do.**

   If you were assertive, what would you do or say? _____

   _____

   If you were aggressive, what would you do or say? _____

   _____

   If you were passive, what would you do or say? _____

   _____

5. **You like a certain boy, and he has finally started to pay attention to you. The two of you are talking outside the school building when a bully comes by and starts pointing at the two of you and yells across the yard to others, "Look, these two losers finally got together. They are both so ugly and stupid that they deserve each other."**

   If you were assertive, what would you do or say? _____

   _____

   If you were aggressive, what would you do or say? _____

   _____

   If you were passive, what would you do or say? _____

   _____

Emotionally Tough

RATIONALE
Because bullies often get reinforced when victims show their vulnerability by crying, cowering, and the like, helping victims develop "emotional toughness" may help stop the bullying cycle. This intervention is intended to address bullying that is primarily verbal.

MATERIALS
▷ A sheet of paper

▷ A pen or pencil

▷ A large sponge

▷ A bucket of water

PROCEDURE
1. When a client is put down, taunted, and teased, or the target of vicious rumors and lies that may lead to exclusion from peer groups, it is important to empower the client so that he can be more resilient against these kinds of attacks.

2. First, ask him to make a list of all the negative things others have said about him and to rate these on a scale of 1 (not very hurtful) to 5 (very hurtful). When he has finished, discuss the list and the ratings, encouraging him to elaborate on how these events have affected him and how he has attempted to deal with the situation.

3. Next, give him the dry sponge and ask him how it feels when he holds it—light, airy, stiff. Then ask him to dip it in the water and describe how it feels—heavier and soft. Explain that people are sometimes like sponges in that when others say things about them, they just "soak it up," as the sponge soaks up water. Then ask him to wring out the wet sponge and describe how it feels— lighter. Explain that this is what he needs to do when others say mean things to him or about him: He needs to "wring out his sponge" by asking himself whether what others say about him is true. For example, if they call him a wimp, is he a wimp? Even if he is, does that make him a bad person? If he is a wimp, is that the only thing he is? Doesn't he have good qualities as well?

4. Invite the client to pick out several words or phrases from the list he made that are most upsetting. Teach him the disputing process, whereby he challenges the validity of the label or accusation by asking himself the following:

> Where's the evidence that what they say about me true? If it's not true, why do I need to get upset?
>
> If it is true, does that mean I am a total loser?
>
> That's their opinion, but aren't there others who think differently about me?
>
> What they are doing is bad, and kids aren't supposed to bully others, but does it help to get upset and show them that they are getting to me?
>
> How logical is it to try to change their minds? Let them think what they want to think.

5. After reviewing the most hurtful words and phrases and applying the disputing process, share the following with the client: "Sticks and stones can break your bones, but words will never hurt you unless you *let* them." Ask the client to talk about how he could apply this piece of wisdom to his own life.

6. Invite the client to rehearse what he will need to do in real-life situations by engaging in a role play. You play the role of the bully, bombarding him with the examples of verbal abuse that he identified on his list. Instruct the client to respond *after* he has gone through the disputing process in his own mind so that he can more effectively deal with the harassment.

7. Have him write three suggestions on the back of his list that he can use the next time he is the victim of verbal bullying.

CHAPTER 5

Interventions for Typical Developmental Problems

In some ways, growing up today is vastly different than it was even 30 or 40 years ago. Although it used to be that people took drugs if they had a physical illness, today many young people use drugs or engage in self-mutilation to numb their emotional pain. Depression among children and adolescents used to be rare. Now it is almost an epidemic. Years ago, suicide was something that rarely occurred among young people. Now it is the second leading cause of death among adolescents (Vernon, 2009b). Levine (2006) expressed concern that there is a mental health epidemic among privileged youth who "defy the stereotypes commonly associated with the term 'at risk'" (p. 17). These teens and pre-teens, from affluent, well-educated families, experience among the highest rates of depression, anxiety disorders, substance abuse, and general unhappiness of any other group in the country, despite their economic and social privilege.

Yet in many respects, children and adolescents today experience many of the same problems growing up as they would have years ago. To varying degrees, young people always have dealt, and probably always will deal, with issues about self-acceptance and belonging, anxiety about their future after high school, and self-consciousness during puberty. Fighting with friends, mourning the breakup of a romantic relationship, and struggling to compete academically or athletically are also problems that cross generational boundaries.

What we must remember, however, is that, even though typical developmental problems haven't changed much over the decades, change has occurred in the cultural and social factors that affect the lives of young people. Children in today's society grow up faster. As Mary Pipher, author of *Reviving Ophelia,* noted over a decade ago, "The protected place in space and time that we once called childhood has grown shorter" (1994, p. 28). If that was the reality then, it is even more complex now. Today, children and adolescents have more to contend with, in addition to typical, normal developmental problems. As noted in chapter 1, distorted thinking and developmental limitations affect children's and adolescents' ability to interpret and respond appropriately to both situational and typical developmental events. Consequently, far too many young people react in unhealthy ways.

If our charge as practitioners is to help children and adolescents "grow up without giving up," it is important that we help them understand what is normal and teach them effective ways to deal with typical developmental problems so that life doesn't seem so overwhelming. The purpose of this chapter is to provide REBT interventions for typical developmental problems concerning self-acceptance, relationships, and transitions. Interventions both for children and for adolescents will be provided.

SELF-ACCEPTANCE

As children and adolescents grow up, many struggle with self-acceptance issues: Am I good enough? Smart enough? Gifted enough? Attractive enough? and so forth. Developmentally, their view of self impacts them in many arenas—academically and socially, as well as in sports, music, drama, and the like. Furthermore, lack of self-acceptance underscores more serious disorders such as substance abuse, anorexia and bulimia, and self-injury. It contributes to depression and anxiety and impacts relationships. Helping young people develop greater self-acceptance facilitates their overall development in various ways.

REBT theory posits that all human beings are fallible and will make mistakes, and it also emphasizes that self-worth is not contingent on one's performance. It promotes the concept of unconditional self-acceptance, which does not involve global self-rating or evaluation (Dryden, DiGiuseppe, & Neenan, 2003) but does allow for rating different aspects of self. Therefore, although it is possible to evaluate and focus on negative aspects and do something to improve them, global rating of self as good or bad is anti-REBT, as is the notion of considering oneself a total failure on the basis of a few negative characteristics. The concept of unconditional self-acceptance (USA) implies that all individuals are multifaceted and have strengths as well as weaknesses, that human beings are complex and are constantly in the process of change, and that it is impossible to render a single legitimate global rating of any person. The concept of USA is in sharp contrast to the notion of self-esteem, which does imply a single rating. For this reason, REBT practitioners use the term self-acceptance rather than self-esteem (Dryden, 2003).

When clients do not understand or practice the concept of self-acceptance, they engage in self-downing: "I'm no good because I didn't pass that test" or "Because I didn't get asked to the party, it must mean no one likes me and I'm a loser." It is particularly easy for children and many adolescents to experience self-downing because, as concrete thinkers, they see things in either/or terms. This view makes it more difficult for them to separate their self-worth from their performance or to understand the difference between global self-rating and the rating of individual aspects of self. Because their self-downing can easily result in depression, anxiety, and guilt, and self-injury, it is critical to start addressing this problem at an early age.

Concepts related to self-acceptance include the following:

Who you are isn't what you do (your behavior does not define who you are as a person).

There is no such thing as an "all good" or an "all bad" person; everyone has strengths and weaknesses.

You are worthwhile just because you exist.

Making mistakes is natural, and each of us can learn from them.

The following interventions can be adapted as needed, depending on the specific age or developmental level of the child or adolescent.

Can I or Can't I?

RATIONALE   Children typically put themselves down if they can't do something. This intervention helps them understand that everyone has things they can do, things they can't do, and things that they can do somewhat or could do better with more practice. Helping them understand and accept their strengths as well as their weaknesses is an important aspect of self-acceptance.

MATERIALS   ▷ 3 hula hoops (or 3 long pieces of rope tied in 3 circles)

▷ A set of Can I or Can't I? Cards (p. 275); adapt the cards depending on age of the client, making sure that there are things in the list that can be done and others that are more challenging and probably can't be done

▷ Sherry Had Some Tasks to Do song (p. 276)

▷ 3 labels written on a sheet of construction paper: *Can Do, Can't Do,* and *Sort of Can Do*

▷ 3 tennis balls

▷ An orange or apple

PROCEDURE   1. When a client presents with self-downing issues, discussing how dumb she feels or how she can't do anything right, engage her in some experiments that prove what she can do, can't do, and can do somewhat.

2. First, place the hula hoops on the floor, side by side, approximately 4 feet away from her. Place one of the following labels inside each hoop: *Can Do, Can't Do, Sort of Can Do.* Invite her to play a game, in which she draws a card, tries to do what it specifies, then hops to the hula hoop representing whether she could do it, couldn't do it, or could do it somewhat, placing that card in the designated hoop. Continue in this manner until all cards have been drawn.

3. After she has completed the tasks, help her analyze her performance: Were there things she could do? Couldn't do? Sort of could do? How realistic would it be to expect that she could do

everything? Discuss what that says about her as a person: Is she bad because she wasn't able to do everything?

4. Process the activity by discussing the fact that all people have strengths and weaknesses. Ask her to think about people in her family or in her neighborhood or school: Does she think that there are things they can do, things they can't do, and things they sort of can do? Invite her to share examples, asking her whether she thinks they are bad people if they can't do everything.

5. Teach her the Sherry Had Some Tasks to Do song (sung to the tune of "Mary Had a Little Lamb") as a way to remember that everyone has strengths and weaknesses.

Can I or Can't I? Cards

Count backward from 100 to 1.

Name the capitals of two states in the U.S.

Sing a short song.

State your address and phone number.

Put a book on top of a bookshelf without a ladder or a chair.

Spell the name of the city or town in which you live.

Hop on one foot for 30 seconds.

Recite the alphabet backward.

Tie your shoe using only one hand.

Juggle three tennis balls without letting them fall.

Without using your hands, pick up the orange or apple.

Name two animals that milk comes from.

From *More What Works When with Children and Adolescents: A Handbook of Individual Counseling Techniques,* © 2009 by Ann Vernon, Champaign, IL: Research Press (800-519-2707, www.researchpress.com)

Sherry Had Some Tasks to Do
(To the tune of "Mary Had a Little Lamb")

Sherry had some tasks to do, tasks to do, tasks to do.
Sherry had some tasks to do that were too hard for her.
So, she thought I am so dumb, am so dumb, am so dumb.
So, she thought I am so bad, how will I ever be smart?
But Sherry knew she had to try, had to try, had to try.
Sherry knew she had to try, and maybe could succeed.
So Sherry tried her very best, very best, very best.
Sherry tried her very best, and did okay with some of it.
Sherry's teacher said that's good, said that's good, said that's good.
Sherry's teacher said good try, that's what it takes to learn.
He also said she could do things, could do things, could do things.
And when she couldn't do some things, that doesn't make her bad.

No, I'm Not; Yes, I Am

RATIONALE
This intervention facilitates children's awareness of their different abilities and the concept of self-acceptance versus self-rating.

MATERIALS
▷ 20 to 30 pieces of wrapped candies, varying in color, size, shape, and taste

▷ 3 jars: one filled with the candies, one labeled *Yes, I Am,* and one labeled *No, I'm Not*

PROCEDURE
1. To increase a client's understanding that people have varying degrees of ability that don't make them "good" or "bad," engage him in the following intervention.

2. First, show him a jar of mixed candies, asking the client whether they are all alike. Assuming that he says no, engage him in a short discussion of how they are different: in size, color, shape, and so forth. Make the comparison to people, asking him whether people he knows come in different sizes, colors, and shapes, and with things they can and can't do.

3. Next, ask him to listen carefully. Inform him that you will be reading him some characteristics that may or may not describe him. When he hears something that is true of him, he takes a piece of wrapped candy from the first jar and places it in the *Yes, I Am* jar. If it is not like him, he places a piece of candy in the *No, I'm Not* jar.

Characteristics

Taller than most kids in my class

Smart in math

A good reader

A fast runner

Friendly to everyone

A good swimmer

A good student

Someone who obeys the rules at home

Someone who obeys the rules at school

Kind to others

A good eater

A good singer

Smaller than most kids in my class

A good speller

A good friend to others

Helpful to others

Popular with my classmates

Good at sports

4. After this part of the intervention is completed, ask the client to count the number of candies in each jar, then put them back in: Were there more things like him (strengths) or unlike him (weaknesses)? Initiate a discussion about this, drawing the analogy that this is how people are: They have strengths, or some things they do well, and they have other things, weaknesses, that they don't do as well. Invite him to share other personal examples of what he does well or not as well.

5. Next, ask him to examine the candies in the *No, I'm Not* jar. Is there something wrong with them? Do they look funny or smell funny? Ask him how this applies to him. Is there something wrong with him because he had some candies in the *No, I'm Not* jar? Ask him whether he thinks he should throw out this jar of candy, as if it were "no good." Draw the analogy to people. Should you get rid of them because there are things they can't do as well as others?

6. Invite him to take several pieces of candy from each jar to help him remember that he has strengths as well as weaknesses.

The Whole Picture

RATIONALE Because of their dichotomous thinking, children often have difficulty understanding that they are complex beings, made up of different characteristics. This intervention addresses that concept.

MATERIALS ▷ A child's puzzle

▷ An 8½ × 11-inch sheet of construction paper, cut into 10 shapes that fit together like a puzzle and put into a manila envelope

▷ A pen or marker

▷ A roll of transparent tape

PROCEDURE 1. When a client presents with self-acceptance issues, engage her in this intervention that helps her look at the "whole picture" as opposed to focusing on one or more weaknesses or negative aspects.

2. First, ask the client to put the puzzle together. As she works, discuss what the object of putting a puzzle together is, and what happens if there are missing pieces. Emphasize the idea of needing all pieces to see the whole picture.

3. Next, give her the manila envelope and invite her to take out the pieces, explaining that this is a personal puzzle. Ask her to think about the different parts ("pieces") of herself and write one of these on each of the puzzle pieces. For example, she might think about her role in the family, her interests and hobbies, what she looks like, what she does well and doesn't do well, and so forth.

4. When she has finished writing something on each shape, ask her to put them together to form a puzzle, taping the pieces together when they all fit. Then invite her to look at the "whole picture": Who is she? What are her interests, hobbies, and strengths? and so forth. Invite her to discuss this with you. Ask her what would happen if she just had one or two pieces of her puzzle: Would that give a very accurate picture of who she is?

---

5. After encouraging discussion about how people aren't just "one thing" or another, give her the personal puzzle to help remind her that she is more than one aspect.

Who, Me? Yes, You

RATIONALE This intervention helps adolescents identify personal characteristics and avoid global self-rating, critical concepts for adolescents who so readily rate themselves negatively.

MATERIALS ▷ Who Me? Yes, You Checklist (p. 282)

▷ A pen or pencil

PROCEDURE 1. When a client presents with self-downing issues, suggest that she complete the Who, Me? Yes, You Checklist.

2. Invite her to discuss her results with you. How many characteristics were like her and how many were unlike her? What does this say about her overall worth as a person: Is she "better" if she had more check marks? If this is a difficult concept for her, ask her to think about one of her friends: If this friend hadn't checked off many of the characteristics, would she think less of her? Encourage her to think about the fact that she is a complex and worthwhile person with many different characteristics that define her.

3. Next, ask the client to read the list of characteristics out loud, in the following format: I am only a good person if I am _____ (have her substitute each of the characteristics on the checklist). When she has finished, ask her to reflect on the exercise. Is it true that she is only a good person if she is smart, a leader, outgoing, and so forth?

4. Work with her to identify some rational thoughts she can use to remind herself that she is a worthwhile person with many different characteristics and that who she is (a leader, etc.) does not define her entire self.

Who, Me? Yes, You Checklist

Directions: Place a check mark beside each item that describes you.

- ❏ A risk taker
- ❏ Studious
- ❏ Smart
- ❏ A good athlete
- ❏ Musically talented
- ❏ A leader
- ❏ Popular
- ❏ Good looking
- ❏ Someone with a good personality
- ❏ Someone with a good sense of humor
- ❏ Fun to be with
- ❏ Responsible
- ❏ Dependable
- ❏ Loyal
- ❏ Respectful
- ❏ Trustworthy
- ❏ Honest
- ❏ A good communicator
- ❏ Outgoing
- ❏ Decisive (makes decisions easily)

Too Perfect?

RATIONALE   Although there are positive outcomes of perfectionism, there are also negative aspects, particularly the physical and emotional consequences. This intervention helps adolescents look more realistically at what they should be expecting of themselves.

MATERIALS   ▷ Too Perfect? Worksheet (p. 284)

▷ Too Perfect? Barriers Worksheet (p. 285)

▷ A pen or pencil

PROCEDURE   1. When a client presents with issues related to perfectionism, ask him to fill out the first column on the Too Perfect? Worksheet, which asks him to list of all the reasons he thinks he must be perfect. Review his reasons with him, discussing where these "shoulds" come from: Are they self-imposed, other-imposed, or are there other sources for the pressure he feels to be perfect?

2. Next, ask him to complete the second column, identifying advantages of his perfectionism. When he has finished his list, discuss it with him, encouraging him to talk more about the perceived advantages.

3. Then, ask him to complete the third column, listing the disadvantages of being too perfect: How does it affect him physically, emotionally, socially, or behaviorally? Review his list and encourage discussion about how his need to be perfect affects him.

4. Finally, invite the client to reflect on how perfect he thinks he needs to be: Are there aspects he would like to change? Explore the barriers that may prevent him from doing this by completing the Too Perfect? Barriers Worksheet. Help him look realistically at his situation. For example, will he really be better than others if he is perfect? Can he withstand the pressure to be perfect? Is he only worthwhile if he is perfect? Work with him to challenge his distorted thinking as it relates to needing to be so perfect.

Too Perfect? Worksheet

Directions: Complete the worksheet by addressing the topics in each column.

Why must I be perfect?	Advantages	Disadvantages
1. _____	_____	_____
_____	_____	_____
2. _____	_____	_____
_____	_____	_____
3. _____	_____	_____
_____	_____	_____
4. _____	_____	_____
_____	_____	_____
5. _____	_____	_____
_____	_____	_____
6. _____	_____	_____
_____	_____	_____
7. _____	_____	_____
_____	_____	_____
8. _____	_____	_____
_____	_____	_____

From *More What Works When with Children and Adolescents: A Handbook of Individual Counseling Techniques,* © 2009 by Ann Vernon, Champaign, IL: Research Press (800-519-2707, www.researchpress.com)

Too Perfect? Barriers Worksheet

Directions: Read the following information and check those that apply to you.

❏ I must be perfect because if I'm not, I'm not as worthwhile.

❏ If I'm not perfect, bad things will happen.

❏ I must be perfect because others expect it of me, and I can't let them down.

❏ I will have better opportunities if everything I do is perfect.

❏ I must be perfect so that I am better than others.

❏ I must be perfect because my life will be better.

❏ Being perfect eases my anxiety.

❏ If I do everything perfectly, I won't have to worry about not getting ahead in life.

❏ Add your own:

_____

❏ Add your own:

_____

Accept Yourself

RATIONALE   Many adolescents are very self-critical and do not accept themselves for who they are. This intervention helps them understand the concept of unconditional self-acceptance (USA).

MATERIALS
▷ 12 index cards

▷ A pen or pencil

▷ 12 blown-up balloons, tied with string (make sure the strings are at least 10 inches long)

▷ A straight pin

PROCEDURE

1. When a client lacks self-acceptance and rates herself as "all good" or "all bad," depending on her successes or failures, discuss the concept of unconditional self-acceptance, which means accepting yourself as a worthwhile person regardless of successes or failures and not rating yourself as either "all good" or "all bad."

2. Next, ask the client to reflect on her week, recalling significant successes or failures in sports, music, drama, academics, relationships, and so forth. Have her write these on individual index cards.

3. Next, give her a blown-up balloon for each index card she completed, tying the strings together to form one bunch. Then ask her to read her index cards. For each one that she considered to be a failure, she should take a straight pin and pop a balloon. Continue in this manner until all cards have been read.

4. Discuss the activity. What it was like for her to think of successes and failures? How many balloons does she have left in the bunch, and how does that affect the overall worth and quality of the bunch of balloons? Ask her to draw an analogy to herself: How is that bunch of balloons like or unlike her self-worth? Is she less than worthwhile if she has some failures? Challenge her to think about accepting herself as a worthwhile person who has both strengths and weaknesses, successes and failures—to accept herself unconditionally, which is the concept of USA.

RELATIONSHIPS

A significant number of the problems that children and adolescents present in counseling involve relationships—with peers, siblings, parents, teachers, romantic partners, or authority figures. Waters (1982) noted that children irrationally believe that it's awful if others don't like them, and adolescents believe that it would be awful to be a social loser and that they must conform to their peers. According to Ellis (1996), two core irrational beliefs relate to relationships: "I absolutely must, at practically all times, be successful at important performances and relationships—or else I, as a person, am inadequate and worthless!" and "Other people absolutely must practically always treat me considerately, kindly, fairly, or lovingly—or else they are no damned good and deserve no joy in their existence" (p. 13).

It is also important to look at relationships from a developmental perspective. According to an expert on child stress (Youngs, 1995), issues involving relationships begin as early as the first and second grades, at which time children identify worries related to peer ridicule, teacher disapproval, or separating from parents. By the third grade, a key stressor is the disappointment in not being chosen for a team, and this problem continues to be a major source of stress through the eighth grade. Fear of losing a friend, being ridiculed or unpopular, or being disliked by a teacher are also significant issues in elementary school. In middle school and high school, adolescents worry about being unpopular or rejected. Romantic involvement, family relationships, and conflict with adults over role definition are pertinent issues for this age group as well.

It is important not to underestimate the anxiety, depression, frustration, anger, and self-downing that occur in response to relationship difficulties. For this reason, it is imperative to identify effective interventions to address typical relationship problems.

Finding Friends

RATIONALE   Children of all ages may lack the skills to make friends or stop themselves from trying to create friendships because of irrational thinking. This intervention addresses these factors.

MATERIALS   ▷ Several sheets of drawing paper

▷ A pencil or pen

▷ Crayons or markers

▷ A set of Finding Friends Cards (p. 290), hidden around the room

PROCEDURE   1. When a child is self- or other-referred because she lacks friends, ask her to draw a picture or series of pictures that depict what that is like for her. Also ask her to draw thought bubbles out of the heads of the characters, writing down her thoughts or verbalizations in interactions in the pictures.

2. After discussing the pictures so that you have a better understanding of the problem and how she feels and reacts, invite her to play a game.

3. Tell her that there are 15 note cards about friendship hidden throughout the room. Ask her to try to find them. Once she has done that, ask her to sit down to read them (or read them to her). If she thinks that what is described on the card is a good way of finding a friend, she should put that card in front of her. If she thinks it is a bad way of finding a friend, she should put the card behind her. Encourage her to verbalize why she rates them as positive or negative.

4. Next, select the cards that specifically rate to self-downing, demanding, or assuming:

    Assumes if she asks to play, others will say no, so she doesn't ask.

    Thinks that she will never be good enough to be a friend.

Is afraid to invite someone over because she thinks they won't come.

Thinks that no one will like her if she tries to be their friend.

Doesn't try to make friends because she thinks they should do it first.

5. Help her learn to challenge these beliefs by asking her to prove to you that she is or would be a bad friend: Has anyone ever told her that? Does she have to be perfect for others to like her? Has she ever invited anyone over and they have come? If so, is there a chance that this could happen again? If she wants to have friends, how is it helping her to think that others should ask first?

6. Engage her in a role play where she plays the role of someone she wants to be friends with and you are the client. Encourage her to act as she thinks they would when you ask her if she wants to play. If the client, acting as the friend, says no, then you (playing the role of the client) can verbalize rational self-statements such as "Just because she said no doesn't mean there's something wrong with me" or "Maybe she had other reasons for saying no, and it doesn't necessarily mean she doesn't like me."

7. Discuss the role plays, then encourage the client to set a goal about what she can do to find friends.

Finding Friends Cards

Sits at home and wishes she had a friend	Asks a group of kids if she can play with them
Says hello to someone she doesn't know	Assumes if she asks to play, others will say no, so she doesn't ask
Says bad things about others	Thinks that she will never be good enough to be a friend
Thinks that no one will like her if she tries to be their friend	Is afraid to invite someone over because she thinks they won't come
Is bossy	Joins Girl Scouts in hopes that she will find some friends
Cooperates with others on group projects	Doesn't try to make friends because she thinks they should do it first
Makes fun of others	Is a tattletale
Sits by herself at lunch rather than joining others	Offers to help a classmate study for a test

From *More What Works When with Children and Adolescents: A Handbook of Individual Counseling Techniques,* © 2009 by Ann Vernon, Champaign, IL: Research Press (800-519-2707, www.researchpress.com)

Risky Relationships

RATIONALE   As children progress through middle childhood, negative peer pressure can become more problematic. This intervention helps them evaluate the risks that can be involved in relationships.

MATERIALS   ▷ Risky Relationships Scenarios (p. 292–293)

▷ A pen or pencil

PROCEDURE   1. When a client is engaging in risky relationships that have the potential to influence him in negative ways, ask him to read the Risky Relationships scenarios and identify the risks in each one.

2. When he has completed this task, invite him to discuss the scenarios with you, focusing on the risks and consequences.

3. Encourage him to speculate on why he might be tempted to associate with kids who do things or try to involve him in things that can be dangerous or risky: wanting their approval, wanting to belong, or perhaps enjoying the challenge of trying to get by with something.

4. Teach him two different ways to respond when relationships involve some risky behavior: being assertive (standing up for what you believe is the right thing to do) or being nonassertive (going along with them because you don't want to risk their disapproval). Role-play each method to illustrate the difference by asking him to be the peer who wants him to engage in something risky, and you model both the assertive and nonassertive responses.

5. Debrief the role play with him, identifying the pros and cons of being assertive and nonassertive. Invite him to think about other ways to handle relationships that might involve some negative risks for him.

Risky Relationships Scenarios

Directions: Read each of the following scenarios and think about the risks. Write these in the space provided.

1. Your friend Tom invites you home with him after school. As you pass a convenience store, he asks you whether you are hungry. You say that you are, and he asks whether you have any money, which you don't. He says he doesn't have any either, but it's okay—he can just steal a couple of candy bars. He asks you to stand close to him so that you block him from the cashier.

   If you do this, what are the risks? _____

   _____

   If you don't do this, what might happen? _____

   _____

2. When one of your classmates gets on the school bus, she sits by you and tells you that she didn't have time to study for her math test but that she has to get a good grade or she will not be able to go to the class skating party over the weekend. She asks whether you would place your paper on the desk where she can see it and copy it.

   If you do this, what are the risks? _____

   _____

   If you don't do this, what might happen? _____

   _____

3. On your way home from school, some older kids that you think are really cool start walking with you. They ask whether you want to go to the park with them. You are supposed to go right home after school, but you agree to go because you want to hang out with them. When you get to the park, they start picking on some little kids who are playing on the jungle gym. They keep saying, "Come on, let's make them sorry they came. We can just take this over and push them off."

   If you do this, what are the risks? _____

   _____

   If you don't do this, what might happen? _____

   _____

From *More What Works When with Children and Adolescents: A Handbook of Individual Counseling Techniques,* © 2009 by Ann Vernon, Champaign, IL: Research Press (800-519-2707, www.researchpress.com)

4. A boy in your class invites you to come over after school. You don't have many friends, and he is pretty cool, so you tell him you will check with your parents and see whether you can come over tomorrow. When you get to his house the next day, his parents aren't home. The two of you hang out for awhile, then he says that he is going to sneak one of his dad's cigarettes and asks you whether you want one, too.

If you do this, what are the risks? _____

_____

If you don't do this, what might happen? _____

_____

5. Your teacher asks you to be the class monitor while several students are making up a test that you have already taken. Just after she leaves, two friends come up and ask you to tell them the answers to a few tough questions that they can't figure out.

If you do this, what are the risks? _____

_____

If you don't do this, what might happen? _____

_____

Family Feud

RATIONALE   Children often personalize family feuding, thinking it is their fault and that they are bad because of it. This intervention addresses these irrational beliefs and helps them identify coping strategies.

MATERIALS
- ▷ A sheet of drawing paper
- ▷ Crayons or markers
- ▷ 3 or 4 large balloons
- ▷ A marker with a thick (not pointed) tip

PROCEDURE

1. When a client presents with anxiety or other upsetting feelings related to a feuding family, invite her to draw a picture of a recent argument and to discuss it in more detail, including how she felt and how she responded to that event.

2. Next, blow up a balloon, asking the client to imagine that it is her head. Ask her what she is thinking when fights occur in her family. As she verbalizes her thoughts, write them on the balloon with a marker. Work with her to identify possible irrational beliefs, such as "It's all my fault," "I should have been able to stop it," "They're fighting about me, so I must be bad," "This will never end," "We'll never be happy," and so forth.

3. Discuss her thoughts in more detail, and blow up another balloon. Work with her to dispute the irrational beliefs listed in step 2: "How can it be all your fault?" "You are only one person in the family. What makes you think that you alone should have been able to stop it?" "Suppose they are fighting about you. How does that make you a bad kid?" As she comes up with more rational responses, write them on the second balloon.

4. Next, ask her to stand up and pretend that she is a robot who will do whatever you tell her to do. Give her several commands, such as walk backward 12 steps, jump up and down, touch the ground, stand on one foot, and so forth. When she has finished, point out that she did everything you told her to do, and ask her is that how

people are in reality? For example, does her friend, brother, or father do everything that she asks them to do? Do her family members stop fighting when she asks them to? Help her conclude that she cannot control her family, and ask whether she can think of anything she can control.

5. Work with her to identify other ways to cope with the feuding in her family, such as using rational coping statements. Share an example: She could think to herself, "I don't like it when they fight, but I need to take care of myself because I am just a kid and I can't stop them." Blow up another balloon, and ask her to think of another example. Write it on the balloon. Then ask what else she thinks she can do when her family fights and write those ideas on the balloon (use the fourth balloon, if necessary). Give her the balloons to help her remember her rational thoughts and her coping methods.

Relationships Rule

RATIONALE   During adolescence, it is not uncommon for adolescents to be "ruled" by their relationships, allowing them to define who they are and how they act. This intervention helps adolescent clients develop a clearer perspective of this issue.

MATERIALS   ▷ Relationships Rule Worksheet (p. 300)

▷ A pen or pencil

PROCEDURE   1. When a client presents with relationship issues, invite her to share more about what is troublesome about the relationship and how it affects her emotionally and behaviorally. Then ask her to write a short description of the "event" on the worksheet under the A (Activating Event) category and to list her emotional and behavioral reactions under the C (Emotional and Behavioral Consequences) category.

2. Next, explore her beliefs about the event that contribute to her emotional and behavioral reactions: If she is angry, does she think that people shouldn't treat her this way? If she is depressed, is she thinking things will never get better, that she will never have friends again, and so forth? Work with her to identify these beliefs and write them on the worksheet in the B (Rational and Irrational Beliefs) category.

3. Explore these beliefs with the client, helping her see that, if she is angry, she has some demands about how others should treat her. Help her examine how much control she has over others and how getting angry helps her deal with the issues. If she is depressed or putting herself down, encourage her to explore whether she is what they say she is if she is being put down, whether she absolutely cannot live without their approval, and whether she wants to give others power over her feelings.

4. Focus on empowering the client to take better charge of herself so that her relationships don't "rule" her. Ask how she has handled relationship problems such as this in the past. Introduce her

to the concept of assertiveness, indicating that being assertive means standing up for your rights without infringing on others' rights. In contrast, aggression develops out of anger and is more of a self-righteous attack on the person ("How dare you do this to me"). Aggression often invites counterattacks and seldom improves the relationship. The third option, nonassertion, is to do or say nothing and let the other person walk all over you or "rule" you and have the power. To reinforce the client's understanding of these three approaches, model them by sharing examples based on issues she previously identified.

5. Next, invite the client to practice being assertive as a way of dealing with her relationship issues. Ask her to select the most troublesome issue involving a peer and describe it to you so that you can play the role of the peer; the client will play herself. Debrief by focusing on how she felt and how being assertive might affect the relationship.

6. Also ask the client to identify barriers to being assertive, such as "This will only make things worse," "It won't help," and "It's too hard." Help her dispute these beliefs: How do you know it will make things worse? Where's the evidence it won't help? Is what you are doing now working for you?

7. As a homework assignment, invite the client to practice being assertive and report back on whether it helped her deal with others who are trying to "rule" the relationship.

Relationships Rule Worksheet

A—Activating Event

C—Emotional and Behavioral Consequences

B—Rational and Irrational Beliefs

Healthy or Unhealthy?

RATIONALE It is often difficult for adolescents to distinguish between healthy and unhealthy relationships. Helping them identify irrational beliefs that keep them stuck in unhealthy relationships is the objective of this intervention.

MATERIALS ▷ Healthy or Unhealthy? Checklist (p. 301)

▷ A pen or pencil

PROCEDURE 1. When a client presents with issues involving an unhealthy relationship, encourage him to talk more about it, then invite him to complete a short checklist identifying what he considers to be healthy or unhealthy aspects of relationships.

2. Discuss the completed checklist with him, encouraging him to share more about how these characteristics apply to the relationship he is currently struggling with.

3. Next, explore what keeps him in this unhealthy relationship, helping him identify irrational beliefs such as "I can change her," "I probably deserve it," "It's better to put up with this than not be in the relationship at all," "There must be something I am doing wrong," "If I end this relationship I may not find someone else I care about as much," and "I need her."

4. Work with the client to dispute these beliefs, using the "best friend" technique. Ask him, "If your best friend told you that he deserved to be mistreated by his girlfriend, what would you say to him?" "If your best friend said that it is better to be in a bad relationship than not be in one at all, what would you say to him?" "If your friend says that there must be something wrong with him, how would you respond?"

5. After he has identified these disputes, explore his difficulties in applying this logic to himself, working on strengthening his self-worth: Where is the evidence that he deserves to be controlled, disrespected, and so forth.

6. Finally, ask him to review his responses on the Healthy or Unhealthy? Checklist and discuss advantages to remaining in an unhealthy relationship.

7. Invite him to set a personal goal, based on what he has discussed during the counseling session, relative to his current relationship.

Healthy Or Unhealthy? Checklist

Directions: Categorize the following as either H (healthy) or UH (unhealthy).

____ Tries to control how you spend your time

____ Lays guilt trips on you

____ Puts you down

____ Stands up for you when others put you down

____ Breaks promises to you

____ Supports your choices

____ Tries to control who you associate with

____ Pressures you into doing things that don't feel right to you

____ Does special things to help you out

____ Makes fun of your values

____ Listens to your opinions

____ Isn't truthful with you

____ Is always dependable

____ Talks about you behind your back

____ Is helpful and supportive of you

____ Add your own: _____

____ Add your own: _____

____ Add your own: _____

From *More What Works When with Children and Adolescents: A Handbook of Individual Counseling Techniques,* © 2009 by Ann Vernon, Champaign, IL: Research Press (800-519-2707, www.researchpress.com)

Reasons for Relationships

RATIONALE   Adolescents are often in relationships for the wrong reasons, such as needing someone else to make them feel important. This intervention addresses that aspect of relationships.

MATERIALS   ▷ Reasons for Relationships Word Cluster (p. 304)

PROCEDURE   1.   When an adolescent presents with concerns about a relationship, encourage her to elaborate some on the main problem, as well as how she feels and how she reacts.

2.   Then ask her to work on the word cluster, identifying as many reasons as she can think of to explain why people want to be in relationships with peers, romantic or otherwise.

3.   Debrief the word cluster activity with her, encouraging exploration of the different variables, with a focus on which ones are positive, which are negative, and which are problematic for her. Also, it may be appropriate to add to what she has identified and include such factors as wanting to feel important, needed, valued, or popular.

4.   Help her connect negative feelings and behaviors with some of the reasons for being in relationships. For example, if she experiences anxiety, it might be because she fears rejection and thinks she needs to belong, or, if she is sad or depressed, it could relate to not feeling important or valued in the relationship.

5.   Next, suggest that she return to the word cluster and put an asterisk beside the reasons for being in relationships that she considers to be healthy, or positive, and an X beside those that she considers to be unhealthy, or negative. Discuss with her what she thinks she can do to avoid being in relationships for the wrong reasons.

6.   To help develop her ability to avoid being in relationships for the wrong reasons, work with her to dispute the belief that she must be in a relationship to feel important or valued, or that it would be awful to be rejected, or that being popular is the most impor-

tant thing in the world. Do this by asking questions such as the following: Where is the evidence that you are valued and important only if you are in a relationship? Is being in a negative relationship better than being in no relationship at all? Can you think of anything worse than being rejected? Have you ever been rejected; if so, were you able to stand it?

7. Encourage the client to reflect on what she has learned about reasons to be in relationships and to set a goal for her own problematic relationship.

Reasons for Relationships Word Cluster

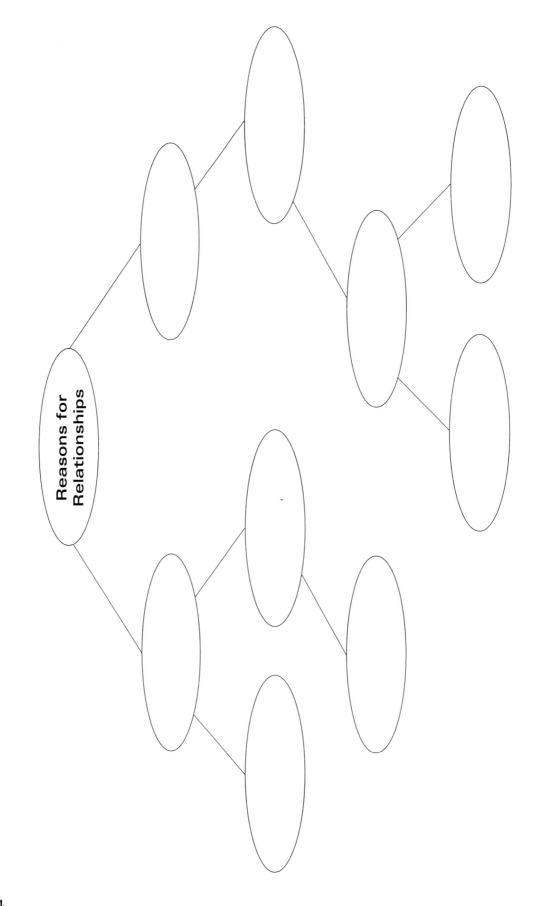

Reasons for
Relationships

From More What Works When with Children and Adolescents: A Handbook of Individual Counseling Techniques, © 2009 by Ann Vernon, Champaign, IL: Research Press (800-519-2707, www.researchpress.com)

TRANSITIONS

Transitions often signify a change in one's roles, routines, relationships, and assessment of oneself. Children and adolescents inevitably experience a variety of transitions as they grow up, and their thoughts about these transitions have a great deal to do with how they feel about them. Common transitions about which children may have varying degrees of anxiety are school related (e.g., changing schools, starting school for the first time, moving to the next grade). Others are family related (e.g., adjusting to parental divorce or remarriage, negotiating their place in the family as a new big brother or sister, coping with the death of a close relative). Still another major transition is that of leaving a familiar environment (e.g., moving to a different school, house, neighborhood, or city and adjusting to new surroundings).

For adolescents, typical transitions include graduating from high school and leaving home, entering the job market, and spending less time with same-sex peers and becoming involved in an exclusive romantic relationship. As with younger children, family-related transitions, such as parental divorce and remarriage or loss associated with death or illness, continue to be very difficult for adolescents to handle. Although anxiety—to varying degrees—may be a common denominator in all transitions, other emotional and behavioral reactions to developmental transitions also are prevalent. They, too, are addressed in this section.

Tough Times

RATIONALE
In this era, many children are forced to deal with issues related to a family member being deployed for military service. In addition to the anxiety regarding the safety of this individual, changes in the family composition also result in a variety of emotional and behavioral reactions that this intervention addresses.

MATERIALS
▷ Tagboard and a brass fastener (to create the Tough Times Wheel, p. 308)

▷ 12 to 15 index cards

▷ A pen or pencil

▷ A sheet of paper

▷ A small box, such as a shoe box

▷ Construction paper

▷ Assorted stickers

▷ Glue and scissors

▷ Markers or crayons

PROCEDURE
1. When a child is referred because a family member has been or is about to be deployed, ask her to spin the Tough Times Wheel to a feeling she has about this event. As she lands on a feeling, invite her to discuss more about it and how she behaves in response to the feeling. Encourage her to continue spinning the wheel until she has identified all feelings related to this situation.

2. Next, specifically zero in on her worry or anxiety, asking her to take some index cards and, on each card, write one of the things she worries about relative to this situation.

3. Then introduce her to the concept of a continuum, in which you take a sheet of paper and draw a line across the middle of it. Explain to the client that at one end is what she worries about or fears the most; ask her to select that from her worry cards and

write it at one end of the continuum. Then ask her to think about the opposite of the fear or worry; for example, if the worst is that Dad or Mom could get killed, the opposite would be that they would return completely uninjured and safe. Help her see that, although it is natural to sometimes think the worst, doing so contributes significantly to her anxiety. Discuss with her the fact that it is possible that, in times of war, the worst can happen—but there are lots of soldiers who aren't harmed, or perhaps are hurt but not killed. Work with her to help her identify six or seven other possibilities and have her write them along the continuum. For instance, someone could be very seriously hurt but not die, someone could break and arm or leg, and so forth.

4. After she completes the continuum, ask whether seeing many different possibilities helps decrease her anxiety. Encourage her to use this strategy for other things she worries about.

5. Next, ask her whether she has ever worried a lot about something that didn't actually happen. After discussing this, explain that it can often be this way with worries: they don't happen, or maybe they do but aren't as bad as we thought they would be. Invite her to make a worry box, decorating it with the construction paper, stickers, and markers. Encourage her to put her worry cards in the box, and, when she wakes up tomorrow, tear up the worry cards that didn't come true. Invite her to use this strategy every day, writing what worries her on cards, putting them in the box, and tearing up the ones that didn't occur.

6. In a follow-up session, ask how the worry box is helping her. Take the worries still existing in the box and help her apply the continuum concept to reduce these concerns.

Tough Times Wheel

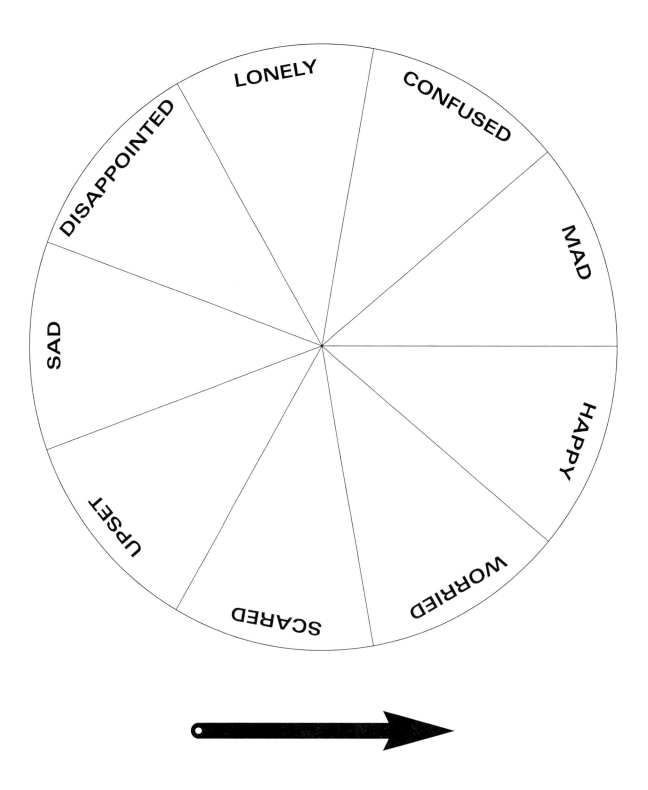

From *More What Works When with Children and Adolescents: A Handbook of Individual Counseling Techniques,* © 2009 by Ann Vernon, Champaign, IL: Research Press (800-519-2707, www.researchpress.com)

Room for One More?

RATIONALE Becoming a new big brother or sister is another transition many young children experience, often with mixed or negative emotions. This intervention addresses that issue and helps children learn coping strategies.

MATERIALS
▷ A toy baby bottle

▷ A baby pacifier

▷ A set of Room for One More? Cards (p. 311), divided into two separate envelopes; put one envelope under the baby bottle and the other under the pacifier

▷ One die from a pair of dice

▷ 2 puppets

PROCEDURE
1. When a client presents with negative feelings related to a new baby in the family, acknowledge that this can be a major change in a family and encourage him to tell you more about the baby: the baby's name and who the baby looks like, how big he or she is, and so forth.

2. Then invite the child to play a game that can help him express his feelings about the changes in his family that have occurred as a result of this baby's arrival.

3. Explain to him how the game is played. He will roll the die. If he rolls a 1, 2, or 3, he takes a card from the envelope under the baby bottle, reads it, and responds. If he rolls a 4, 5, or 6, he takes a card from the pacifier pile and does the same.

4. As he plays, encourage him to elaborate about the statement written on each card he draws.

5. When he has completed this task, ask him whether he knows anyone who has felt differently about a new baby in the family. Does he know anyone who was excited or happy? Invite him to participate in a puppet play, where you are the child who is happy about being a big brother or sister and he is the puppet who isn't. As the

---

puppet play ensues, elicit irrational beliefs and model rational thoughts in your puppet (for example, saying something like "Do you ever feel jealous because you think your parents love the baby more than you? I did, too. Now, I know that they love me, too; it's just that they have to give the baby more attention because he can't do anything for himself now" and so forth). As much as possible, your puppet should elicit irrational beliefs from his puppet, and your puppet should probe for evidence to support or refute the client's beliefs.

6. After the puppet play, ask the client whether he feels any differently about having the new baby. Encourage him to identify remaining negative thoughts, such as "It's not fair that my parents pay more attention to the baby." Then work with him to identify more rational thoughts, such as "They pay more attention to him now because he is helpless, just like they did with me when I was a baby."

7. As a homework assignment, invite your client to practice his new thinking and see whether he can find anything positive about being a new big brother.

Room for One More? Cards

When I found out we would have a new baby in the family, I felt . . .	I don't like being a big brother or sister because . . .
When the baby came home from the hospital, I felt . . .	When the baby gets older, it will be . . .
The way I feel about this baby now is . . .	In my family, the one who gets most of the attention is . . .
The reason I don't like having a new baby in the house is because . . .	It is hard for me to have a new baby brother or sister because . . .
A bad thing about this new baby is . . .	Something I liked about my life before this baby was . . .
I feel jealous because . . .	I wish my mom or dad would . . .
One way this baby has changed things in our house is . . .	I don't like it when the baby . . .
How I think my parents feel about the baby is . . .	If I could give some advice to a friend about having a baby brother or sister, it would be . . .
I get tired of the baby because . . .	I wish . . .

From *More What Works When with Children and Adolescents: A Handbook of Individual Counseling Techniques,* © 2009 by Ann Vernon, Champaign, IL: Research Press (800-519-2707, www.researchpress.com)

Switching Schools

RATIONALE   Moving to a new school can be a difficult transition for children. This intervention is designed to facilitate this adjustment.

MATERIALS

▷ 10 blank index cards with green dots on them

▷ A pen or pencil

▷ A game board (see appendix; spaces on the game board should be color coded with alternating dots—green, yellow, and red)

▷ A set of Switching Schools Cards (p. 314) with a green dot on each card.

▷ 2 different coins or other markers

▷ One die from a pair of dice

PROCEDURE

1. When a client presents with issues related to moving to a new school, discuss how she feels about this transition and ask her to tell you what she knows about the new school.

2. Next, ask her to think about her concerns or worries relative to this transition. Have her write these thoughts on the index cards and mix them in with the set of Switching Schools Cards.

3. Next, invite her to play a game with you. First, select a marker. Then explain that the two of you will take turns rolling a die, moving a marker the designated number of spaces, and then following these instructions: If either of you lands on a space with a green dot, draw a Switching Schools Card, read it, and identify something you could do to deal with that concern. If either of you lands on a space with a yellow dot, state something that might be positive about this change. If either of you lands on a red space, identify a personal strength that will help with this transition.

4. As the game progresses, you should model coping strategies when it is your turn. For example, if the worry is that you might not be able to find your way around the new school, you can suggest that it might be helpful to do a trial run—visiting the school a day or

two before you start classes just to make sure you know where the classroom is, where the lunchroom is, and so forth. If the worry is that the teacher might be mean, you can model that that is just an assumption and, in fact, the teacher might be really nice.

5. Continue playing the game until you both reach the end. Throughout the event, work with her to challenge any assumptions she may be making about this transition. Debrief by asking her whether any of the things she was worried about aren't as much of a concern now and which coping strategies or strengths she can use to deal with the worries that remain.

Switching Schools Cards

What if the teacher is mean?	What if nobody sits by me on the bus?
What if the work is harder than at my old school?	What if the teacher calls on me and I don't know the answer?
What if I get lost because it is a bigger school?	What if I don't like my teacher?
What if nobody talks to me?	What if we have to change clothes for physical education?
What if kids stare at me because I'm new?	What if we have to switch classes and have several different teachers?
What if I don't like the school lunch?	What if kids say mean things about me?
What if nobody sits by me at lunch?	What if nobody from my old school keeps calling me?

From *More What Works When with Children and Adolescents: A Handbook of Individual Counseling Techniques,* © 2009 by Ann Vernon, Champaign, IL: Research Press (800-519-2707, www.researchpress.com)

Troubling Transitions

RATIONALE   Friendships are all-consuming for young adolescents in particular, but friendship patterns change rapidly as peer pressure and varying rates of maturation impact relationships. This intervention helps adolescents deal with these peer group transitions.

MATERIALS   ▷ Troubling Transitions story (p. 317)

▷ A pen or pencil

▷ An envelope

▷ Several strips of paper or index cards

PROCEDURE   1. When a client presents with relationship issues resulting from a transition out of a peer group, explore the issue in some detail, noting whether this was an elected or an imposed transition.

2. Invite her to read the Troubling Transitions story, underlining anything that is similar to her situation. When she has finished, ask her to share how she did or did not identify with the issues presented in this story.

3. Next, explore different things she can do to handle a transition of this nature. Help her understand that there are things she can do internally and externally. Internally, she needs to identify what she is telling herself about not being part of this peer group: Does she feel like there is something wrong with her? That she will never be included in a group again? That it wasn't fair? and so forth. Have her write these thoughts on the paper strips; discuss her responses in more detail, then put the paper strips in the envelope. Help her learn to dispute irrational beliefs: How is she a bad person just because she was excluded? Where's the evidence that she will never find a peer group again? And, although it might not be fair, does it help her to dwell on the situation, because unfair things do happen?

4. Then discuss the fact that, although she cannot control what these friends did, there are some things she can do behaviorally, or

---

externally, to help herself. Ask her to think about what advice she might give herself about how she could deal with this situation more effectively. Invite her to write those ideas on the outside of the envelope.

5. Finally, suggest that, as a homework assignment, she make a transition "tool kit": Take a shoe box or a plastic box and inside it put things that might help her feel better, such as CDs of upbeat songs, quotations or short stories that she enjoys reading when she is down, and other mementos that remind her of happier times.

Troubling Transitions

When I first started hanging out with a group of kids at the beginning of the summer, I thought it was just perfect. We could all just act like ourselves, and no one was judging anyone else. We rode our bikes all over town, played video games and watched movies at each other's houses, and spent time at the pool. We didn't badmouth others in the group, and we could trust each other with our secrets.

But that all changed when school started. On weekends two of my best friends started hanging out with kids from different schools, and they stopped calling me. If I called them, they always had an excuse for why they didn't want to be with me. At first it wasn't so bad because there were still others in the group that I liked to do things with, so even though I would have liked being with my best friends better, I still thought things were all right.

About a month into the school year, my parents were going to be gone for the afternoon, but they said I could have a friend over. We were just hanging out in my room drinking Cokes, when my friend asked me whether my parents had any liquor. I said I didn't know, and she said she was going to check around because it would be fun to get drunk. I felt really uncomfortable; I didn't want to get in trouble, but I didn't want her to think I wasn't cool, so I told her where it might be if we had any. I really hoped she wouldn't find any, but she did, and she poured some in her Coke. She tried to get me to try it, too, but I said no. I was really nervous for the rest of the afternoon, and I kept telling her that she couldn't have any more or my parents would find out. She said I didn't know how to have fun, and she got mad and left. I actually felt sort of relieved, but also I worried what she might tell the other kids.

The next weekend there was a party at her house, and I got invited. Because she had asked me, I just assumed that she hadn't told anyone about the drinking episode at my house. But it didn't take long for me to figure out that that wasn't the case. We were all sitting in a circle, and she announced that there were some new "rules" for our group, which included drinking. She said that she had given me my one and only chance and I had blown it, but she was going to let the group decide whether they wanted to keep me or not. She called for a vote, and only one person stuck up for me. Majority ruled, so they told me to get out.

I felt terrible. I had trusted them to be my friends, and I couldn't believe that they had kicked me out because of this. I didn't agree with what they were doing, and it didn't seem fair that just because I didn't want to drink that I couldn't be in their group. I had never felt so left out and lonely in my life, and I wondered what I would do now without any friends. I would look pretty stupid showing up all alone, and I was scared that they would start saying bad things about me so that others wouldn't want to be my friend. This was the first time I hadn't had a group of good friends, and I felt lost. I couldn't even imagine going to school on Monday, but I knew my parents would make me go. It's not like I could hole up in my room forever, but it just didn't seem like there were good alternatives. How would I go about making new friends again? Would everyone think I was just a reject? How would I get through this?

On My Own

RATIONALE   Becoming more independent is a gradual transition that occurs during adolescence and becomes more of a reality after high school graduation. Being less dependent, particularly on parents, is exciting for some clients. For others, this transition may be anxiety provoking. This intervention helps clients learn to deal more effectively with negative feelings and low frustration tolerance associated with being more on their own.

MATERIALS   ▷ A sheet of paper

▷ A pen or pencil

PROCEDURE   1. When a client presents with some anxiety about being more independent after graduation, ask him to make a list of all the things he now depends on others to do for him, at least in part. This list should be broken into the following categories: parents, teachers or school personnel, and friends. For example, he may depend on his parents to do his laundry and cook his meals, on his teachers to remind him about deadlines, and on his friends to initiate social activities.

2. When he has completed the list, encourage him to share it with you and elaborate more on what he has written.

3. Next, ask him to close his eyes and imagine himself living on his own. Ask him to visualize himself going through his day: What will he need to do for himself that he isn't doing now? After several minutes, invite him to verbalize what he visualized and identify and discuss feelings associated with this image of being on his own.

4. Then help him identify irrational beliefs associated with being more independent and responsible for himself, such as "It's too hard for me to remember to do things when I need to," "I can't stand doing household chores that used to be done for me," "It's too hard to manage my own money and pay all my own bills; what happens if I don't have enough money?" "What happens if I am

late for work or class?" After he has identified these irrational beliefs, have him imagine that it is just too overwhelming to be on his own and ask him to visualize not ever being independent—that because it might be too challenging or anxiety provoking, he is going to live at home for the rest of his life, having others take care of him until old age. After he has had some time to visualize this scenario, ask how he would feel about this option and what it would mean for him if, in fact, it was his reality.

5. Next, help him identify ways to challenge any low frustration tolerance or beliefs that it is too hard to be independent: "How logical is it for you to depend on others for everything?" "Is it possible to go through life and never have to be responsible for things yourself?" "Is it realistic to think that things will never be difficult or frustrating?" Help him challenge the anxiety: "What's the worst that will happen if you are late for work or class?" "What's the worst that will happen if you don't have enough money to pay your bills?" "How likely is it that the worst will happen, and, if it does, does it mean that you don't have any control over the outcome?"

6. After he has learned the concept of disputing, ask him to make a list of the five most challenging things he has to face when he is on his own. Work with him to identify practical problem-solving strategies, such as making lists, keeping a calendar, developing a budget, and so forth.

7. As a homework assignment, encourage him to select some of the practical problem-solving strategies and start using them now to practice being more independent.

Alone Again

RATIONALE   A difficult transition for many adolescents occurs after an unelected break-up of a romantic relationship, leaving them single again and dealing with these adjustments. This intervention helps them identify irrational beliefs that make their adjustment more difficult.

MATERIALS   ▷ Alone Again Worksheet (p. 323)

▷ A pen or pencil

PROCEDURE   1. When a client presents with adjustment issues after a relationship break-up that she did not choose to terminate, invite her to discuss the situation so that you have a better understanding of the issues and her feelings.

2. Then ask her to use the Alone Again Worksheet to help her identify her thoughts about what this break-up means to her.

3. When she has completed the worksheet, discuss her responses, encouraging elaboration to help you understand more about her irrational beliefs and how they are affecting her.

4. After some discussion, ask her to imagine that she is her best friend who is in a similar situation. Have her read out loud each of the items that she checked, as applicable to herself, starting with "Because the relationship ended against your wishes, you ..."

5. Ask what it was like for her to read these as if the qualities applied to her friend: Would she in fact think her friend was a failure, a reject, destined to be unhappy forever, and so forth? Most likely she will say no—she would not think her friend was a failure or a reject, for example. Ask, "If you wouldn't describe your friend this way, why would you describe yourself in this way?"

6. Then teach her how to dispute her irrational beliefs using three types of disputes.

   Functional: How is it helping you deal with your loss and adjust to being alone if you continue to dwell on these negative thoughts?

Logical: How much sense does it make to describe yourself in this way? How logical is it for you to assume you are no good just because this relationship was terminated?

Empirical: Where is the evidence that you are a loser, that everyone is gossiping about you, or that you can never have fun again?

7. After discussing these disputes, have her practice applying them to the items she checked on the worksheet. Discuss the effect that disputing can have—helping her put the issue in perspective and reducing the intensity of the negative emotions.

8. Finally, on the back of her worksheet, have her make a list of all the adjustments she has to make as a result of this transition, such as being single when many of her friends are in relationships, being in charge of her own time when previously her time had been consumed by the relationship, and so forth. Ask her to try to reframe these negative aspects to positives, such as "There are some things I can do now that I couldn't do then because I have more time to myself" and "Even if most of my friends are in relationships, maybe I can meet other people who aren't in relationships and broaden my circle of friends."

9. Ask the client what she learned and how she can apply the disputing and reframing processes to her personal transition.

Alone Again Worksheet

Directions: Read this list and check off the thoughts that apply to your situation.

Because my relationship ended against my wishes, I . . .

- ❏ am a loser
- ❏ will always be alone
- ❏ am unworthy of a relationship
- ❏ will be the subject of lots of gossip
- ❏ will never have a relationship as good as the one that ended
- ❏ am a failure
- ❏ will be ridiculed
- ❏ won't have any fun again
- ❏ am a reject
- ❏ am a fool
- ❏ am unattractive to the opposite sex
- ❏ will never be able to forget this rejection
- ❏ am destined to fail in other relationships
- ❏ am stupid when it comes to romance
- ❏ will always think I should have done something to save this relationship
- ❏ cannot stand being alone, not being in a relationship
- ❏ am not as important because I am single again
- ❏ Add your own: _____
- ❏ Add your own: _____

CHAPTER 6

Applications for Parents and Teachers

Few would argue that being a parent is sometimes as frustrating and challenging as it is rewarding. The same can be said for teaching. Both at home and at school, parents and teachers often struggle in their attempts to nourish happy and productive young people. Unfortunately, this task has become increasingly difficult, given the growing number of children who could be considered "at risk" and whose social and emotional needs often interfere with their ability to learn and develop in healthy ways.

Parents and educators alike cannot help but be alarmed and disheartened by current child-related concerns such as homicide, suicide, street violence, substance abuse, eating disorders, academic underachievement, depression, conduct and attentional disorders, and promiscuous sexual behavior. Not only do these issues make parents' and educators' jobs increasingly difficult, they also heighten the awareness that now, more than ever, parents and teachers need skills that increase their effectiveness as educators, role models, and nurturers of young people. At the same time, we must recognize that adults living and working with children have issues in their own lives that can interfere with their competence. Furthermore, adults frequently exhibit negative emotional and behavioral reactions that are based on irrational beliefs; it is those negative reactions that contribute to a deterioration in the adult–child interaction.

Although parents and teachers might wish for ready-made answers or cure-all approaches that will "fix" the child, such methods often do not work. The reason they don't is that the adults themselves frequently have negative feelings about the youngster or the problem that can sabotage their ability to deal calmly with the situation. After all, parents and teachers are human, and sometimes when they get angry and upset about a child's behavior, they act out as well. Suppose Johnny has been throwing temper tantrums at home and at school.

His parents and his teachers are at their wit's end trying to figure out what to do. As Johnny is on the classroom floor, kicking and screaming, his teacher is trying to keep 28 other children quiet, is frustrated beyond belief, and is screaming at him to stop. When he does the same thing at church, his father becomes so angry that he brusquely grabs Johnny by the arm and practically drags him down the aisle. In both instances, emotions clouded these adults' ability to think clearly and caused them to overreact, in turn likely causing them to feel guilt and embarrassment.

Although traditional approaches to teaching and parenting offer practical suggestions for dealing with problems, rational emotive behavior therapy (REBT) goes beyond that. It is a skills-based approach that offers solutions and, more important, helps adults identify irrational beliefs that cause the ineffective emotional and behavioral reactions that interfere with good parenting and teaching. REBT proposes that there are actually two types of problems in dealing with children: *practical problems,* such as determining which rules to apply or how to communicate effectively with youngsters; and *emotional problems,* such as feeling angry when children don't follow rules or becoming depressed about a child's physical disabilities. Addressing both types of problems is essential for long-lasting solutions.

This chapter explains how negative emotions prevent parents and educators from implementing effective strategies with children. It then goes on to discuss how practitioners can teach these adults to identify and dispute irrational beliefs—which will have a positive impact on how adults relate to children. The chapter also presents beliefs that are specific to parents and teachers and describes the effects these beliefs have on parenting, teaching styles, and approaches to discipline. In addition, it describes effective communication and discipline strategies and offers suggestions for solving practical problems. The chapter concludes with a case study that illustrates how these principles can be applied to parents.

PROBLEM ASSESSMENT

When parents or teachers seek assistance from helping professionals about a problem they are having with a child, it is, of course, necessary to gather information about the child. This information should relate to the nature and severity of the problem; the onset of the problem and when it typically occurs; any significant changes or transitions or traumatic events that may have precipitated the problem; and other relevant data regarding the intensity of the problem. Equally important is that practitioners ask about the role the parents or teachers play, specifically searching for how they have dealt with the problem—which strategies have or have not worked well and how the child responded to these interventions. Eliciting parents' or teachers' feelings about the problem or how they have dealt with it—as well as discovering their irrational beliefs—is essential in problem assessment.

To form a comprehensive picture of the problem, it is helpful to use the BASIC ID, a multimodal approach developed by Lazarus (1976, 1997, 2002). BASIC ID is an acronym for "behavior, affect (physiological), sensation, imagery, cognitions, interpersonal relationships, and drugs/biology/health." Keat (1990) adapted this model for use with children. His HELPING model includes the following dimensions, which spell out the acronym HELPING: health; emotions; learning/school performance; personal relationships; imagery/interests; need to know/think; and guidance of actions, behaviors, and consequences. These assessment models emphasize a holistic approach that involves parents and teachers in the data-gathering process, as illustrated in the following example of the BASIC ID:

> Mr. Hernandez, a sixth-grade teacher, sought the assistance of the school counselor because he was having difficulty with Jackson. According to Mr. Hernandez, Jackson was belligerent and uncooperative most of the time. He refused to participate in class activities and was extremely unmotivated. Most of the time he failed to turn in homework assignments; consequently, he was failing several of his classes.

> After determining that the problem had been ongoing throughout the school year and that various interventions had been tried, albeit unsuccessfully, the counselor asked Mr. Hernandez to first describe Jackson's behaviors (B) in greater detail, including how he behaved in response to Jackson's actions. The counselor then asked Mr. Hernandez whether he had any ideas about Jackson's affect (A): Did it appear that he was angry, which might relate to his belligerence? Was Mr. Hernandez able to identify any other emotions this child might be experiencing? And what about his own emotional reactions to Jackson?

> By asking Mr. Hernandez to discuss Jackson's situation first and then gently leading him into a discussion of his own behaviors and emotional reactions, the counselor lessened any resistance the teacher might have and gained important information about the consultee (the teacher) as well as the student. After Mr. Hernandez described Jackson's behaviors in detail, he said that he had tried numerous behavior management strategies that had worked well with other students, but hadn't

with Jackson. "I'm about at my wit's end," he said. "I don't understand what I'm doing wrong . . . why aren't these things working? Sometimes I just get so frustrated that I know I have a short temper with the other students, and I feel guilty about that. They don't deserve that . . . Jackson is the problem, and he is driving me up a wall."

"Obviously," the counselor said, "Jackson's behavior is having a negative effect on you, and I think we can work together to find better ways for you to respond, which in turn will hopefully bring about some changes in Jackson's behavior as well. Getting back to our assessment, let me ask whether you have had any physiological sensations (S) or know of any that Jackson might be having."

"Well, I don't know about Jackson, but I feel tense whenever I am around him . . . my stomach feels like it's in knots," said Mr. Hernandez.

"That's definitely not a pleasant condition," said the counselor. "I'm wondering, does this affect your image of yourself?"

"You bet," replied Mr. Hernandez. "I have always considered myself to be a good teacher, but now I'm having second thoughts. I just can't seem to get through to this kid."

"Do you have any idea about how this is impacting Jackson's view of himself?" asked the counselor.

Mr. Hernandez thought for a minute. "Not really—he acts like he doesn't care. Who knows? Maybe he sees himself as pretty powerful since it is obvious that he is getting to me."

"And when you see yourself as incompetent because you can't find the right strategies to change Jackson's behavior, and when you get frustrated at times to the point of anger, are you aware of your cognitions? What thoughts go through your head?"

Mr. Hernandez responded that when he tried something that had worked in the past but didn't with Jackson, he found himself thinking, "This kid *should* respond." He shared that sometimes he was so discouraged that he considered getting out of teaching because he couldn't seem to do anything right this year.

The counselor continued to elicit more cognitions before moving on to the final two areas of the assessment: interpersonal relationships (I) and drugs/biology/health (D). Mr. Hernandez said that Jackson didn't have many friends and that he didn't know of any health problems. As for himself, he thought his relationship with other students was being negatively affected because of his frustration with Jackson, and he often left school with a headache.

As the example shows, BASIC ID helps practitioners systematically gather relevant data, including an assessment of irrational beliefs. Identifying parents' and teachers' irrational beliefs relative to the child's problem is an essential first step in problem resolution.

IDENTIFYING IRRATIONAL BELIEFS

Because the ultimate goal in working with parents and teachers is to help them be more effective with children, it is essential that we improve parents' and teachers' stability so they are able to achieve *their* goals. Parenting and teaching are stressful jobs, and, although educators receive more training than parents, both parties are often not as well prepared as they would like to be to handle daily challenges.

Like children, adults think that the *activating event* (A) causes their emotional and behavioral *consequences* (C), and they work hard to change this activating event. According to REBT theory, although activating events may serve as important contributors to the consequence, the *beliefs* (B) about the A actually cause the C. Four general categories of irrational beliefs that interfere with effective parenting and teaching are uncertainty (anxiety), self-condemnation, demanding, and low frustration tolerance.

Uncertainty (anxiety). It is not at all uncommon for parents and teachers to lack parenting and teaching skills, because children do not come with operating instructions. Unfortunately, there is often no "best way" to handle certain situations, and it is hard to predict outcomes. Many parents and teachers think they *should* know what to do and what the outcomes will be, feeling anxious and uncertain because they don't have access to a crystal ball. Part of the true test in working with children is for adults to do their best without ever knowing for sure what is right.

Self-condemnation. When children have problems at home or in the classroom, the adults in their lives are often quick to blame themselves. If children score poorly on basic skills tests, teachers assume it is because they themselves were inadequate and didn't do enough to prepare their students. If children turn to drugs and alcohol or become troublemakers at school, parents blame themselves, thinking that if their children turn out poorly, then they are bad parents. In reality, teachers and parents are not the only influences in youngsters' lives. Furthermore, adults won't always do the right thing, but they are worthwhile people regardless.

Demanding. When parents and teachers believe that children *must* turn out a certain way but don't, they think it is awful, and they fall into the trap of demanding. It is perfectly normal to *want* children to develop certain traits or abilities, and it is important to encourage this development. Demanding parents and teachers, however, have little tolerance for children who do not always put forth their best effort; consequently, they feel angry and resentful about the children's inadequacies. Furthermore, these relationships often become controlling and conflictual when absolutistic demands are placed on children always to perform in specific ways.

Low frustration tolerance. Parents in particular, especially in today's society, may think that children should not have to endure hardship or discomfort. In fact, there is growing concern by educators that more and more parents are becoming "helicopter parents," hovering over their children and their children's teachers to make sure their offspring don't experience failure. Mize (2008) adamantly stated that parents must learn how to let their children fail because overprotected children won't be prepared for the workforce or life. Helicopter parents who may think they are helping their children are actually depriving them of opportunities to stand on their own feet. In fact, children who are allowed to fail are more resilient and courageous. Parents who believe that children should never be frustrated are constantly rescuing them, interrupting their own busy schedules to take gym clothes or lunches to school because their youngsters forgot them; they do not want their children to be punished for this negligence, nor do they want them to experience any discomfort. Parents with low frustration tolerance are the ones who immediately take their son or daughter out of a class if the child complains that the teacher is "mean," or deliver the child's newspapers when he or she complains about having to get up early in the morning to do the job. Furthermore, parents often think that they themselves cannot stand to be uncomfortable. They avoid dealing with problems because they do not want conflict. This same phenomenon can apply to classroom teachers as well. Because these adults want children to like them, or because they think they cannot tolerate confrontations with their students, they fail to establish or enforce rules and consequences.

Bernard and Joyce (1984) identified specific irrational beliefs of parents, categorizing them according to emotional reactions: anger, depression, discomfort anxiety/low frustration tolerance, anxiety, and guilt. These beliefs are described as follows:

Anger

My child must always behave the way I want her to behave. It is horrible and awful when children do not behave well.

My child must do as I say.

My child must be fair to me at all times.

It should be easier to help my child.

My partner should always be in agreement with me.

Children should always do well and behave correctly. Children who act badly must be punished.

Depression

I am a worthless parent because my child has so many problems.

I am a terrible parent for being annoyed with my child, who cannot help having the problem.

My worth as a parent depends on the performance of my child.

If others think I'm a poor parent, I'm worthless.

If my child misbehaves frequently, it is awful, and I'm a failure as a parent.

If my child does not love me or approve of me, I am worthless.

When I don't perform as I think a good parent should, I am a complete failure as a person.

If you really want others to know that you care for them, you must become upset about their problems. If you're too calm, you don't care.

Unkind words, gestures, and behaviors from kids can just hurt us emotionally.

If you are not an outstanding parent, or, if you make mistakes, it is awful, and you are worthless.

My child's problems are all my fault.

When my child misbehaves, he is doing it because he doesn't love me.

Discomfort Anxiety/Low Frustration Tolerance

I can't stand it when something bad happens.

I can't stand my child's behavior.

I can't stand my child's attitude.

If something is frustrating or difficult, it must be avoided.

It is best to avoid dealing with difficult issues for as long as possible.

Anxiety

I couldn't bear it if something bad or painful happened to my child.

The world is a dangerous place, and you must be aware of this at all times.

Painful experiences must be avoided at all costs.

I *must* worry about my child (I can't help it).

Worrying is a sign of good parenting.

Guilt

If I make a mistake, it will always affect my child.

I am the sole cause of my child's problems.

I could have and should have done something to prevent my child's disability/problem.

I am totally responsible for everything that happens to my child.

Because of my own inadequacies, my child will always suffer.

It is awful for my child to suffer, and I must prevent it at all costs.

I must never do anything wrong to my child.

Although many of these irrational beliefs pertain to teachers, Bernard, Joyce, and Rosewarne (1983) also identified beliefs specific to teachers:

Students should behave properly at all times.

You can judge the worth of students by their behavior.

I generally need someone's advice at school to help me overcome problems with students.

I must have my students' approval.

I should know how to solve all the problems I encounter with my students.

I should have the power to make my class do what I want.

It is easier to avoid problems or difficulties than to confront them.

I can't stand it when students are being unpleasant.

Students should not be frustrated.

My worth as a teacher is determined by the effectiveness of my students.

I must have control of my students at all times.

I should have the respect of my students at all times.

I shouldn't have to perform unpleasant tasks at school.

I should be a perfect teacher.

Parents should do a better job of raising their children.

When parents and teachers think irrationally and are intensely emotional about a problem they are having with a child, the practitioner must resist the temptation to offer practical solutions to the problem instead of identifying and disputing irrational beliefs. The following personal experience illustrates the practitioner's dilemma:

> I clearly recall working with a mother who was overwhelmed by the multiple responsibilities she had caring for her three children. She was experiencing a great deal of stress and felt very guilty about taking it out on her children by nagging, yelling, and occasionally spanking. As she talked about her role as a parent, it became evident that Connie was one of those parents who felt she had to "do everything" for her children in order to qualify as a "good mother." However, in her case, the price she had to pay was getting to be too much, even though she was reluctant to look at it that way.
>
> Because she wanted to reduce her stress, I asked her to describe how she spent her time, focusing specifically on the activities she did with and for the children.
>
> When she explained that she spent an hour each day with each of her three children, helping them practice the piano, I could see why she was overwhelmed: This task alone took up so much of her time. However, rather than helping this client identify her irrational beliefs that good parents always help their children with homework, lessons, and so forth—that her worth as a parent depended on her children's performance; that if she did not spend time helping them, she was being selfish; and that if her children did not perform well, others would certainly think she was a bad parent, and that would be awful—I mistakenly jumped to what I thought was an ideal solution to relieve her stress.
>
> "Connie," I said, "why not just practice with one child per day? You would free up two hours a day that you could use for relaxation or enjoyment to help relieve

your stress. By doing that, you would be less likely to feel so overwhelmed and frustrated and take this out on your children." At the time, this client agreed that she could try this approach, but I should have known she would not be successful because I had failed to dispute the irrational beliefs about being a good mother that were preventing this client from changing her behavior.

As this example illustrates, effective problem resolution must address what is perpetuating the problem. Sometimes, however, parents and teachers are reluctant to look at themselves, and, therefore, they become defensive. Their resistance may relate directly to their guilt and shame about not being perfect because they can't "fix" the child's problem themselves. It is important to address this issue by pointing out that teaching and parenting can be very challenging and that there is no such thing as a perfect parent or teacher (or a perfect child). On the other hand, informing them that their job may be easier if they learn to handle *their* feelings about the child's problem often facilitates self-disclosure, which in turn helps them to identify irrational beliefs.

To reduce resistance further, it is also helpful to educate parents and teachers about how their negative emotions, such as anger, depression, guilt, discomfort anxiety, and the like can affect their behavior. Strong feelings such as anger, for example, transform the most reasonable adults into mean-spirited people who say things they don't mean and do things they wish they hadn't done. Parents or teachers with high degrees of discomfort anxiety fail to establish reasonable rules and don't follow through on consequences, and this failure only perpetuates problems. Guilty parents who feel responsible for their children's unhappiness may overindulge them and later have to deal with the negative results, as their spoiled, manipulative children assume the upper hand.

Recognizing that parents and teachers have other stressors in their lives besides the children they live and work with is also a good way to establish a solid working alliance. Teaching and parenting are not easy roles, and there are no easy answers.

Dispelling myths is also effective (Vernon & Al-Mabuk, 1995). For some reason, there is an assumption that parents have an innate ability to know what to do and can intuitively solve whatever problems their children are having. Although this myth does not apply as strongly to teachers, we often hear that "good teachers are born, not made." In either case, intuition can play a role, but there is more to these roles than innate ability.

Another common myth is that, once adults have figured out how to parent or teach properly, it will be smooth sailing from then on.

Realistically, that is not the case, because there are always new challenges to face. Additionally, many parents and teachers believe that their jobs should be easy, that they should not have to work so hard to find the right strategies. Unfortunately, children do not automatically respond appropriately, and there will be failures and setbacks that necessitate renewed efforts.

Finally, it is important to dispel the myth that what works with one child will work with another. Because children have different temperaments and personalities and also have different needs at various developmental stages, the "one size fits all" approach does not work, and this reality makes teaching and parenting more difficult.

DISPUTING IRRATIONAL BELIEFS

Helping parents and teachers understand the connection between their thoughts and feelings and behavioral consequences (the B–C connection) is an important step in identifying, and consequently disputing, irrational beliefs. Although some adults stubbornly hold on to the notion that the activating event (e.g., a child's refusal to do her homework or follow rules) causes them to feel upset, the practitioner can correct this misunderstanding by pointing out that two sets of parents or teachers could be faced with the same problem (e.g., Annie refusing to comply with the rules). The first set of teachers or parents is extremely frustrated and angry about this lack of compliance—because these adults believe that Annie should follow rules, and they cannot stand it when she doesn't—but the second set of individuals is more relaxed about it. Although the more laid-back parents or teachers would like Annie to behave differently, they just keep trying different approaches and do not let their irritation about her behavior rule their lives. These two sets of individuals respond differently because of what they are telling themselves about this child's behavior.

Adults, like children, often minimize the strength of their emotional reactions, so it is helpful to ask them how they behave when they have negative feelings about something concerning a child. Once the intensity of the feelings has been correctly identified, it is not difficult to uncover the irrational beliefs, because anger relates to demanding; guilt or anxiety relates to discomfort anxiety and low frustration tolerance; and guilt and depression relate to self-downing. The following case illustrates how to help parents see the B–C connection and identify and dispute irrational beliefs:

> Roberta and Todd initiated counseling, seeking help with their 17-year-old daughter, whose behavior was causing them some anxiety. Allison had always been an

honor roll student, and throughout high school she had been very involved in extracurricular activities: concert and marching band, chorus, and basketball. She had been class president last year and was initiated into the National Honor Society. She had always had a good group of friends that her parents approved of, because they knew most of the parents, and they had never had concerns about where Allison was, who she was with, or what she was doing. They described her as being very responsible and somewhat mature for her age.

However, in recent months, Allison was showing very little interest in school. Her grades were still good, but she had recently dropped out of band and chorus and had informed her parents that she was not going out for basketball. She was also associating with a different crowd . . . older students who had graduated last year. At first, Todd and Roberta thought this was just "senioritis," but now they weren't sure. Roberta in particular wondered whether Allison would even apply for college because she had not filled out one application and it was almost the end of the first semester. If they mentioned it, Allison flew into a rage and told them to get off her back. In fact, when Roberta was in Allison's room, she noticed several articles about Tasmania, which concerned her because one of the girls she was associating with had been there as an exchange student last year. At this point, Roberta wouldn't put it past them to leave the country and live there, which in her mind was totally unacceptable. Another thing that concerned Todd and Roberta was that Allison refused to wear the nice clothes she had always enjoyed and was now wearing things she bought at the Salvation Army. Not only that, but she had just applied for a job there. She didn't need to work . . . they gave her plenty of money. None of it made sense.

When I asked Todd and Roberta how they felt about these recent changes, they shared that they were confused, anxious, and very frustrated. Their daughter had always been a "good girl" whom they hadn't needed to worry about, in contrast to her older brother, who had been a bit more of a challenge.

After listening to Roberta and Todd's concerns about Allison and gathering more information about her to assess for possible depression or substance abuse, which neither parent felt pertained to their daughter, it seemed to me that Allison might just be searching for herself, a normal developmental task. However, when I shared this with Allison's parents, they assured me that this was not the case . . . they also had another concern, and that had to do with the fact that Allison had never had a boyfriend, but now she was spending all of her time with one particular girl and being very secretive. Roberta worried that maybe her daughter was gay. This was totally unacceptable to them, and they felt it would be absolutely devastating to the family. They wanted me to visit with Allison and figure out what was going on with her.

When I met Allison, I was very impressed with her maturity. Just as I had suspected, she was bored with school, her classmates seemed immature, and she was tired of the usual "high school drama." Instead, she had become close friends with a couple of young college students and spent her time over coffee with them discussing philosophical ideas that were far more interesting to her than what she was going to wear to the school dance. The more I talked to Allison, the more normal I thought she was, and I had to silently agree with her when she said that she thought her parents, especially her mother, were the problem. "They just want me to fit into their upper middle class mold," she said. "My mother's biggest disappointment is that I'm not going to homecoming and that I don't have a date. Who cares . . . it's so stupid. I did that high school thing for three years, and I've had enough." As I probed more about her relationships, she said that she knew her mother thought she was a lesbian, and she played that to the hilt. "It's not like that at all," she explained, "but it is fun to see my mother's reaction because she is so straight-laced and conservative. I am really close to Tara, but we don't have a relationship . . . we're just good friends."

I asked Allison where we should go from here, and she asked whether I could meet with her parents and try to help them understand where she was coming from. I agreed but stated that I preferred to have her there because I didn't know if I could speak for her. She reluctantly agreed to participate.

At the next session, there appeared to be considerable tension between Allison and her parents. I thanked them all for coming and indicated that the fact they were all there demonstrated their commitment to each other, even if they were experiencing some difficulty at this time. I explained that the purpose of our meeting was for both parties to share their concerns and, I hoped, arrive at some new understandings. I established some ground rules and then invited them all to take a few moments to write three to five concerns about their relationship at the current time.

I asked who would like to share first, and, not surprisingly, Roberta volunteered. Her concerns were that Allison was a lesbian, that she would never go to college and might even drop out of high school because she was so unmotivated, and that she would be an embarrassment to the family because she was outwardly rejecting their values. Allison could barely stifle a laugh when she heard the list, but she went on to read her own list—which amounted to the fact that her parents didn't trust her to make her own best judgments and that they worried too much. Her father then shared his list, which was very similar to his wife's.

I then explained to the parents that the senior year in high school is a time of transition and that it is not at all uncommon for young people to reject family values as they search for self. I described a continuum to help put Allison's behaviors in perspective: At one end was the teenager who dropped out of school, did drugs, amounted to nothing, and had no association with her family. At the other end was the teen who continued to be the honor roll student, involved in all the same activities as she had throughout high school, did everything her parents requested, and so forth. I asked the parents where they would place Allison, and they both agreed that she was somewhere in the middle. I next asked Roberta and Todd to explain to Allison what the indicators of their concern were, and they spoke in particular about her association with the girlfriend, being secretive, seeing the articles about Tasmania, and dropping out of her old peer group. Allison very clearly explained to them, as she had to me, that she was bored, her old friends were immature, she had no interest in silly boys who didn't act their age, and she had a close intellectual relationship with her college-aged friend but was definitely not a lesbian. She also shared that this friend was helping her get a science scholarship for study abroad in Tasmania, and, although that might mean she would delay college a semester, she had no intention of not going. As Allison talked, I could see her parents breathing sighs of relief. When she finished, I pointed out to them that they had allowed their concern to escalate because they had jumped to erroneous conclusions, overgeneralizing about things that had very little basis. I encouraged them to consider looking hard and fast at facts rather than making assumptions and asked how it helped them to draw conclusions without having evidence that what they thought was true. I also helped them see the connection between what they felt and what they believed: When they had new evidence that Allison was applying for a science scholarship, they were happy, but when they assumed she was just leaving the country and wouldn't be attending college, they felt anxious. I gave them handouts on cognitive distortions and encouraged them to study them, think before jumping to conclusions, and check out the facts by assertively communicating with their daughter. I shared some information with Roberta on the differences among assertion, aggression, and nonassertion so she understood how to talk to her daughter about her anxiety rather than avoid and assume.

At the end of the session, I felt that Allison's parents had a better understanding of what their daughter was going through and were better able to put the issues in perspective. Allison felt more understood, and I was hopeful that this situation would continue. A follow-up session was scheduled to check on progress.

As this case illustrates, being overly anxious or angry did not help these parents solve their problems and, in fact, prevented them from functioning effectively. Although it was normal for them to be concerned and dislike the situation, they could accomplish more by calmly and realistically assessing the problem. These parents finally learned that exaggeration is self-defeating and that the more they exaggerated, the more likely they were to become angry or anxious and to catastrophize. Consequently, their ability to problem solve was adversely affected.

These same disputing principles apply to teachers. Bernard and Joyce (1984) identified the following examples for several commonly held irrational beliefs:

1. Teachers who think they must be in total control of their classes at all times can challenge this irrational belief by recognizing that they will never have total control—and to insist on it will be counterproductive. Students are not all alike: Some will behave, and others will not.

2. Teachers who avoid unpleasant or uncomfortable tasks and interpersonal situations can learn that life isn't easy; that their effectiveness will decrease by avoiding these situations; and that they can tolerate these situations, even if they don't like them.

3. Teachers who believe that students who misbehave must be severely punished can dispute this belief by seeing that children sometimes misbehave out of ignorance and that severe punishment usually does not work—in fact, it only exacerbates the problem.

4. Teachers who think they have to be perfect, can never make a mistake, and must know how to handle every problem can challenge these beliefs by understanding that there is no such thing as a perfect teacher, that all teachers make mistakes, and that one mistake does not mean that they are total failures.

5. Teachers who believe that children should know better and should never misbehave need to challenge this thinking by realizing that, although it would be nice if all children knew how to behave, this certainly is not always the case. Besides, even if all children did behave themselves, they would still make mistakes or poor choices.

Irrational beliefs not only contribute to the way parents and teachers respond emotionally to children, they also influence how these adults behave and how they relate to youngsters. Different styles of teaching and parenting affect the way youngsters are treated.

TEACHING AND PARENTING STYLES

Two characteristics that help identify teaching and parenting styles are warmth and control (Vernon & Al-Mabuk, 1995). High control and low warmth are associated with an *authoritarian* style, whereas low control and high warmth are related to a *permissive* style. A reasonable degree of warmth and a reasonable degree of control reflect an *authoritative* style.

Authoritarian Style

Authoritarian parents and teachers believe that children should not misbehave or disagree with them and that bad behavior should be punished. They also see themselves as having the power to make children do what they want them to do. Furthermore, they think that children must do well without needing praise and rewards. Because these parents and teachers mistakenly assume that getting angry is an effective way to modify others' behavior, they often discipline through punishment, some of which is very harsh (Bernard & Joyce, 1984).

Although children may respond to this style of parenting or teaching by being well behaved and outwardly compliant, the relationship between child and adult is often very tense, and little respect or caring is evident. These children tend to be inhibited and fearful. Although they may not express their anger directly, this anger simmers beneath the surface and is commonly displayed as general unhappiness. Children who have been subjected to authoritarian parenting or teaching have self-esteem problems and look to authority figures for "right and wrong." They also lack spontaneity, fail to take initiative, and have poor social and communication skills.

Permissive Style

Permissive parents and teachers have low frustration tolerance. They believe that children should never be frustrated, that they should be free to do what they want, that it is easier to give in than to argue, and that all punishment is wrong (Bernard & Joyce, 1984). They see conflict as bad and consider it something that just creates more problems. In their minds, it is easier to let things go so that everyone can be happy. Adults who adopt this laissez-faire style make unclear and inconsistent rules—an approach that results in anxiety on the part of the child. And because children need parameters in their lives, they often act out in varying degrees to reestablish an appropriate hierarchy of authority.

Children who live in permissive homes or have permissive teachers know that, if they misbehave, their behavior will often be overlooked; they know that threats of consequences and punishment are just that—threats. They know that if punishment is in fact meted out, it won't last long. Although at first glance we might think that this situation is what children want, it is not the case: They need structure, and, when it exists, they experience relief, even though they may initially rebel against it. The permissive style has a negative impact on children in that they tend to lack self-control, may have difficulty accepting responsibility for their actions, and can be immature.

Authoritative Style

Parents and teachers who practice the authoritative style have rational beliefs. They know that children will sometimes make mistakes and misbehave, but these adults do not become extremely upset about it or allow their anger to overrule their reasoning ability. They recognize that children need to learn to be independent—that as fallible human beings, they will occasionally make poor choices. Authoritative parents and teachers set reasonable limits and rules; they have clear expectations and are prepared to hand out appropriate consequences. Children in these environments are competent, confident, self-reliant, and responsible. They are less likely to be rebellious and self-destructive because their parents and teachers demonstrate that they respect and care about them and work collaboratively with them to solve problems.

Practitioners working with parents and teachers can help them become more effective by teaching them how to identify and dispute the irrational beliefs that affect their teaching and parenting style. Once practitioners have succeeded in doing this, it is much easier to work on the practical problem by teaching parents and teachers various discipline and communication strategies that can also improve their relationships with children.

SOLVING THE PRACTICAL PROBLEM

Years ago, Hauck (1967) noted that, when parents encounter emotional problems with their child, it is not a good idea to work on resolving the child's emotional problems first and reducing the parents' emotional upset later. Instead, it is much wiser to help parents use cognitive strategies to calm themselves first, then work on helping the child. Hauck also stated that, in many cases, children will not change until their parents do. This sound advice, which is also applicable to teachers, still holds true today. Not until adults are more rational can practitioners introduce practical problem-solving strategies that will have a positive effect on children's behavior.

If you were to poll parents and teachers, many would admit that a majority of the problems they have in working with children relate to discipline or communication. Out of frustration or a lack of knowledge or skill, some revert to what they experienced as children at home or in the classroom, employing techniques that their own parents and teachers used. Unfortunately, these methods were often strict and harsh and could be classified as authoritarian. Teaching today's parents and teachers more appropriate strategies will help resolve current and future problems at home and in the classroom.

Nelsen and Lott (2000) identified long- and short-range parenting and distinguished between the two, stating that long-range parenting is farsighted and results in responsible children who have skills that will serve them well throughout life. On the other hand, they noted, short-range parenting results in children who become codependent, unhealthy, and rebellious. Although Nelsen and Lott described these methods as they related to parenting, they seem equally applicable to teaching.

The goal of the long-range approach is to develop responsible children. It involves listening but not "fixing it for them," providing structure and follow-through, and allowing for mistakes. In practicing this approach, parents and teachers offer encouragement to children and teach them how to make their own decisions as well as how to live with the consequences. They also give children an opportunity to share their own perspectives, thus fostering open communication.

The short-range approach does not teach children the skills they need to become independent adults. By doing things for or to children, parents and teachers try to "fix" their problems instead of encouraging the children to do so. This approach has arbitrary rules with little or no follow-through, and the adults are in control. There is no room for mistakes. Rewards (more likely, punishments) are the main forms of behavioral control.

Basing their work on these approaches, Nelsen and Lott developed two lists of practices—one that will work with children and one that will not.

Practices That *Will* Work

Appreciation and respect

Logical consequences and follow-through

Reasonable structure

Consistent rules, including limits and routines

Joint problem solving and compromise

Support and validation

Talking with (instead of talking more); listening more

Letting go of anger and resentment; not taking things personally

Empowering, encouraging, and letting children assume responsibility

Practices That *Will Not* Work

Sarcasm and disrespect

Punishment

Permissiveness

Arbitrary rules and lack of follow-through

Control and too many no's

Put-downs, criticism, and name-calling

Lecturing, not listening

Hanging on to issues, resentments; personalizing problems

Overprotecting, doing for

These two categories identify discipline and communication techniques that parents and teachers can employ (or not employ) to increase their effectiveness with children. Many of the suggestions refer to logical consequences (as opposed to punishment).

Logical Consequences

The logical consequences approach to discipline was developed by Dreikurs, who believed that all misbehavior is the result of children's mistaken assumptions about how to fit in and gain status. Dreikurs and Soltz (1964) identified four goals of misbehavior: (1) to get attention, (2) to gain power, (3) to seek revenge, and (4) to use disability to avoid doing something.

When children's goal is to gain attention, they think they count only when they are being noticed. If their goal is to achieve power, they dominate and manipulate because they think it is the only way they matter. Vengeful children think they are unlikable and have no power, but they also think they have the right to hurt others because they have been hurt. Children who adopt the goal of inadequacy think they cannot do anything right and that it is easier not to try at all.

For adults to employ logical consequences effectively, it is imperative first to identify the child's goal. One way is to ask parents or teachers to consider how they feel when the child does something they think is inappropriate. According to Dreikurs and Soltz (1964), if adults feel annoyed, the child's goal is probably attention. If they are angry and frustrated and feel that they are in a win–lose situation, the youngster's goal is most likely power. If they feel hurt and attacked, the child's goal is usually revenge. If they feel hopeless and discouraged, the child's goal is probably avoidance through inadequacy.

It is also helpful for parents and teachers to observe children's reactions when they are corrected. For example, if their goal is to get power, youngsters will overtly defy the rules and utter, "You can't make me," under their breath. If their goal is to get revenge, youngsters may continue the misbehavior and become violent when adults attempt to stop it. Yelling, screaming, and threatening, as well as hitting and kicking, may occur because the children want to inflict physical or emotional hurt.

Logical consequences do not constitute a form of punishment. Rather, they are behavioral interventions directly related to the misbehavior, and they help children recognize their misbehavior as a mistake. These interventions teach children how to be more responsible by allowing them to make choices so they can avoid negative consequences. They also do not involve threat or coercion and deal only with current behavior; they do not involve punishment, which is often a response to the accumulation of all past wrongdoings by the children. In employing logical consequences, it is important to be kind and firm and to avoid argument. Follow-through is critical. Adults should present the concept of logical consequences as a choice between continuing to behave inappropriately or changing the behavior. For example, if a child is messing around with her food at the table, the parent might say, "You can either stop playing with your food or excuse yourself from the table. If you choose to leave, you cannot have anything to eat until breakfast." If the child chooses to stay, but in a few minutes resumes the behavior, the parent can say, "I see that you cannot stop this behavior, so you need to leave now." In the classroom, when several children are whispering and not listening to a story, the teacher can say something like "I don't like it when you whisper and interrupt the story. You can choose to stay and listen or go back to your seats. What is your choice?"

Logical consequences are interventions that teach children how to change their behavior and learn from their mistakes. This approach helps avoid power struggles and, for this reason, is effective with adolescents, who naturally seek power. Adolescents who consistently come home past curfew can be given the choice either to adhere to the curfew or to come in earlier the next night. Those who conveniently "forget" to do their homework can choose to bring it home and do it during the week or not go out on weekends because they will need to study.

Communication Techniques: What Doesn't Work and What Does

Although most parents and teachers do not intentionally block communication, it is easy to fall into such ineffective habits. Gordon (2000) identified the following communication roadblocks.

Ordering, directing, and commanding. "Do it because I said so" often provokes anger and resistance. Ordering, directing, and commanding put children on the defensive and invite argument.

Warning, admonishing, and threatening. "If you don't stop that, you will have detention for a week." Certainly, those who misbehave need to be advised of the consequences of their actions, but there are better ways to communicate this idea, such as stating, "I want you to stop disrupting the classroom, and, if you don't, you will need to serve detention."

Moralizing, preaching. "You should know better than to skip class." Children probably already know this, and most often they will tune out the preaching and moralizing because it is demeaning. It is far better simply to state that there are consequences for skipping class.

Advising, giving solutions or suggestions. It is impossible for parents and teachers not to advise, but heavy doses of it can interfere with youngsters' ability to learn problem-solving techniques. If adults advise too much, children may become overly reliant on the advice or blame the advice giver if things do not turn out as they wished. Obviously, problem-solving ability improves with age, so it is more appropriate to give advice in limited doses to younger children.

Lecturing, making logical arguments. "If you had done what I told you to, you wouldn't be in this mess now." To say that children resent lectures and logical arguments is probably an understatement. Because adults usually end up inviting resentment when they use this tactic, they would be better off to zip their lips whenever they are tempted to deliver a lecture. Besides, the lecture usually does not affect positive behavior change and may, in fact, do the opposite.

Judging, criticizing, disagreeing, and blaming. It is impossible not to disagree with some things children do, but when adults do, they can express their disagreement in the form of an opinion rather than a judgmental, critical, blaming comment. Note the difference between "That was a stupid thing to do" and "I don't think spending all your allowance on candy was the best choice you could have made."

Praising. At first glance, it seems as though this might be a good strategy, but actually it is not helpful, because no amount of praise will make children feel confident if they are uncertain about their abilities. It is better, for example, to offer encouragement that separates children from their behavior: "I have confidence in you" or "I like what you did" versus "You did a good job" (because, if the next time the children do not do a good job, it confirms, in their minds, their incompetence).

Name-calling, ridiculing, and shaming. No one likes to be demeaned, and these types of communication can result in problems with self-esteem, humiliation, and resentment for the child on the receiving end.

Interpreting, analyzing, and diagnosing. "You're just dating that boy because you don't feel good enough about yourself to find someone better." A statement like that will only lead to a counterargument. Rather than using these techniques, express your concern in a straightforward manner: "I worry that you are dating him because maybe you don't feel good about yourself."

Reassuring, sympathizing, consoling, and supporting. This is another case in which, at first glance, the techniques employed might seem useful. However, reassurance can backfire. There is no guarantee that telling children they will do well on an exam will make it happen; if they fail, they might feel worse. Sympathy implies a "you poor thing" attitude. (Empathy works better because you are feeling *for* the children rather than feeling sorry for them.) Consolation and support are appropriate as long as they do not make children feel inadequate and incapable of dealing with the problem.

Probing, questioning, and interrogating. "Why didn't you do your homework?" "Why weren't you home on time?" "Why were you with them?"—"Why" questions put youngsters on the defensive and may provoke arguments. Adolescents in particular resent being bombarded by questions and will be less likely to converse under those circumstances.

Withdrawing, distracting, diverting, and being humorous. Although these may be temporary solutions, when children are upset, it is best to deal with the problem as soon as it arises. Humor can sometimes be taken the wrong way, particularly by younger children, and distracting and diverting techniques sometimes convey the message that you do not think they are capable of handling the problem.

The most effective communication technique involves "I" messages—nonjudgmental statements based on feelings. "I" messages are intended to invite open communication and cause less resentment than "you" messages, which are accusations or evaluations of someone's behavior, attitudes, or motives (Gordon, 2000). Unfortunately, "you" messages are easy to deliver and very familiar: "You should study for tests" or "You should come home on time." Children usually know they are being evaluated negatively, and these messages invite defensiveness. A typical example of "I" versus "you" messages in a classroom might sound like this:

"Jason, I would really appreciate it if you would stop talking to Justin."

"Jason, you had better stop talking to Justin and get to work *now!*"

The adult's tone of voice is an important ingredient in delivering messages to children. "I" messages should be stated in a calm, firm, but friendly tone, whereas "you" messages are often conveyed in an angry, demanding tone. To deliver an effective message, adults have to set aside their tendency to judge, assume, and blame. They need to stay calm. A simple formula that adults can use to improve the way they send a message to a youngster involves stating a feeling, then following up by describing the bothersome behavior. The message should be delivered in a nonjudgmental manner. Sharing the effects of the behavior and making a request for a change complete the formula. Adults should be specific in describing the behavior, and they should not exaggerate. Instead, they should be objective and brief, as in the following example.

> **Parent to child:** I am feeling frustrated because I have asked you several times to clean your room, and it still has not been done. It is hard for me to get the laundry done when your dirty clothes are still on the floor. I would like you to have it cleaned by tomorrow night; if you don't, you will not be able to go out with your friends until it is done.

Contrast that approach with the one used in the following classroom example.

> **Teacher to class:** You had all better shut your mouths and pay attention during this lecture, or you'll all be sent to the principal. Your behavior disgusts me, and I have had enough of it.

Clearly, the second example will do nothing to enhance the relationship the teacher has with these students and will more than likely result in frequent power struggles and a more disruptive classroom.

RATIONAL EMOTIVE EDUCATION

Obviously, as you consult with parents and teachers about problems they are having with children, you are in the business of educating them. This form of consultation is ordinarily done on a one-to-one basis and serves to remedy an existing problem. In addition to this type of intervention, REBT can be offered in the form of *prevention* to parents and teachers through educational programs. In these sessions, which can occur in either small- or large-group formats, participants learn the principles and practices of REBT and how to apply them both to themselves and to children. An important part of this education should also be information about child and adolescent development. Educators and parents need to know how development affects children's ability to conceptualize and respond to situational and developmental tasks, as well as what typically to expect from children at various stages of their development. Practical suggestions related to communication and discipline are also helpful, along with age-appropriate modifications. In addition, teachers can be taught how to apply these principles in the classroom with children through rational emotive education (REE).

Because of the educational nature of REBT, its principles can easily and systematically be incorporated into a classroom or small-group setting. When REBT is used in this manner, its primary emphasis is on prevention. REE is a systematic, curricular approach to emotional education, with the goal being to teach rational thinking skills so children can gain emotional insight and learn sensible coping strategies to apply to current as well as future problems.

In the classroom setting, REE is typically implemented through a series of structured emotional education lessons that are experientially based, allowing for student involvement and group interaction. Several programs have been developed (Bernard, 2001; Knaus, 1974; Vernon, 1998a, 1998b, 1998c, 2006a, 2006b) that typically incorporate the following components into their lessons (Vernon & Bernard, 2006).

Self-acceptance. REE lessons stress the concept of unconditional self-acceptance rather than self-esteem because the latter implies a rating of self. Core ideas in the curricula include developing an awareness of personal strengths and weaknesses; accepting imperfection; learning not to equate performance with self-worth; and understanding that children, like all humans, are fallible and will make mistakes.

Feelings. Understanding the connection among thoughts, feelings, and behaviors is a critical component of REE lessons. It is also important to develop a feeling vocabulary, learn to deal with emotional overreactions, assess the intensity of feelings, and identify appropriate ways to express feelings. Recognizing that feelings change according to how one thinks is a core concept.

Beliefs. REE lessons teach children to differentiate between rational and irrational beliefs and to understand how beliefs affect emotions and behaviors. Distinguishing facts from assumptions is also critical because, as concrete thinkers, children and many adolescents readily misconstrue events by failing to distinguish between a fact (he didn't ask me to his party) and an assumptions (he doesn't like me anymore).

Disputing beliefs. The concept of disputing entails replacing irrational beliefs with rational beliefs. As a result of disputing, children feel more moderate emotions and are able to engage in more self-enhancing behavior. Many different types of disputing strategies can be modified to make them developmentally appropriate for children and adolescents (Vernon, 2002).

REE lessons begin with a short, age-appropriate stimulus activity, such as reading a rational story, completing a problem-solving task, participating in a simulation game, or completing a worksheet or art activity. This stimulus activity is designed to introduce the objectives of the lesson and is followed by a directed discussion about the concepts introduced in the stimulus activity. The discussion is the most important part of the lesson and is organized around two types of questions: (1) content questions, which emphasize the cognitive learnings from the activity, and (2) personalization questions, which help students apply the learnings to their own experiences.

REE concepts can also be presented in a small-group format. There are two types of REE groups: (1) problem centered, in which members raise current concerns and are taught to apply REBT principles to problem resolution, and (2) preventative groups. The approach taken by the preventative groups is similar to that taken by the REE classroom groups, except that the process occurs in groups of six to ten members. Smaller preventative groups offer a better opportunity for members to interact and deal with the concepts introduced in the lessons on a personal level.

By participating in classroom or small-group sessions, children learn rational thinking principles, presented in a creative manner, that invite group participation and discussion. This approach enables children to apply these principles to current problems; even more important, it equips them with skills they can use to deal with future problems—and to reach new understandings and resolutions. For specific activities, consult Bernard (2001), Knaus (1974), and Vernon (1998a, 1998b, 1998c, 2006a, 2006b).

CASE STUDY

This case study illustrates the application of REBT concepts by a single parent concerned about her 16-year-old son. The boy is failing in school, and his mother suspects he has substance abuse problems. The following conversation is from the counselor's first session with this client.

Counselor: Hello, Mrs. Goman. It's nice to see you. What brings you to counseling?

Client: Well, I'm really worried about my son, Jeremy. He's 16 and has been having a lot of problems lately, and I don't know what to do.

Counselor: What sorts of problems is he having, and when did you first become concerned?

Client: I've been noticing little things for about a year. He started getting moody and argumentative, and at first I just figured it was a teenage thing, but this year he has been having major problems at school. He never wants to go and is always trying to get me to write excuses for him. He is really smart, but now he is failing almost all his classes. He has also started hanging out with a different bunch of kids. I don't know them well because he doesn't bring them to the house much, but I am pretty sure they are into drugs and alcohol.

Counselor: And are you thinking this is something your son does, too?

Client: I think so. I noticed a big behavior change around the time he started hanging out with these new friends. And, although he was moody and argumentative last year, lately it has been much worse. He is very disrespectful and disobedient. I know he lies. Nothing I say or do seems to have any effect on him.

Counselor: It sounds like you have noticed some major changes that are of concern. How are his problems affecting you?

Client: Where do I start? First of all, I feel guilty. I just wanted him to grow up happy and healthy, and now things are such a mess. I don't know what I did wrong.

Counselor: So you are blaming yourself for your son's problems?

Client: I must have done something wrong, or he wouldn't be this way.

Counselor: So it's all your fault that he is flunking his classes and smoking dope?

Client: I don't know. Something went wrong. Maybe it's because his dad and I got a divorce, and I didn't have a lot of money, so he couldn't have the kind of clothes he needed to fit in. I don't know.

Counselor: It's certainly possible that the divorce could have affected him, but do all children from divorced families have problems like this? Or do all kids who don't have the right kind of clothes act like your son?

Client: I don't think so, but I keep feeling that this is my fault.

Counselor: So you feel guilty, and you are telling yourself that you should have done things differently. And it could be true—maybe there were things you could have done differently. But did you deliberately do things that you knew were hurtful and damaging, or did you do the best you could at the time?

Client: I did the best I could. It isn't easy being a single parent, especially when my ex-husband hardly helps out at all and acts like he doesn't even care about his son.

Counselor: Well, it is obvious that you care about Jeremy, but I want you to get past this notion that you are a failure as a parent. Just because your son has problems, how does it figure that you failed? Certainly, what you do influences him, but are you the only influence in his life?

Client: No, I'm sure I'm not.

Counselor: And even if you failed, are you a rotten person?

Client: It sometimes feels that way.

Counselor: But are these feelings of guilt and depression helping you help your son?

Client: No.

Counselor: What can you tell yourself so you don't continue to beat yourself up about this?

Client: I guess I can just say that I did the best I could to raise him, and now he has problems that aren't all my fault.

Counselor: That's better. Now, tell me how you have responded to Jeremy's problems.

Client: Well, I try to get him up to go to school, and he just yells at me, so I back off and write a note to excuse his absence. Then I'm mad at myself for doing that. And I have talked to him about his friends and how I think he is using drugs, and he just goes ballistic and threatens to move out.

Counselor: You mentioned that you feel angry with yourself for backing off. And you back off because you think you can't stand to hear him yell and threaten to leave home?

Client: Right. I just don't know how to respond.

Counselor: I'm sure it is uncomfortable when he behaves this way, but do you really think you can't stand it?

Client: If you put it that way, I can stand it—I just don't like it. It seems easier to back down.

Counselor: But when you back down, you then get angry with yourself. So it doesn't sound like either alternative is great. But in the long run, will you be doing him any good by backing down because you think you can't stand the discomfort?

Client: I don't think so. But it's so hard, because when he's angry, he calls me names, and that hurts so much.

Counselor: Yes, but you must be telling yourself that words can hurt. Of course, it isn't nice to hear someone you love say these things, but do you really think that he means everything that he says to you when he is angry?

Client: Probably not; I know I just let it get to me.

Counselor: To keep yourself from becoming more depressed about this, you need to develop some "emotional muscle" so his words don't hurt as much.

Client: And how do I do that?

Counselor: By remembering that "sticks and stones may break my bones, but words will never hurt me unless I let them." In other words, you have to ask yourself, "Am I what he says I am? Where is the proof that I am an awful, horrible, mean mother?" And even if you were some of those things, would that make you a totally worthless person?

Client: No.

Counselor: Of course, you won't be happy about what he says, but you don't have to be so hurt and devastated.

Client: You're right—it's just hard to do.

Counselor: Parenting is hard work. But as we have been discussing today, there are things you can tell yourself to take some of the emotional distress away and thus increase your effectiveness. I just noticed that our time is up, but before we close, I'm wondering whether this has been helpful and what made the most sense to you.

Client: I do feel better. You helped me see that I did the best I could to raise Jeremy and that I can't take on all the responsibility for his problems. I might have done some things wrong, but I'm not a bad parent.

Counselor: That's right. And it certainly isn't helping you to deal with his problems when you feel guilty and depressed. For a homework assignment, I would like to recommend that you make a list of all the things you have done for

Jeremy over the years. You can then refer to this list whenever he berates you so you can keep yourself from being hurt by his words.

Summary of Case Study

As this case illustrates, parents' emotional problems about their children's problems affect their behavior and can compound their emotional upset. Dealing with this mother's guilt and depression by disputing her irrational beliefs about her bad parenting and helping her develop more emotional muscle to handle her son's verbal attacks was a major, positive step. As a result of this counseling, Mrs. Goman eventually got to the point where she was able to become less enabling and insist on counseling for Jeremy. After a few more sessions and months of therapy, including substance abuse treatment for Jeremy, this family's relationship improved.

Game Board

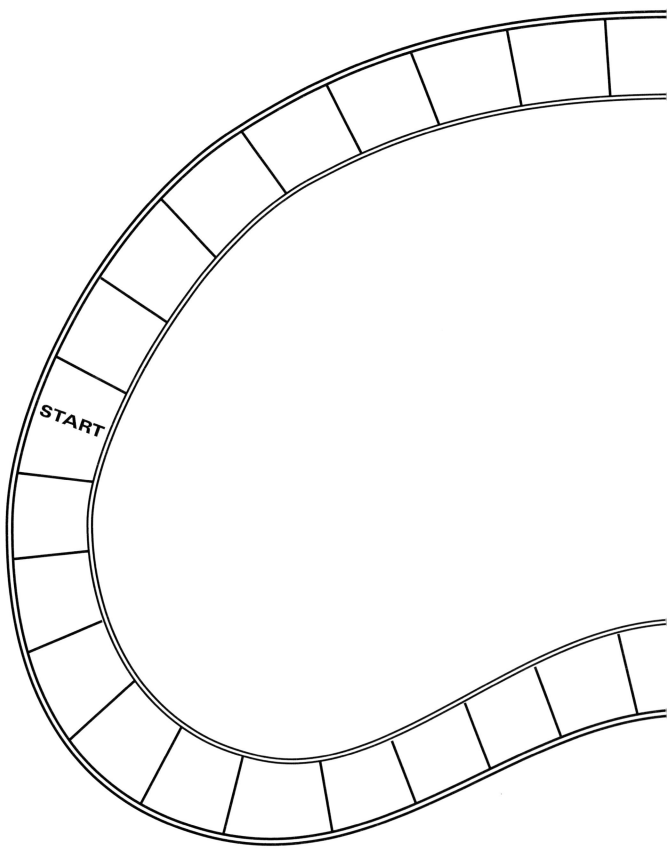

START

From *More What Works When with Children and Adolescents: A Handbook of Individual Counseling Techniques,* © 2009 by Ann Vernon, Champaign, IL: Research Press (800-519-2707, www.researchpress.com)

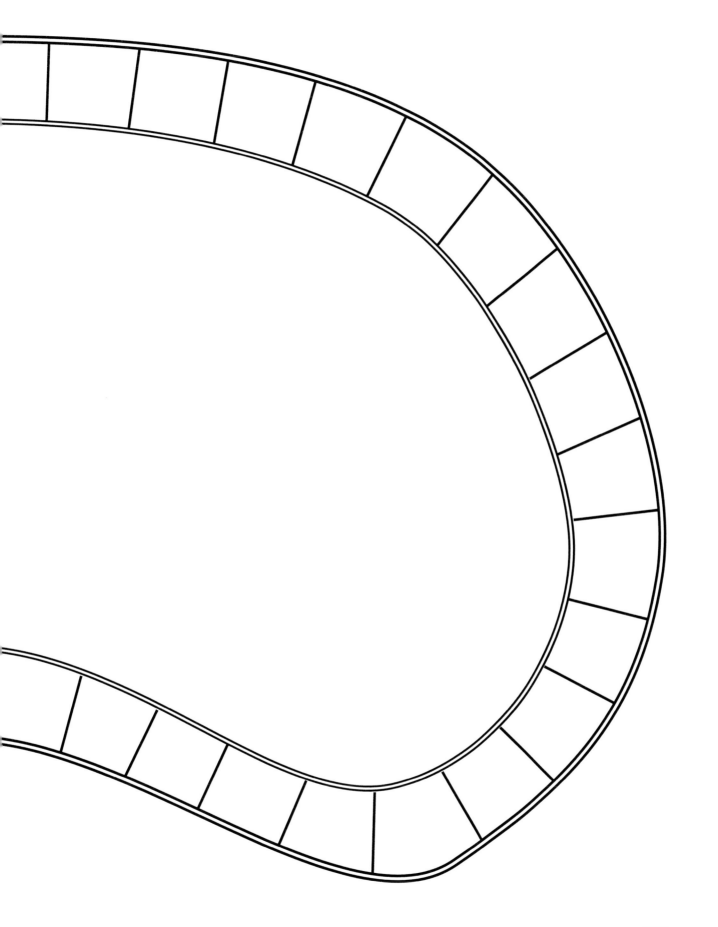

357

References

Ando, M., Asakura, T., & Simons-Morton, B. (2005). Psychosocial influences on physical, verbal, and indirect bullying among Japanese early adolescents. *Journal of Early Adolescence, 25,* 268–297.

Antony, M. M., & Swinson, R. P. (2000). *The shyness & social anxiety workbook: Proven techniques for overcoming your fears.* Oakland, CA: New Harbinger Publications.

Bauman, S., & Del Rio, A. (2006). Preservice teachers' responses to bullying scenarios: Comparing physical, verbal, and relational bullying. *Journal of Educational Psychology, 98,* 219–231.

Beck, J. (1995). *Cognitive therapy: Basics and beyond.* New York: Guilford.

Bedford, S. (1974). *Instant replay.* New York: Institute for Rational Living.

Bee, H. (2000). *The developing child* (9th ed.). Needham Heights, MA: Allyn & Bacon.

Berger, K. (2003). *The developing person through childhood* (3rd ed.). New York: Worth.

Berger, K., & Thompson, R. (1991). *The developing person through childhood and adolescence.* New York: Worth.

Berk, L. E. (2003). *Child development* (6th ed.). Needham Heights, MA: Allyn & Bacon.

Bernard, M. E. (1981). Private thought in rational-emotive psychotherapy. *Cognitive Therapy and Research, 5,* 125–142.

Bernard, M. E. (2001). *Program Achieve: A curriculum of lessons for teaching students how to achieve and develop social-emotional behavioral well-being,* Vols. 1–6. Laguna Beach, CA: You Can Do It! Education.

Bernard, M. E. (2004). *The REBT therapist's pocket companion for working with children and adolescents.* New York: Albert Ellis Institute.

Bernard, M. E., & Joyce, M. R. (1984). *Rational-emotive therapy with children and adolescents: Theory, treatment strategies, preventative methods.* New York: Wiley.

Bernard, M. E., Ellis, A., & Terjesen, M. (2006). Rational-emotive behavioral approaches to childhood disorders: History, theory, practice and research. In A. Ellis & M. E. Bernard (Eds.), *Rational emotive behavioral approaches to childhood disorders: Theory, practice and research* (pp. 3–84). New York: Springer.

Bernard, M. E., Joyce, M. R., & Rosewarne, P. M. (1983). In A. Ellis & M. E. Bernard (Eds.), *Rational-emotive approaches to the problems of childhood* (pp. 415–466). New York: Plenum.

Bloomgarden, A., Mennuti, R., Conti, A., & Weller, A. B. (2007). A relational-cultural, cognitive-behavioral approach to treating female adolescent eating disorders. In R. W. Christner, J. L. Stewart, & A. Freeman (Eds.), *Handbook of cognitive-behavior group therapy with children and adolescents: Specific settings and presenting problems* (pp. 447–464). New York: Routledge.

Broder, M. S. (2001). Dr. Albert Ellis—in his own words—on success. *Journal of Rational-Emotive and Cognitive Therapy, 19*(2), 77–78.

Broderick, P. C., & Blewitt, P. (2006). *The life span: Human development for helping professionals* (2nd ed.). Upper Saddle River, NJ: Pearson Education.

Carlson, N. (1994). *What if it never stops raining?* New York: Penguin.

Carney, J. V. (2008). Perception of bullying and associated trauma during adolescence. *Professional School Counseling, 11* (3), 179–188.

Carter, L., & Minirth, F. (1995). *The freedom from depression workbook.* Nashville: Thomas Nelson.

Chernicoff, E. R., & Fazelbhoy, S. R. (2007). Cognitive-behavioral groups for substance-abusing adolescents. In R. W. Christner, J. L. Stewart, & A. Freeman (Eds.), *Handbook of cognitive-behavior group therapy with children and adolescents: Specific settings and presenting problems* (pp. 349–366). New York: Routledge.

Christner, R. W., & Walker, M. L. (Eds.). (2007). Mediating depression in youth: A cognitive-behavior group therapy approach. In R. W. Christner, J. L. Stewart, & A. Freeman (Eds.), *Handbook of cognitive-behavior group therapy with children and adolescents: Specific settings and presenting problems* (pp. 293–316). New York: Routledge.

Cobb, N. J. (2001). *Adolescence: Continuity, change, and diversity* (4th ed.). Mountain View, CA: Mayfield.

DiGiuseppe, R. (1999). Rational emotive behavior therapy. In H. T. Prout & D. T. Brown (Eds.), *Counseling and psychotherapy with children and adolescents: Theory and practice for school settings* (pp. 252–293). New York: Wiley.

DiGiuseppe, R., & Bernard, M. E. (2006). REBT assessment and treatment with children. In A. Ellis & M. Bernard (Eds.), *Rational emotive behavioral approaches to childhood disorders: Theory, practice and research* (pp. 85–114). New York: Springer.

DiGiuseppe, R., & Kelter, J. (2006). Treating aggressive children: A rational-emotive behavior systems approach. In A. Ellis & M. E. Bernard (Eds.), *Rational emotive behavioral approaches to childhood disorders: Theory, practice and research* (pp. 257–280). New York: Springer.

Dreikurs, R., & Soltz, V. (1964). *Children: The challenge.* New York: Duell, Sloan, and Pearce.

Dryden, W. (2002a). Rational emotive behaviour therapy. In W. Dryden (Ed.), *Handbook of individual therapy* (4th ed., pp. 347–372). London: Sage.

Dryden, W. (2002b). Idiosyncratic REBT. In W. Dryden (Ed.), *Idiosyncratic rational emotive behaviour therapy* (pp. 2–14). Ross-on-Wye, UK: PCCS Books.

Dryden, W. (2003). *Rational emotive behaviour therapy.* New York: Brunner-Routledge.

Dryden, W., DiGiuseppe, R., & Neenan, M. (2003). *A primer on rational emotive behavior therapy* (2nd ed.). Champaign, IL: Research Press.

Dryden, W., & Ellis, A. (2001). Rational emotive behavior therapy. In K. S. Dobson (Ed.), *Handbook of cognitive behavioral therapies* (pp. 295–348). New York: Guilford.

Dusek, J. B. (1996). *Adolescent development and behavior* (3rd ed.). Upper Saddle River, NJ: Prentice Hall.

Elkind, D. (1984). *All grown up and no place to go: Teenagers in crisis.* Reading, MA: Addison Wesley.

Elkind, D. (1988). *The hurried child: Growing up too fast too soon.* Reading, MA: Addison Wesley.

Ellis, A. (1957). *How to live with a "neurotic": At home and at work.* New York: Crown.

Ellis, A. (1994). *Reason and emotion in psychotherapy: A comprehensive method of treating human disturbances.* New York: Institute for Rational-Emotive Therapy.

Ellis, A. (1996). *Better, deeper, and more enduring brief therapy.* New York: Brunner/Mazel.

Ellis, A. (1998). *How to control your anxiety before it controls you.* Secaucus, NJ: Carol.

Ellis, A. (2000). Rational emotive behavior therapy. In R. J. Corsini & D. Wedding (Eds.), *Current psychotherapies* (pp. 168–204). Itasca, IL: Peacock.

Ellis, A. (2001a). *Overcoming destructive beliefs, feelings, and behaviors.* Amherst, NY: Prometheus.

Ellis, A. (2001b). *Feeling better, getting better, staying better.* Atascadero, CA: Impact.

Ellis, A., & Bernard, M. E. (Eds.). (2006). *Rational emotive behavioral approaches to childhood disorders: Theory, practice and research.* New York: Springer.

Ellis, A., & Dryden, W. (1997). *The practice of rational emotive behavior therapy* (2nd ed.). New York: Springer.

Ellis, A., & MacLaren, C. (1998). *Rational emotive behavior therapy: A therapist's guide.* Atascadero, CA: Impact.

Ellis, A., & Wilde, J. (2002). *Case studies in rational emotive behavior therapy with children and adolescents.* Upper Saddle River, NJ: Prentice Hall.

Evans, J. R., Van Velsor, P., & Schumacher, J. E. (2002). Addressing adolescent depression: A role for school counselors. *Professional School Counseling, 5,* 211–218.

Fiorini, J. J., & Mullen, J. A. (2006). *Counseling children and adolescents through grief and loss.* Champaign, IL: Research Press.

Foa, E. B., & Andrews, L. W. (2006). *If your adolescent has an anxiety disorder.* New York: Oxford.

Frey, K. S., Hirchstein, M. K., Snell, J. E., Edstrom, L., MacKenzie, E. P., & Boderick, C. J. (2005). Reducing playground bullying and supporting beliefs: An experimental trial of the Steps to Respect program. *Developmental Psychology, 41,* 479–491.

Fryxell, D., & Smith, D. C. (2000). Personal, social, and family characteristics of angry students. *Professional School Counseling, 4*(2), 86–94.

Genest, M., & Turk, D. C. (1981). Think-aloud approaches to cognitive assessment. In T. V. Merluzzi, C. R. Glass, & M. Genest (Eds.), *Cognitive assessment.* New York: Guilford.

Gladding, S. T. (2005). *Counseling as an art.* (3rd ed.). Alexandria, VA: American Counseling Association.

Grieger, R. M., & Boyd. J. D. (2006). Childhood anxieties, fears, and phobias. In A. Ellis & M. E. Bernard (Eds.), *Rational emotive behavioral approaches to childhood disorders: Theory, practice and research* (pp. 232–256). New York: Springer.

Gordon, T. (2000). *Parent effectiveness training: The proven program for raising responsible children.* New York: Three Rivers Press.

Hauck, P. (1967). *The rational management of children.* New York: Libra.

Jaffe, M. L. (1998). *Adolescence.* Danvers, MA: Wiley.

James, J. W., & Friedman, R. (1998). *The grief recovery handbook.* New York: HarperCollins.

Jones, A. (2007). Self-injurious behavior. In R. W. Christner, J. L. Stewart, & A. Freeman (Eds.), *Handbook of cognitive-behavior group therapy with children and adolescents: Specific settings and presenting problems* (pp. 367–388). New York: Routledge.

Kang, S. M., & Shaver, P. R. (2004). Individual differences in emotional complexity: Their psychological implications. *Journal of Personality, 72,* 687–726.

Kaplan, P. S. (2000). *A child's odyssey* (3rd ed.). Belmont, CA: Wadsworth.

Kasen, S., Berenson, K., Cohen, P., & Johnson, J. G. (2004). The effects of school climate on changes in aggressive behavior and other behaviors related to bullying. In D. L. Espelage & S. M. Swearer (Eds.), *Bulling in American schools: A social-ecological perspective on prevention and intervention* (pp. 187–210). Mahwah, NJ: Erlbaum.

Keat, D. (1990). *Child multimodal therapy.* Norwood, NJ: Ablex.

Knaus, W. J. (1974). *Rational-emotive education: A manual for elementary school teachers.* New York: Institute for Rational Living.

Knaus, W. J. (2006). Frustration tolerance training for children. In A. Ellis and M. E. Bernard (eds.), *Rational emotive behavioral approaches to childhood disorders: Theory, practice, and research* (pp. 133–155). New York: Springer.

Koplewicz, H. S. (2002). *More than moody: Recognizing and treating adolescent depression.* New York: Berkley.

Lazarus, A. A. (1976). *Multimodal behavior therapy.* New York: Springer.

Lazarus, A. A. (1997). *Brief but comprehensive psychotherapy: The multimodal way.* New York: Springer.

Lazarus, A. A. (2002). The multimodal assessment therapy approach. In F. W. Kaslow & J. L. Lebow (Eds.), *Comprehensive handbook of psychotherapy: Integrative/eclectic* (pp. 241–254). New York: Wiley.

Levine, M. (2006). *The price of privilege: How parental pressure and material advantage are creating a generation of disconnected and unhappy kids.* New York: HarperCollins.

Lochman, J. E., Powell, N., Boxmeyer, C., Deming, A. M., & Young, L. (2007). Cognitive-behavior group therapy for angry and aggressive youth. In R. W. Christner, J. L. Stewart, & A. Freeman (Eds.), *Handbook of cognitive-behavior group therapy with children and adolescents: Specific settings and presenting problems* (pp. 333–348). New York: Routledge.

Malkinson, R. (2007). *Cognitive grief therapy: Constructing a rational meaning to life following loss.* New York: W. W. Norton.

Martin, D. G. (2003). *Clinical practice with adolescents.* Pacific Grove, CA: Brooks/Cole.

McAdams, C. R., & Schmidt, C. D. (2007). How to help a bully: Recommendations for counseling the proactive aggressor. *Professional School Counseling 11*(2), 120–128.

McDevitt, T. M., & Ormrod, J. E. (2002). *Child development and education.* Upper Saddle River, NJ: Pearson Education.

McWhirter, E., & Burrow-Sanchez, J. (2009). Counseling at-risk children and adolescents. In A. Vernon (Ed.), *Counseling children and adolescents* (pp. 335–358). Denver: Love Publishing.

Merrell, K.W. (2001). *Helping students overcome depression and anxiety.* New York: Guilford.

Meece, J. L. (2002). *Child and adolescent development for educators* (2nd ed.). New York: McGraw Hill.

Mize, S. (2008). Grounding helicopter parents. *ASCA School Counselor,* pp. 39–43.

Nelsen, J., & Lott, L. (2000). *Positive discipline for teenagers: Empowering your teen and yourself through kind and firm parenting* (2nd ed.). Roseville, CA: Prima.

Newman, B. M., & Newman, P. R. (2006). *Development through life: A psychosocial approach* (9th ed.). Belmont, CA: Thompson Wadsworth.

Owens, K. B. (2002). *Child and adolescent development: An integrated approach.* Belmont, CA: Wadsworth.

Piper, W. (1986). *The little engine that could.* New York: Platt and Munk.

Pipher, M. (1994). *Reviving Ophelia: Saving the selves of adolescent girls.* New York: Ballantine.

Potter-Effron, R. (1998). *How to control your anger before it controls you.* Center City, MN: Hazelden.

Rathus, S. A. (2004). *Voyages in childhood.* Belmont, CA: Wadsworth.

Reynolds, W. M. (1992). *Internalizing disorders in children and adolescents.* New York: Wiley.

Riley, P. L., & McDaniel, J. (2000). School violence prevention, intervention, and crisis response. *Professional School Counseling, 4*(2), 120–125.

Seligman, M. E. (1995). *The optimistic child.* New York: HarperCollins.

Siris, K., & Osterman, K. (2004). Interrupting the cycle of bullying and victimization in the elementary classroom. *Phi Delta Kappan,* 288–291.

Vernon, A. (1980). *Help yourself to a healthier you: A handbook of emotional education exercises for children.* Washington, DC: University Press of America.

Vernon, A. (1998a). *The Passport Program: A journey through emotional, social, cognitive, and self-development* (Grades 1–5). Champaign, IL: Research Press.

Vernon, A. (1998b). *The Passport Program: A journey through emotional, social, cognitive, and self-development* (Grades 6–8). Champaign, IL: Research Press.

Vernon, A. (1998c). *The Passport Program: A journey through emotional, social, cognitive, and self-development* (Grades 9–12). Champaign, IL: Research Press.

Vernon, A. (2002). *What works when with children and adolescents: A handbook of individual counseling techniques.* Champaign, IL: Research Press.

Vernon, A. (2006a). *Thinking, feeling, behaving: An emotional education curriculum for children* (Grades 1–6). Champaign, IL: Research Press.

Vernon, A. (2006b). *Thinking, feeling, behaving: An emotional education curriculum for adolescents* (Grades 7–12). Champaign, IL: Research Press.

Vernon, A. (2006c). Depression in children and adolescents: REBT approaches to assessment and treatment. In A. Ellis & M. Bernard (Eds.), *Rational emotive behavioral approaches to childhood disorders: Theory, practice and research* (pp. 212–231). New York: Springer.

Vernon, A. (2007). Application of rational emotive behavior therapy to groups within classrooms and educational settings. In R. Christner, J. Stewart, & A. Freeman (Eds.), *Cognitive behavior group therapy with children and adolescents: Specific settings and presenting problems* (pp. 107–127). New York: Routledge.

Vernon, A. (2009a). Rational emotive behavior therapy. In A. Vernon & T. Kottman (Eds.), *Counseling theories: Practical applications with children and adolescents in school settings* (pp. 153–184). Denver: Love Publishing.

Vernon, A. (2009b). Applications of rational emotive behavior therapy with children and adolescents. In A. Vernon (Ed.), *Counseling children and adolescents* (4th ed., pp. 175–202). Denver: Love Publishing.

Vernon, A. (2009c). Working with children, adolescents, and their parents: Practical application of developmental theory. In A. Vernon (Ed.), *Counseling children and adolescents* (4th ed., pp. 1–38). Denver: Love Publishing.

Vernon, A., & Bernard, M. (2006). Applications of REBT in schools. In A. Ellis & M. Bernard (Eds.), *Rational emotive behavioral approaches to childhood disorders: Theory, practice and research* (pp. 415–460). New York: Springer.

Vernon, A., & Clemente, R. (2005). *Assessment and intervention with children and adolescents: Developmental and multicultural approaches.* Alexandria, VA: American Counseling Association.

Walen, S. R., DiGiuseppe, R., & Dryden, W. (1992). *A practitioner's guide to rational-emotive therapy* (2nd ed.). New York: Oxford University Press.

Waters, V. (1979). *Color us rational.* New York: Institute for Rational Living.

Waters, V. (1980). *Rational stories for children.* New York: Institute for Rational Emotive Therapy.

Waters, V. (1981). The living school. *RET Work, 1,* 1–6.

Waters, V. (1982). Therapies for children: Rational-emotive therapy. In C. R. Reynolds & T. B. Gutkin (Eds.), *Handbook of school psychology* (pp. 37–57). New York: Wiley.

Weisfeld, G. (1999). *Evolutionary principles of human adolescence.* New York: Basic.

Whitted, K. S., & Dupper, D. R. (2005). Best practices for preventing or reducing bullying in schools. *Children & Schools, 27,* 167–175.

Wigfield, A., Lutz, S. L., & Wagner, A. L. (2005). Early adolescents' development across the middle school years: Implications for school counselors. *Professional School Counseling, 9,* 112–119.

Wilde, J. (1996). *Treating anger, anxiety, and depression in children and adolescents: A cognitive-behavioral perspective.* New York: Taylor and Francis.

Youngs, B. B. (1995). *Stress and your child: Helping kids cope with the strains and pressures of life.* New York: Ballantine.

About the Author

ANN VERNON, Ph.D., NCC, LMHC, is professor emerita, University of Northern Iowa, where she served as professor and coordinator of the School and Mental Health Counseling programs for many years. During her tenure there, she taught courses related to counseling children and adolescents, specializing in school counseling. Dr. Vernon has published numerous books, including *What Works When with Children and Adolescents: A Handbook of Individual Counseling Techniques* (the predecessor to this book); *Thinking, Feeling, Behaving: An Emotional Education Curriculum for Children; Thinking, Feeling, Behaving: An Emotional Education Curriculum for Adolescents; The Passport Program: A Journey Through Emotional, Social, Cognitive, and Self-Development; Assessment and Intervention with Children and Adolescents: Developmental and Multicultural Approaches* (with R. Clemente); and *Counseling Children and Adolescents.* In addition, she is the sole author of more than 30 book chapters dealing primarily with counseling children and adolescents, developmental counseling, and applications of REBT with children and adolescents, as well as many journal articles on a variety of topics. In addition to her teaching and writing, Dr. Vernon had a private practice where, for many years, she applied REBT concepts with her clients.

Dr. Vernon has held numerous leadership positions in state, regional, and national counseling associations and is the vice president of the Albert Ellis Institute Board of Trustees. She presents workshops throughout the United States, Canada, South America, Australia, Holland, and Romania on applications of REBT with children and adolescents, as well as on other topics pertaining to counseling young clients. Presently, Dr. Vernon is a visiting professor in the school counseling program at the University of Oradea, Romania, and at the University of Buffalo, Singapore campus.